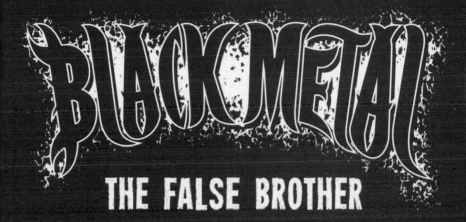

THE FALSE BROTHER

WRITTEN BY
RICK SPEARS

ILLUSTRATED BY
CHUCK BB

EDITED BY
CHARLIE CHU

LETTERED & DESIGNED BY
DOUGLAS E. SHERWOOD

TONING ASSISTS BY
CASEY HUNT

LOGO DESIGNED BY
STEVEN BIRCH
AT SERVO GRAPHICS

PUBLISHED BY ONI PRESS, INC.
JOE NOZEMACK, PUBLISHER
JAMES LUCAS JONES, EDITOR IN CHIEF
CORY CASONI, DIRECTOR OF MARKETING
KEITH WOOD, ART DIRECTOR
GEORGE ROHAC, OPERATIONS DIRECTOR
JILL BEATON, EDITOR
CHARLIE CHU, EDITOR
DOUGLAS E. SHERWOOD, PRODUCTION ASSISTANT

ONI PRESS, INC.
1305 SE MARTIN LUTHER KING JR. BLVD.
SUITE A
PORTLAND, OR 97214
USA

ONIPRESS.COM
RICKSPEARS.COM
CHUCKBB.COM

FIRST EDITION OCTOBER 2011
LIBRARY OF CONGRESS CONTROL NUMBER: 2011906142
ISBN 978-1-932664-99-7

10 9 8 7 6 5 4 3 2 1

PRINTED IN U.S.A. BY LAKE BOOK MANUFACTURING.

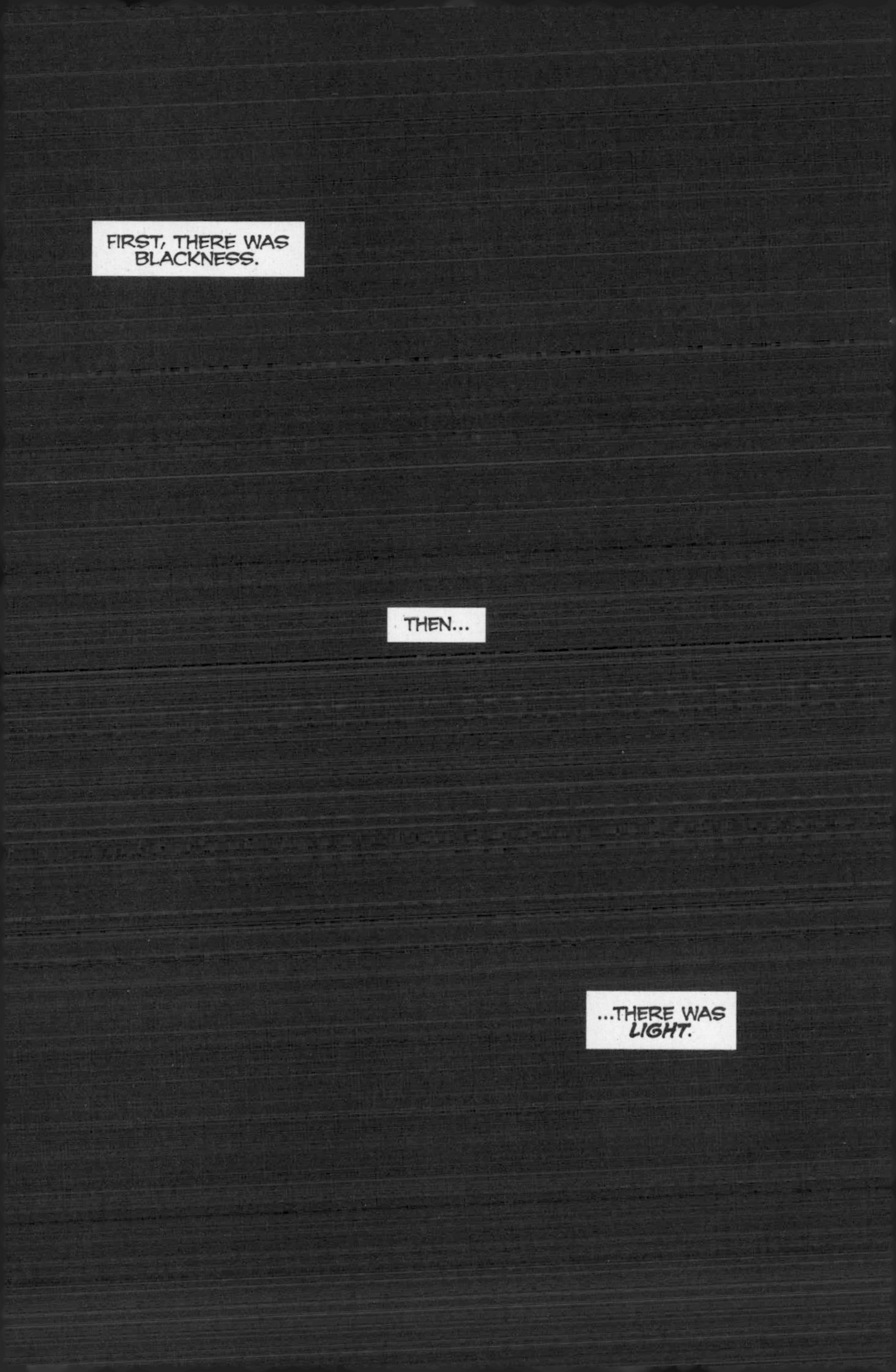
FIRST, THERE WAS BLACKNESS.
THEN...
...THERE WAS *LIGHT*.

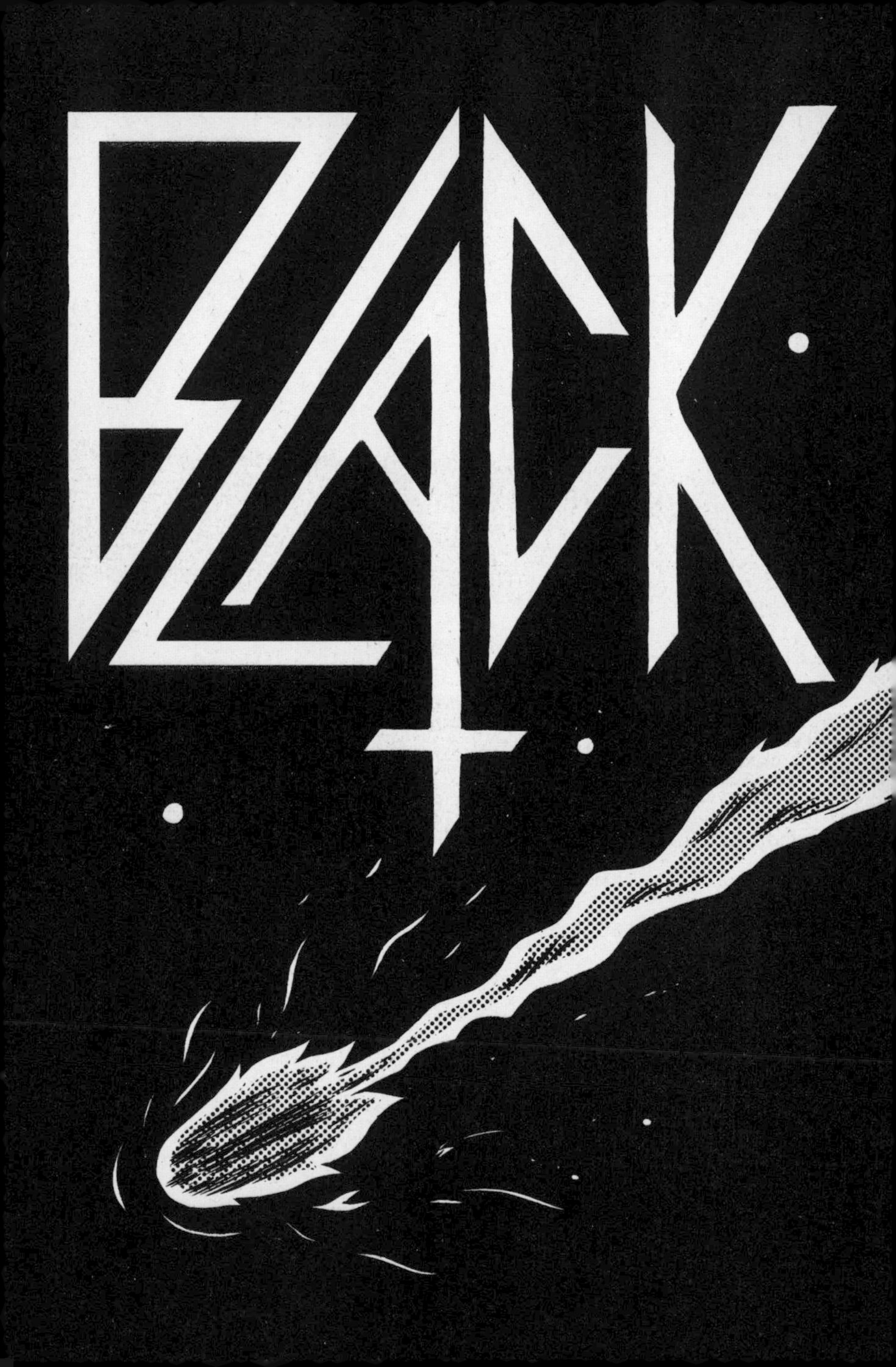
BLACK

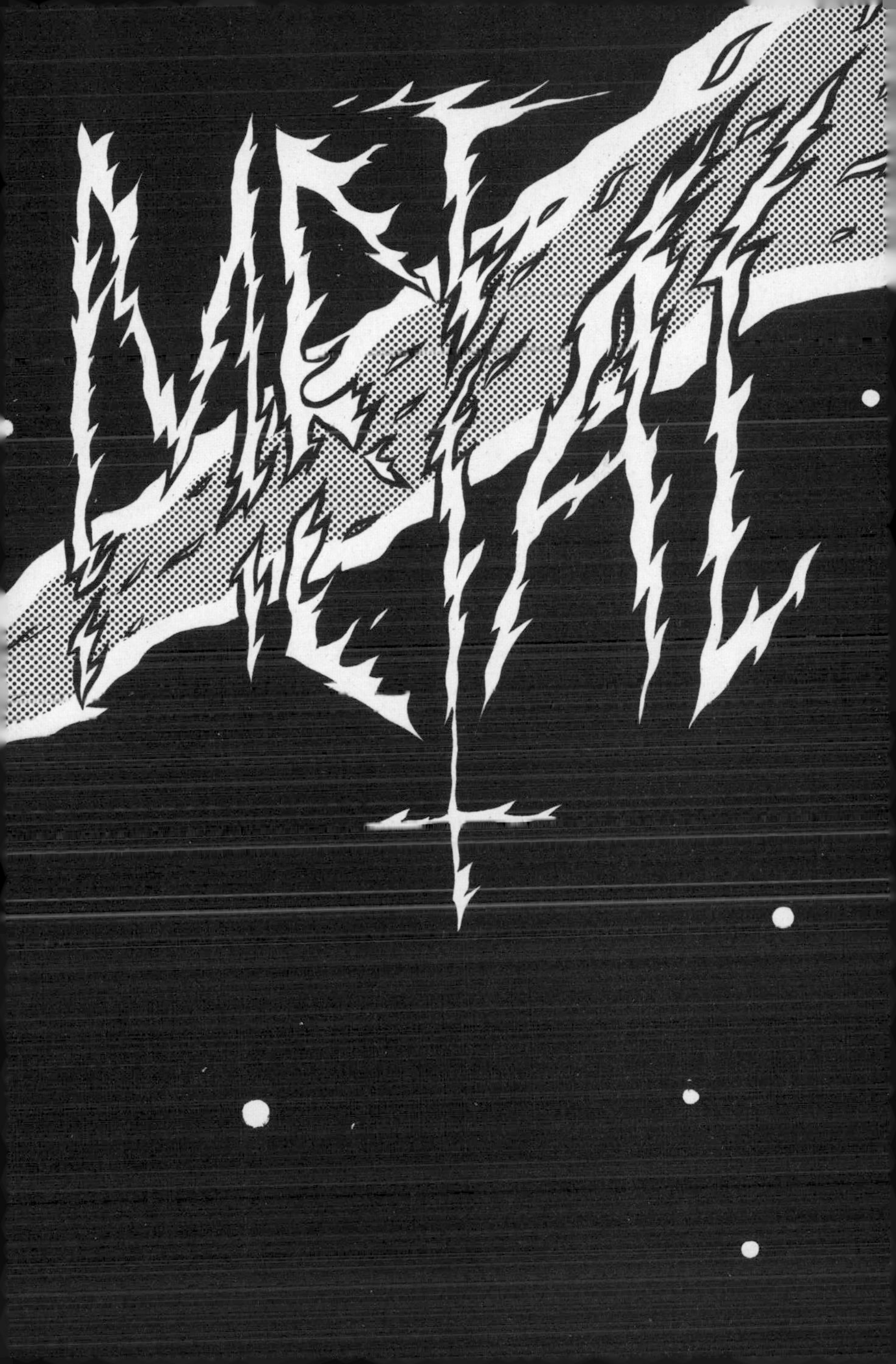

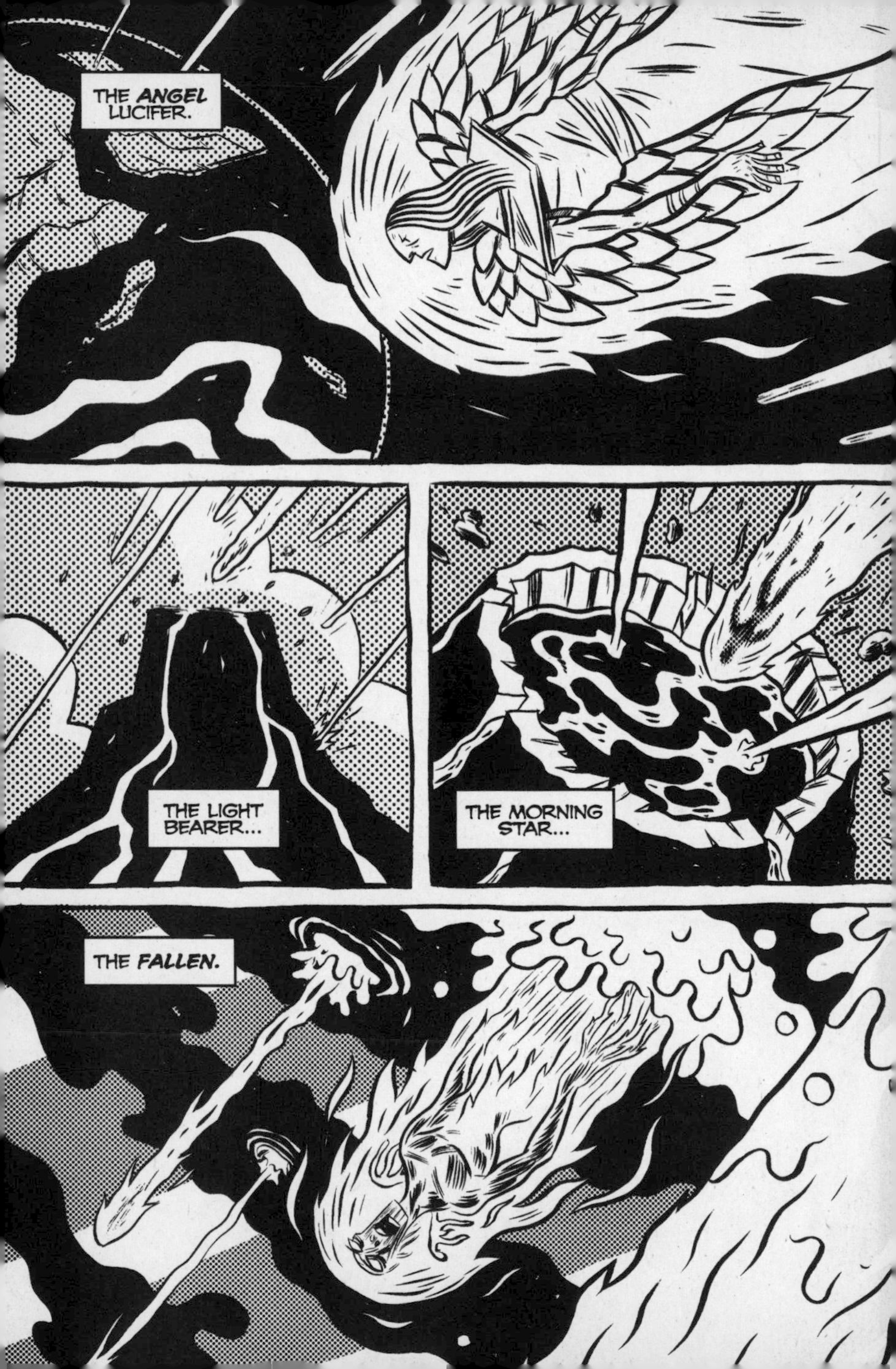
THE *ANGEL* LUCIFER.
THE LIGHT BEARER...
THE MORNING STAR...
THE *FALLEN.*

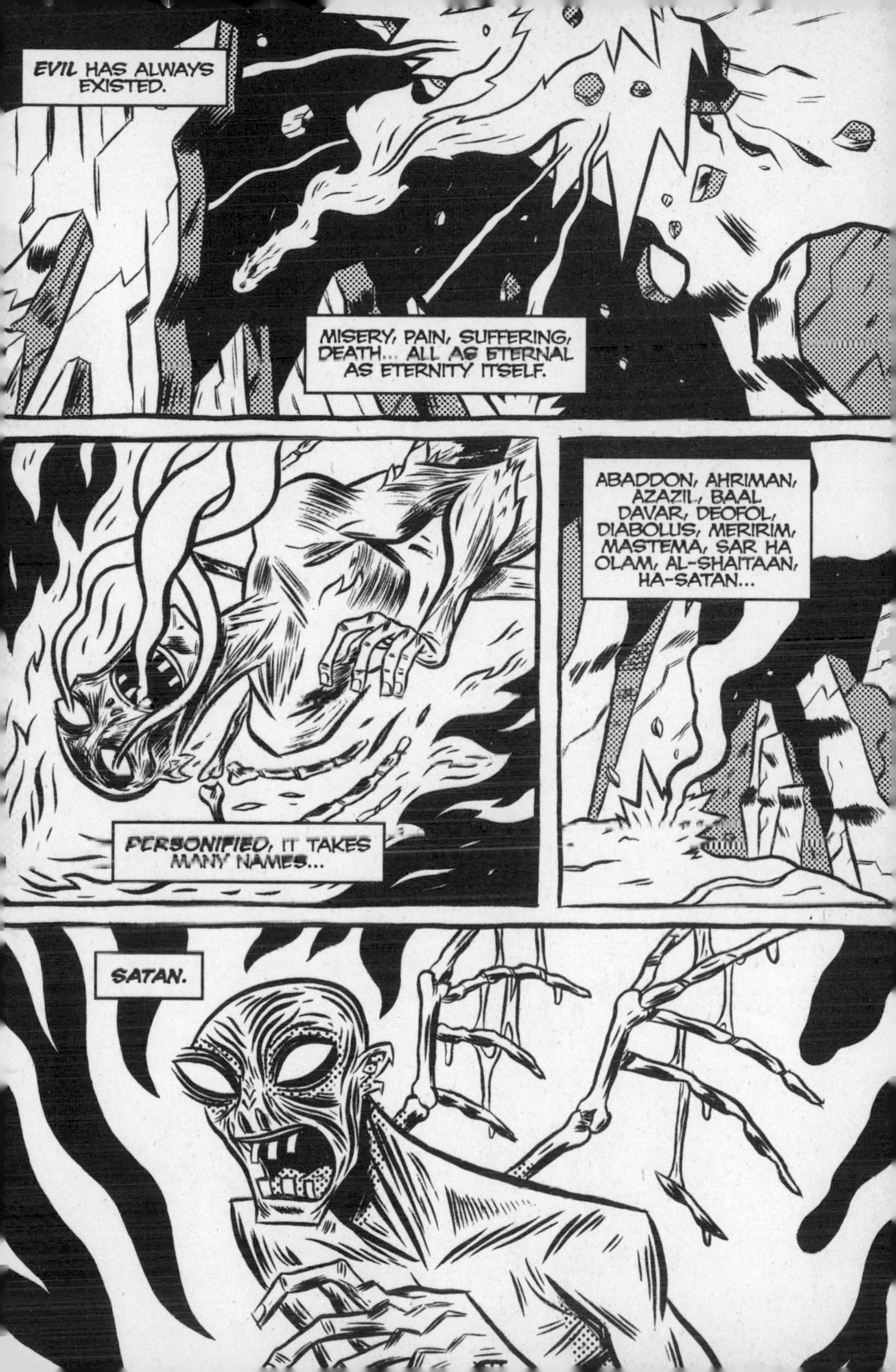
EVIL HAS ALWAYS EXISTED.
MISERY, PAIN, SUFFERING, DEATH... ALL AS ETERNAL AS ETERNITY ITSELF.
PERSONIFIED, IT TAKES MANY NAMES...
ABADDON, AHRIMAN, AZAZIL, BAAL DAVAR, DEOFOL, DIABOLUS, MERIRIM, MASTEMA, SAR HA OLAM, AL-SHAITAAN, HA-SATAN...
SATAN.

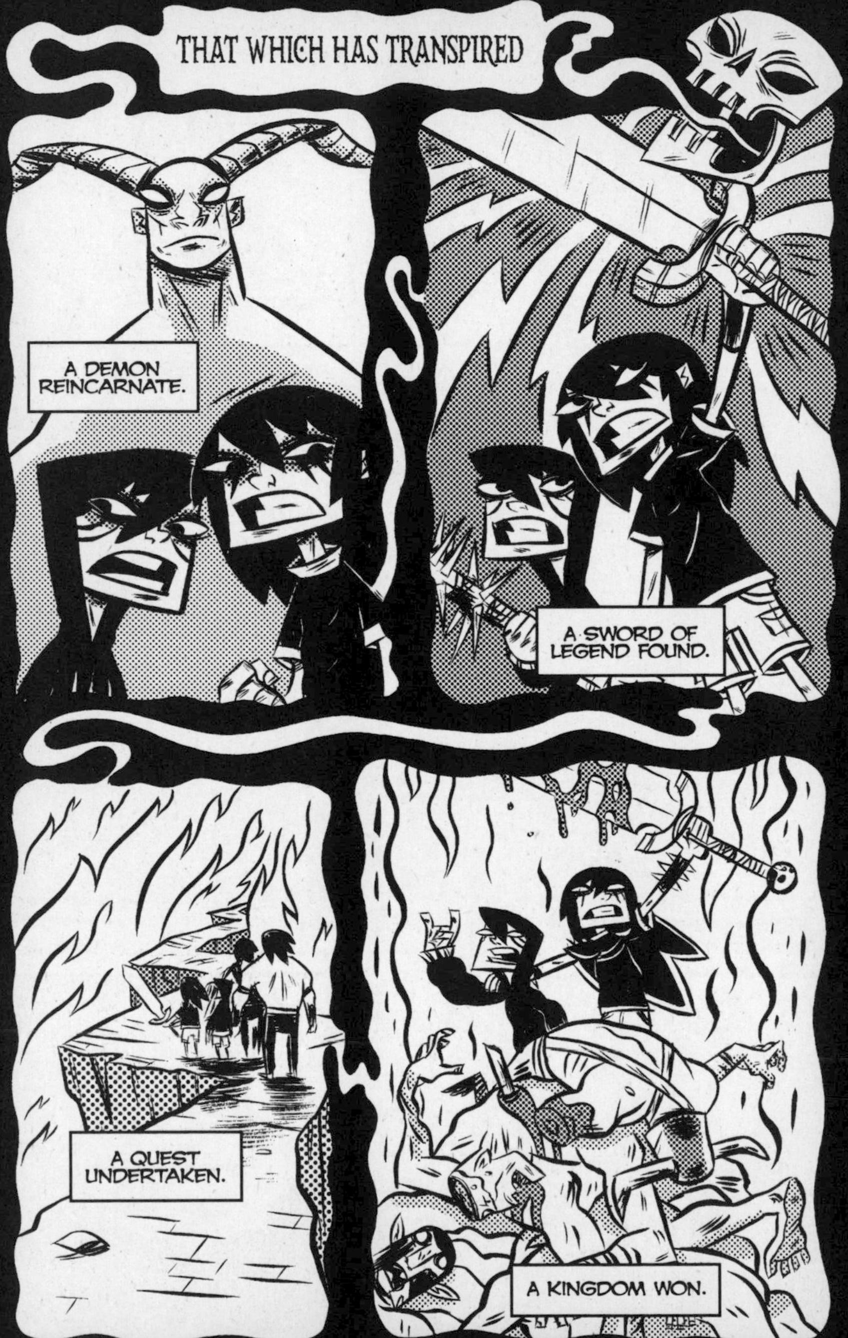
THAT WHICH HAS TRANSPIRED
A DEMON REINCARNATE.
A SWORD OF LEGEND FOUND.
A QUEST UNDERTAKEN.
A KINGDOM WON.

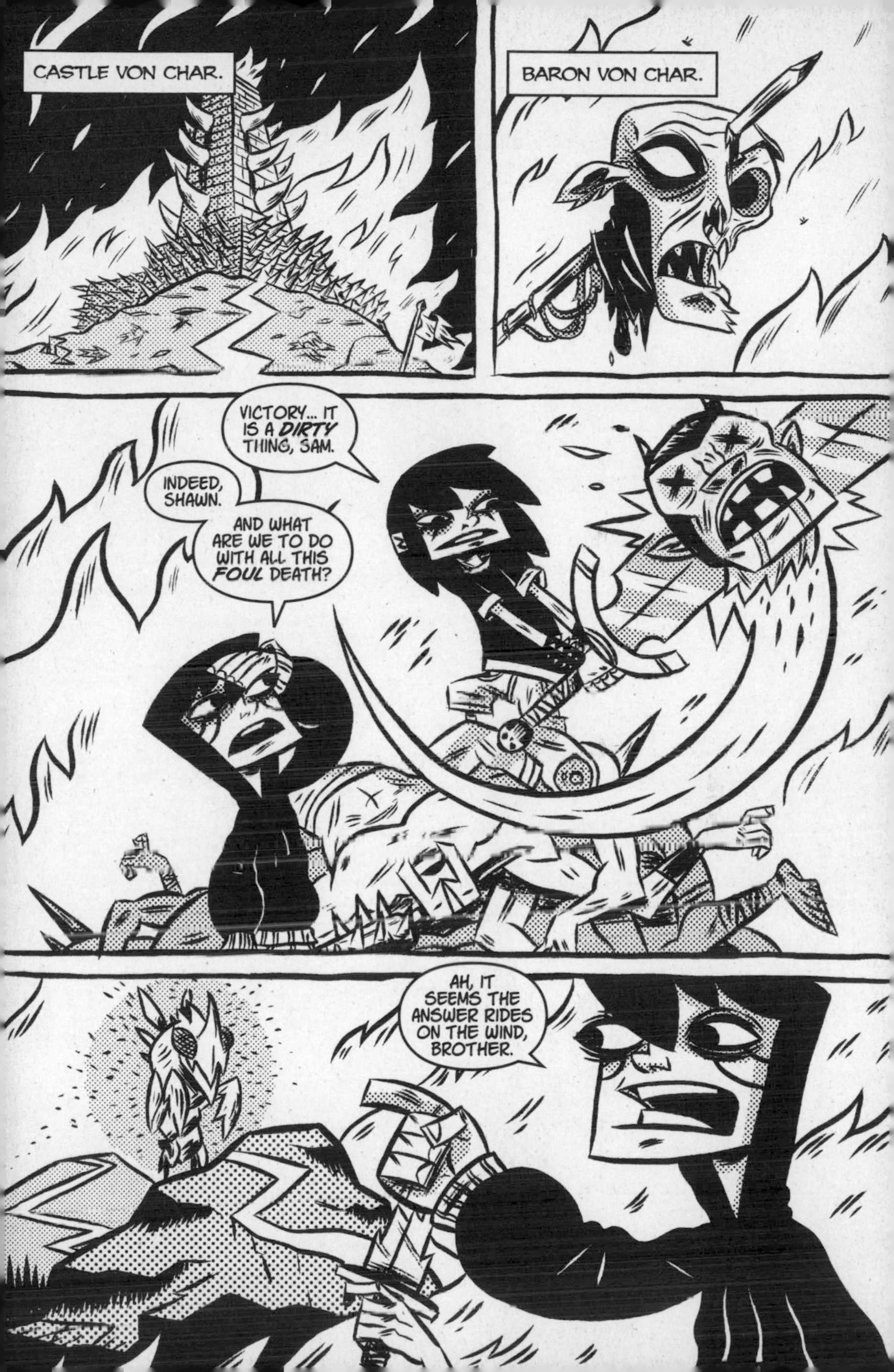
CASTLE VON CHAR.
BARON VON CHAR.
VICTORY... IT IS A *DIRTY* THING, SAM.
INDEED, SHAWN.
AND WHAT ARE WE TO DO WITH ALL THIS *FOUL* DEATH?
AH, IT SEEMS THE ANSWER RIDES ON THE WIND, BROTHER.

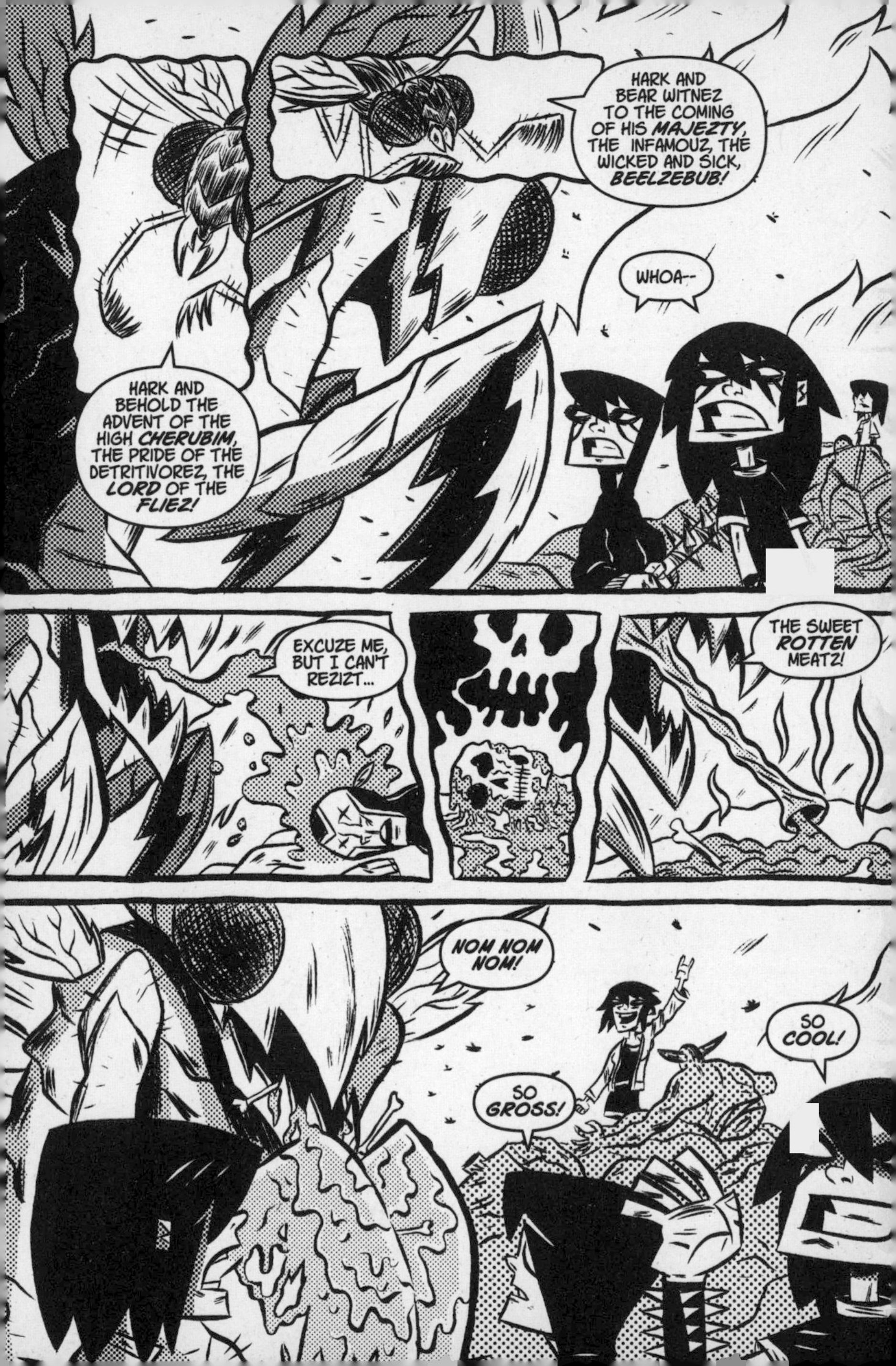
HARK AND BEAR WITNEZ TO THE COMING OF HIS MAJEZTY, THE INFAMOUZ, THE WICKED AND SICK, BEELZEBUB!
HARK AND BEHOLD THE ADVENT OF THE HIGH CHERUBIM, THE PRIDE OF THE DETRITIVOREZ, THE LORD OF THE FLIEZ!
WHOA--
EXCUZE ME, BUT I CAN'T REZIZT...
THE SWEET ROTTEN MEATZ!
NOM NOM NOM!
SO GROSS!
SO COOL!

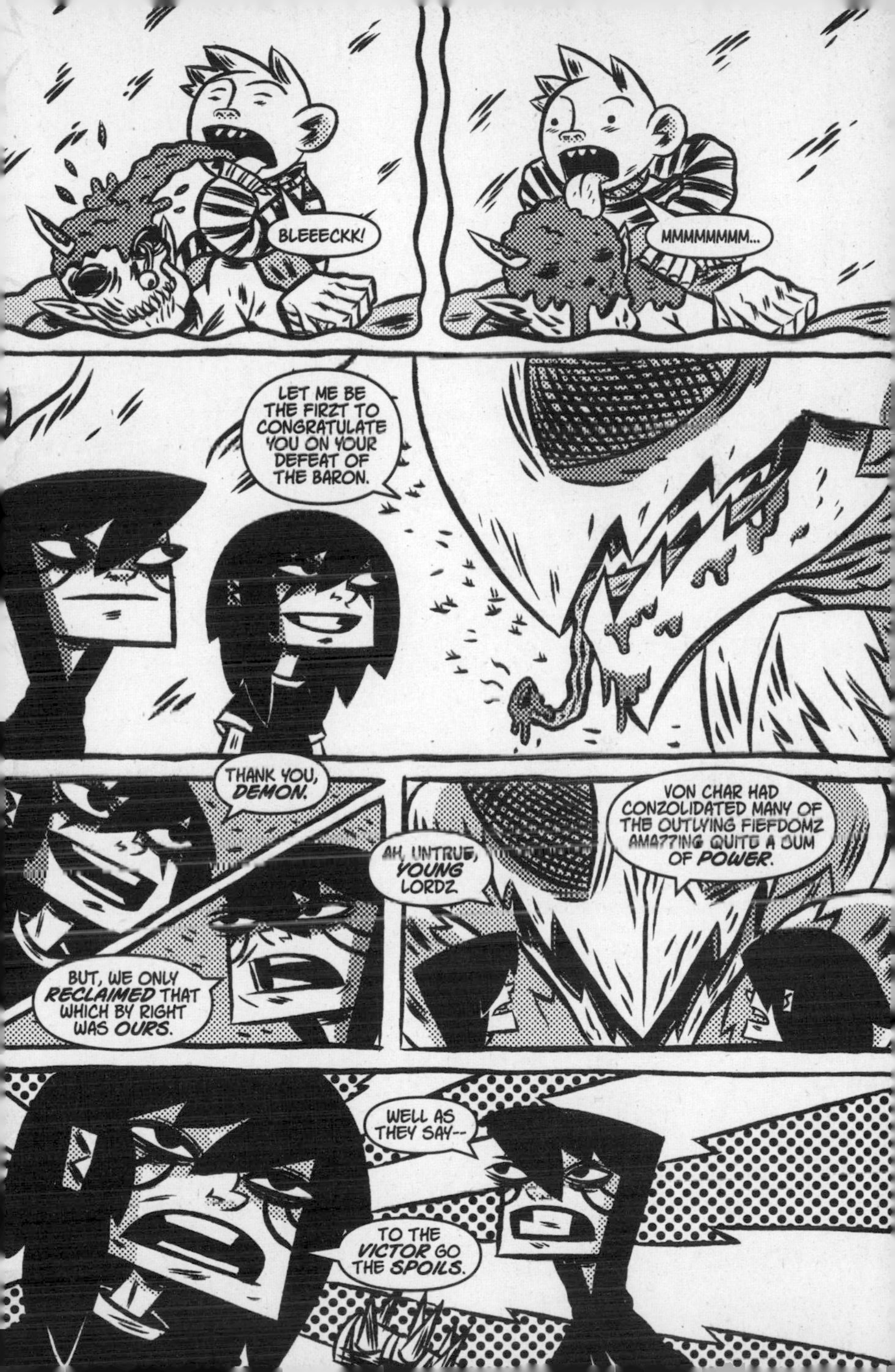
BLEEECKK!
MMMMMMMM...
LET ME BE THE FIRZT TO CONGRATULATE YOU ON YOUR DEFEAT OF THE BARON.
THANK YOU, *DEMON*.
BUT, WE ONLY *RECLAIMED* THAT WHICH BY RIGHT WAS *OURS*.
AH, UNTRUE, *YOUNG* LORDZ
VON CHAR HAD CONZOLIDATED MANY OF THE OUTLYING FIEFDOMZ AMAZZING QUITE A ZUM OF *POWER*.
WELL AS THEY SAY--
TO THE *VICTOR* GO THE *SPOILS*.

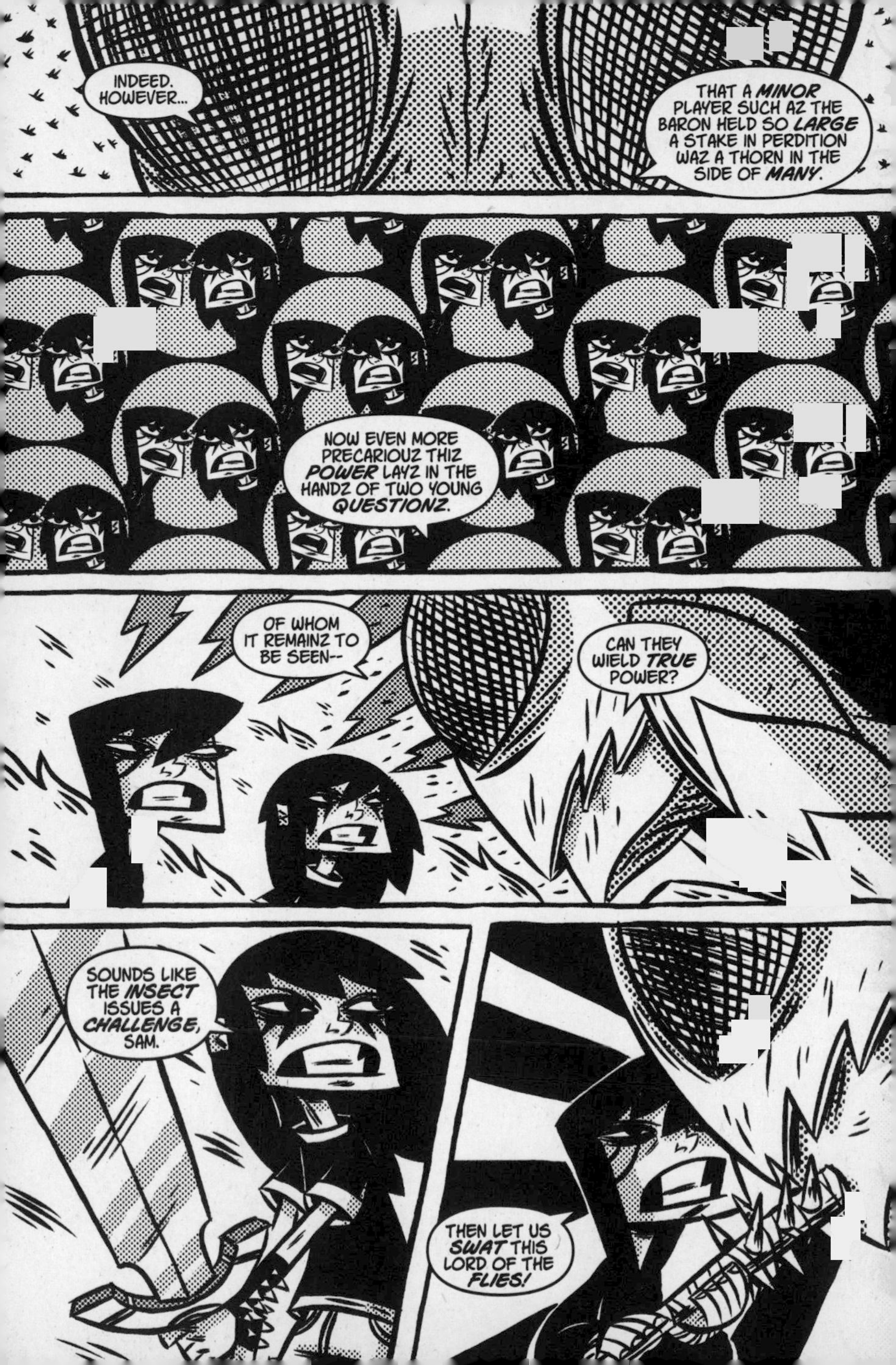

INDEED. HOWEVER...
THAT A MINOR PLAYER SUCH AZ THE BARON HELD SO LARGE A STAKE IN PERDITION WAZ A THORN IN THE SIDE OF MANY.
NOW EVEN MORE PRECARIOUZ THIZ POWER LAYZ IN THE HANDZ OF TWO YOUNG QUESTIONZ.
OF WHOM IT REMAINZ TO BE SEEN--
CAN THEY WIELD TRUE POWER?
SOUNDS LIKE THE INSECT ISSUES A CHALLENGE, SAM.
THEN LET US SWAT THIS LORD OF THE FLIES!

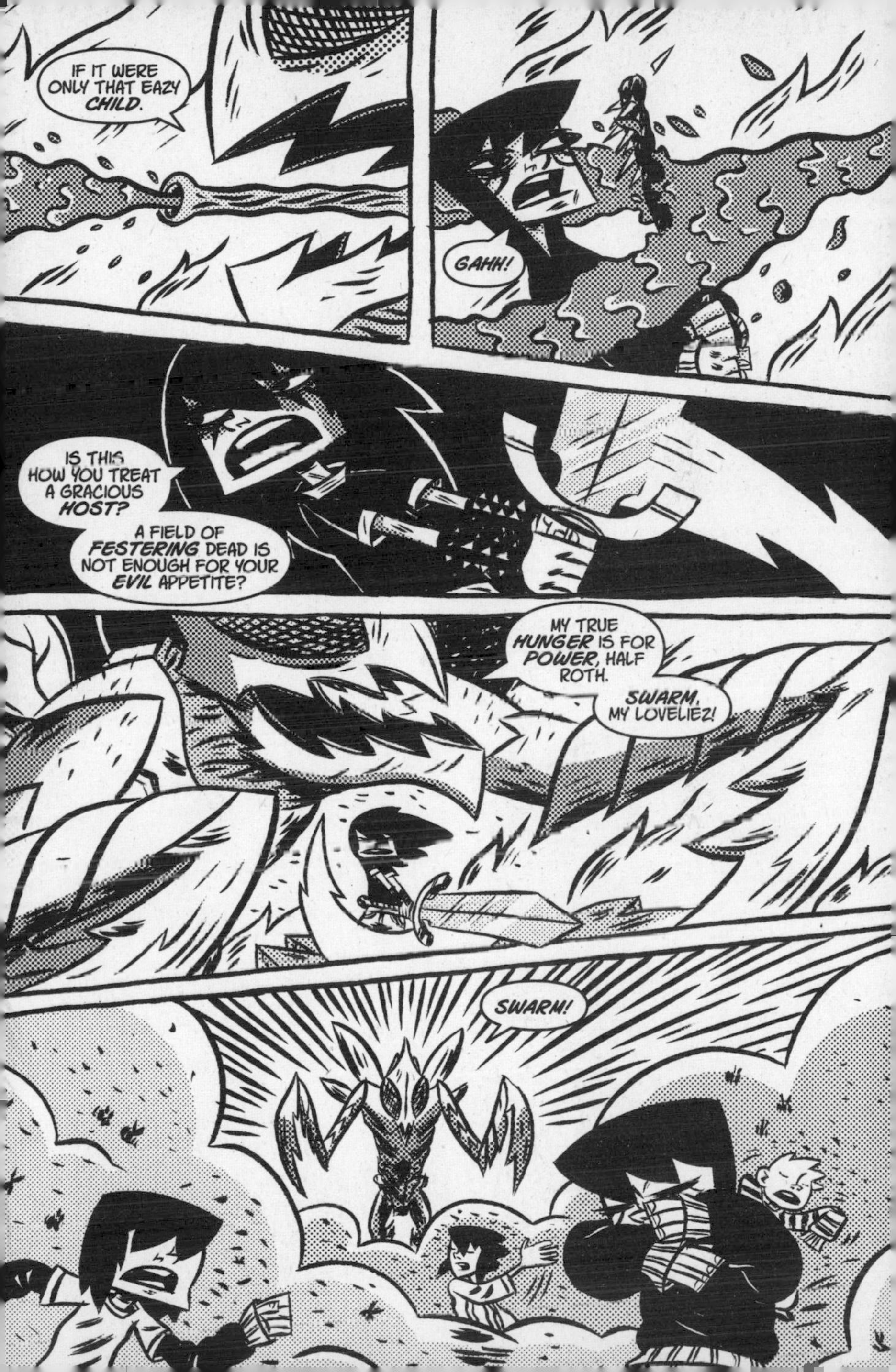
IF IT WERE ONLY THAT EAZY CHILD.
GAHH!
IS THIS HOW YOU TREAT A GRACIOUS HOST?
A FIELD OF FESTERING DEAD IS NOT ENOUGH FOR YOUR EVIL APPETITE?
MY TRUE HUNGER IS FOR POWER, HALF ROTH.
SWARM, MY LOVELIEZ!
SWARM!

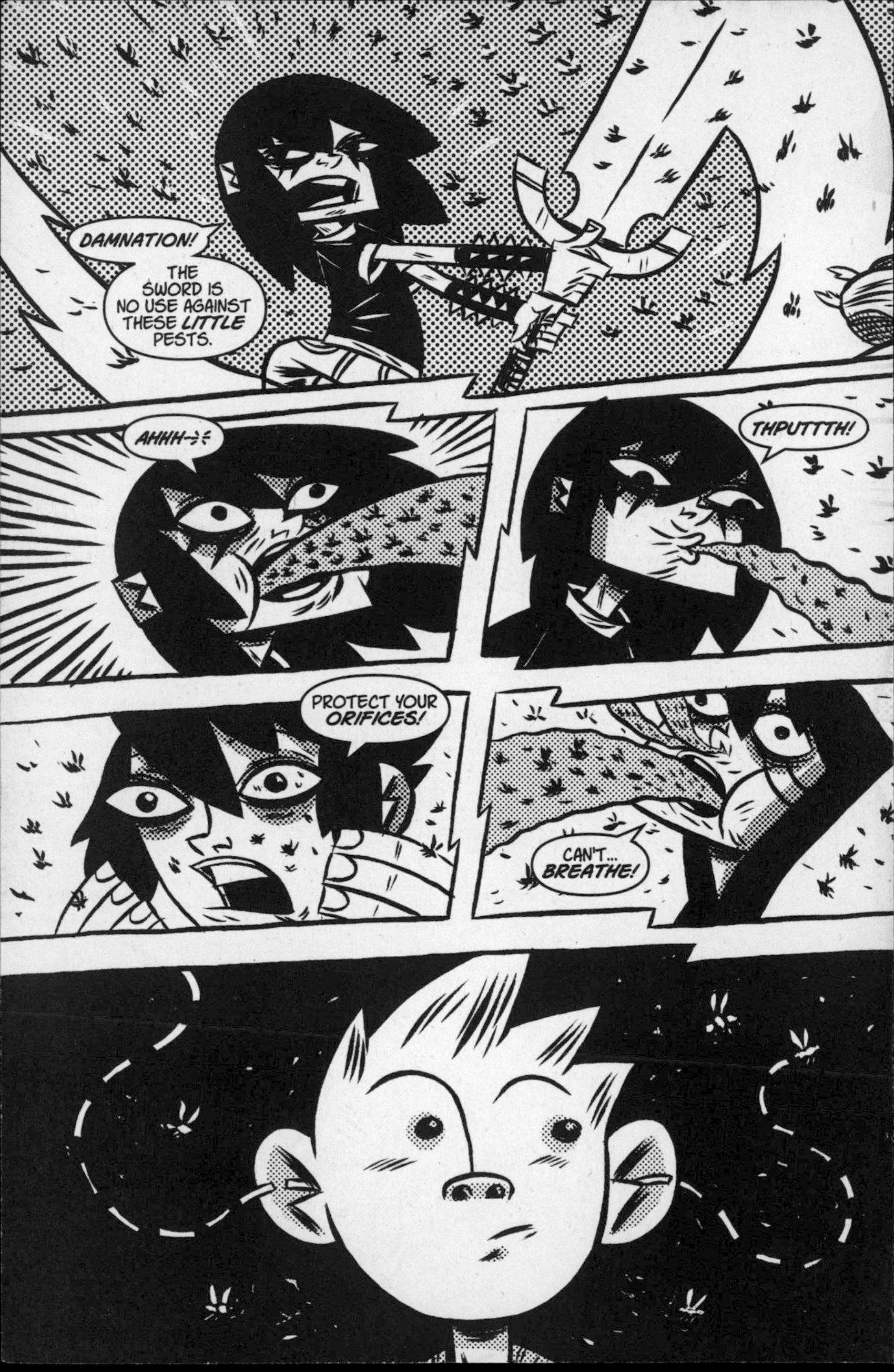
DAMNATION!
THE SWORD IS NO USE AGAINST THESE *LITTLE* PESTS.
AHHH-
THPUTTTH!
PROTECT YOUR *ORIFICES!*
CAN'T... *BREATHE!*

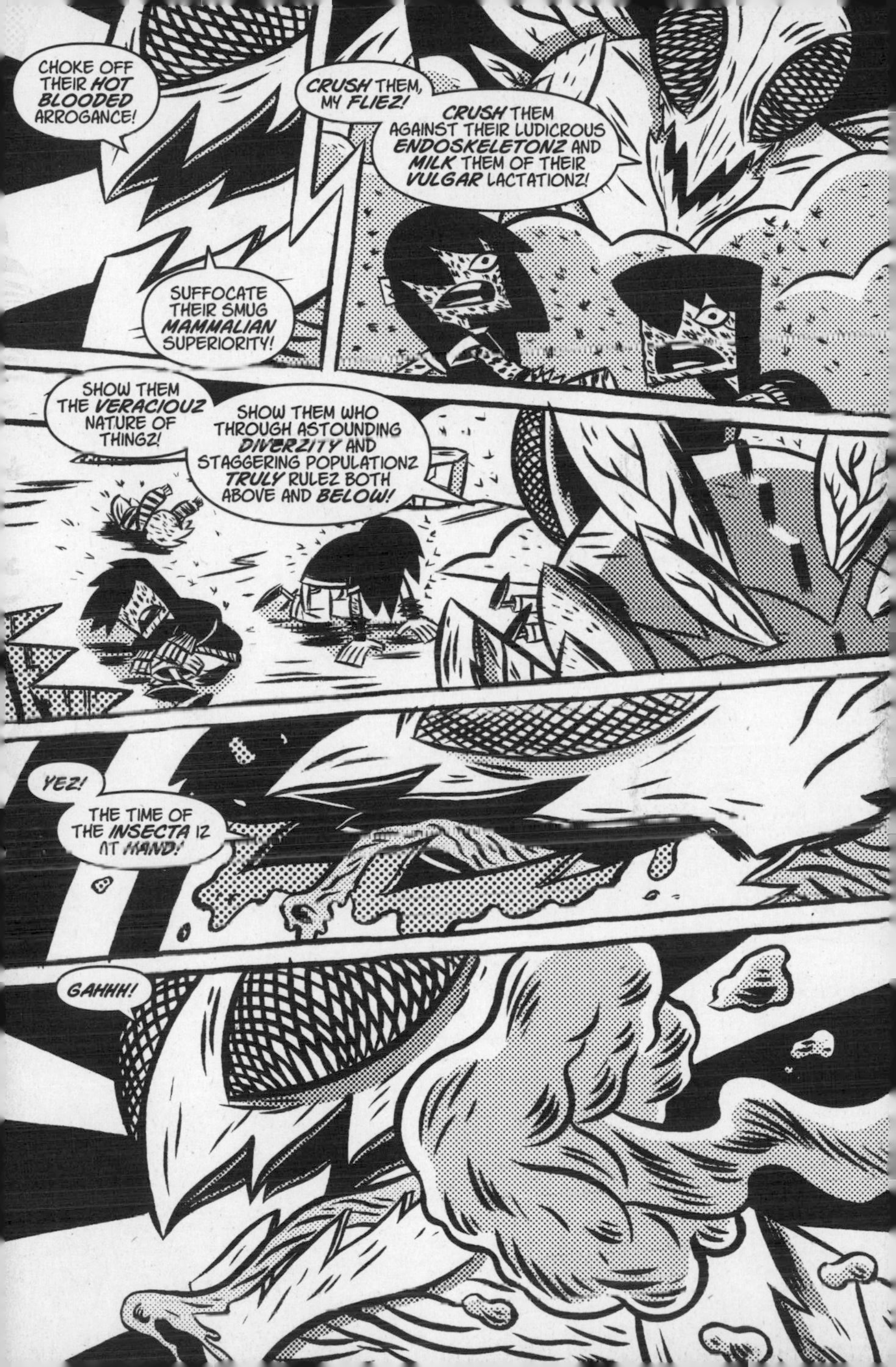
CHOKE OFF THEIR HOT BLOODED ARROGANCE!
CRUSH THEM, MY FLIEZ!
CRUSH THEM AGAINST THEIR LUDICROUS ENDOSKELETONZ AND MILK THEM OF THEIR VULGAR LACTATIONZ!
SUFFOCATE THEIR SMUG MAMMALIAN SUPERIORITY!
SHOW THEM THE VERACIOUZ NATURE OF THINGZ!
SHOW THEM WHO THROUGH ASTOUNDING DIVERZITY AND STAGGERING POPULATIONZ TRULY RULEZ BOTH ABOVE AND BELOW!
YEZ!
THE TIME OF THE INSECTA IZ AT HAND!
GAHHH!

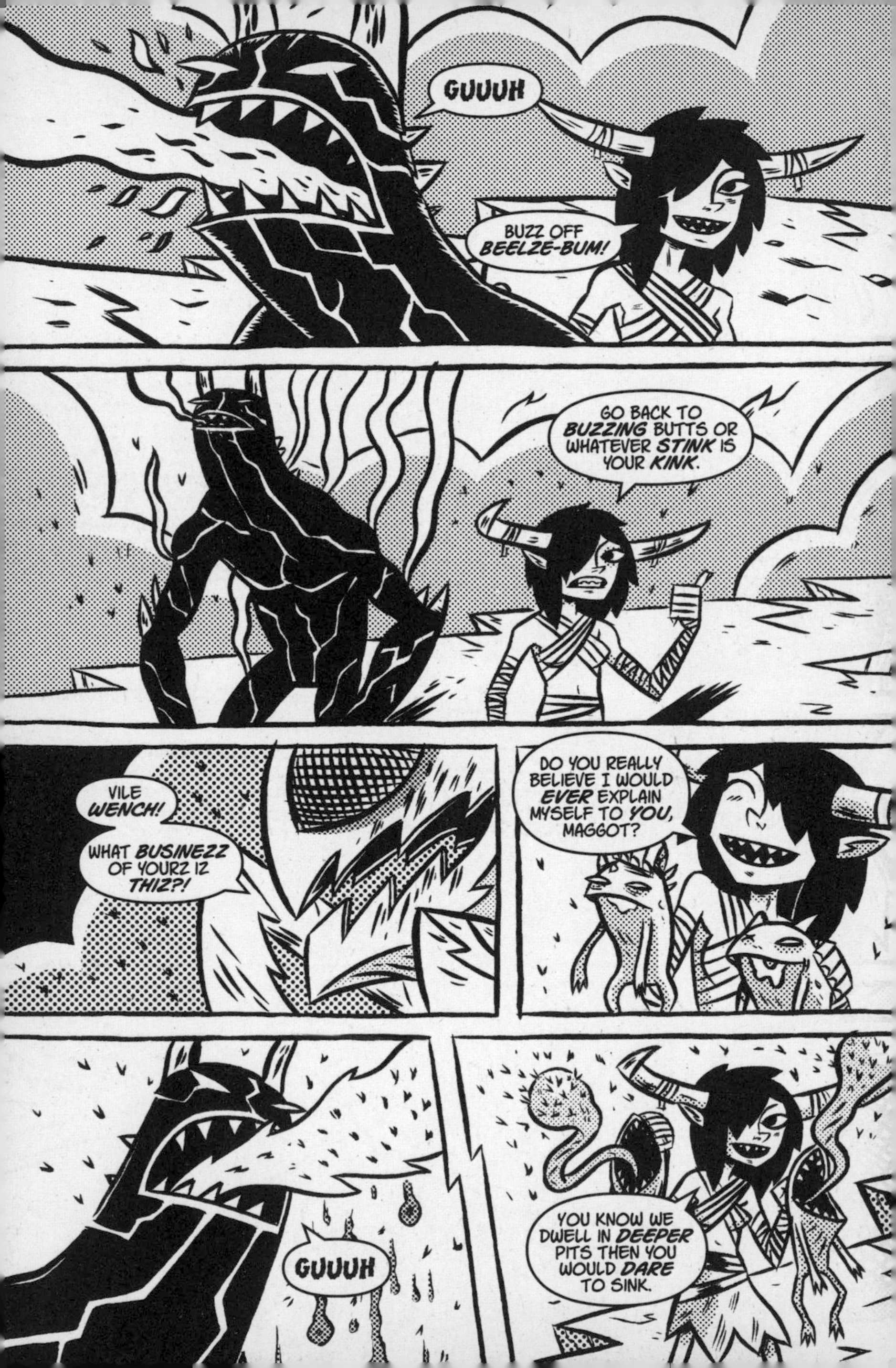
GUUUH
BUZZ OFF BEELZE-BUM!
GO BACK TO BUZZING BUTTS OR WHATEVER STINK IS YOUR KINK.
VILE WENCH!
WHAT BUSINEZZ OF YOURZ IZ THIZ?!
DO YOU REALLY BELIEVE I WOULD EVER EXPLAIN MYSELF TO YOU, MAGGOT?
GUUUH
YOU KNOW WE DWELL IN DEEPER PITS THEN YOU WOULD DARE TO SINK.

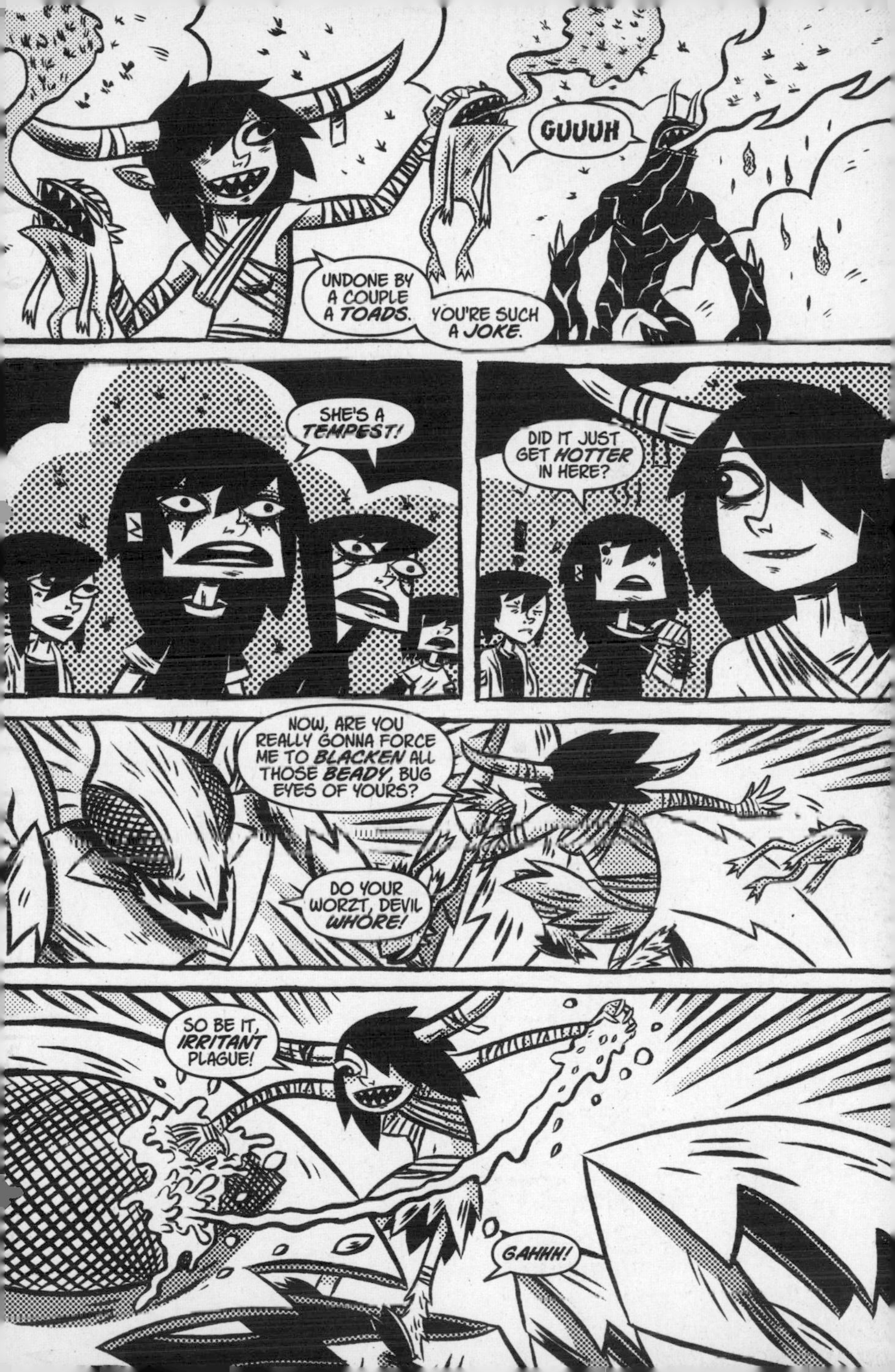
GUUUH
UNDONE BY A COUPLE A TOADS.
YOU'RE SUCH A JOKE.
SHE'S A TEMPEST!
DID IT JUST GET HOTTER IN HERE?
NOW, ARE YOU REALLY GONNA FORCE ME TO BLACKEN ALL THOSE BEADY, BUG EYES OF YOURS?
DO YOUR WORZT, DEVIL WHORE!
SO BE IT, IRRITANT PLAGUE!
GAHHH!

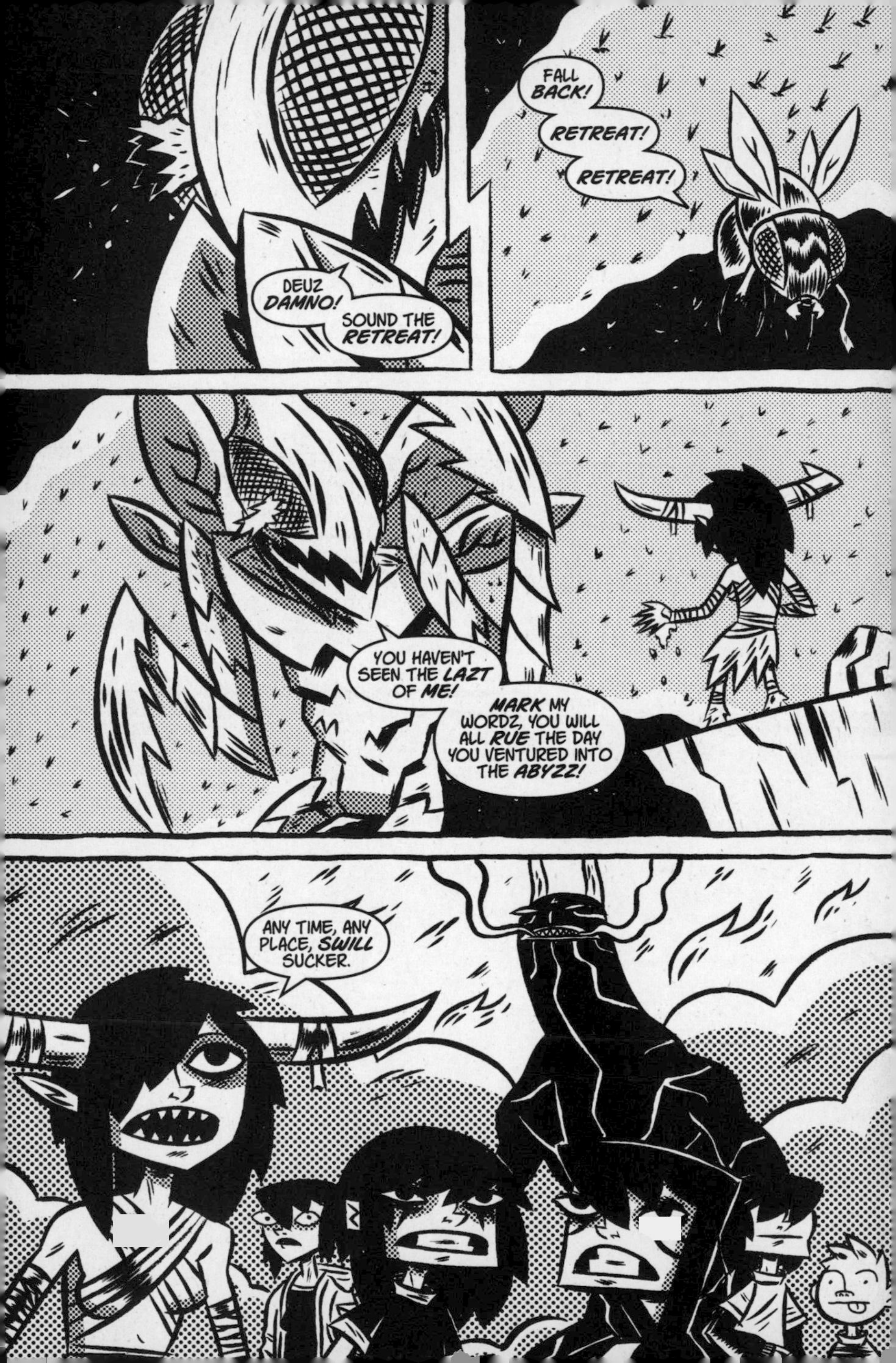
DEUZ DAMNO! SOUND THE RETREAT!
FALL BACK!
RETREAT!
RETREAT!
YOU HAVEN'T SEEN THE LAZT OF ME!
MARK MY WORDZ, YOU WILL ALL RUE THE DAY YOU VENTURED INTO THE ABYZZ!
ANY TIME, ANY PLACE, SWILL SUCKER.

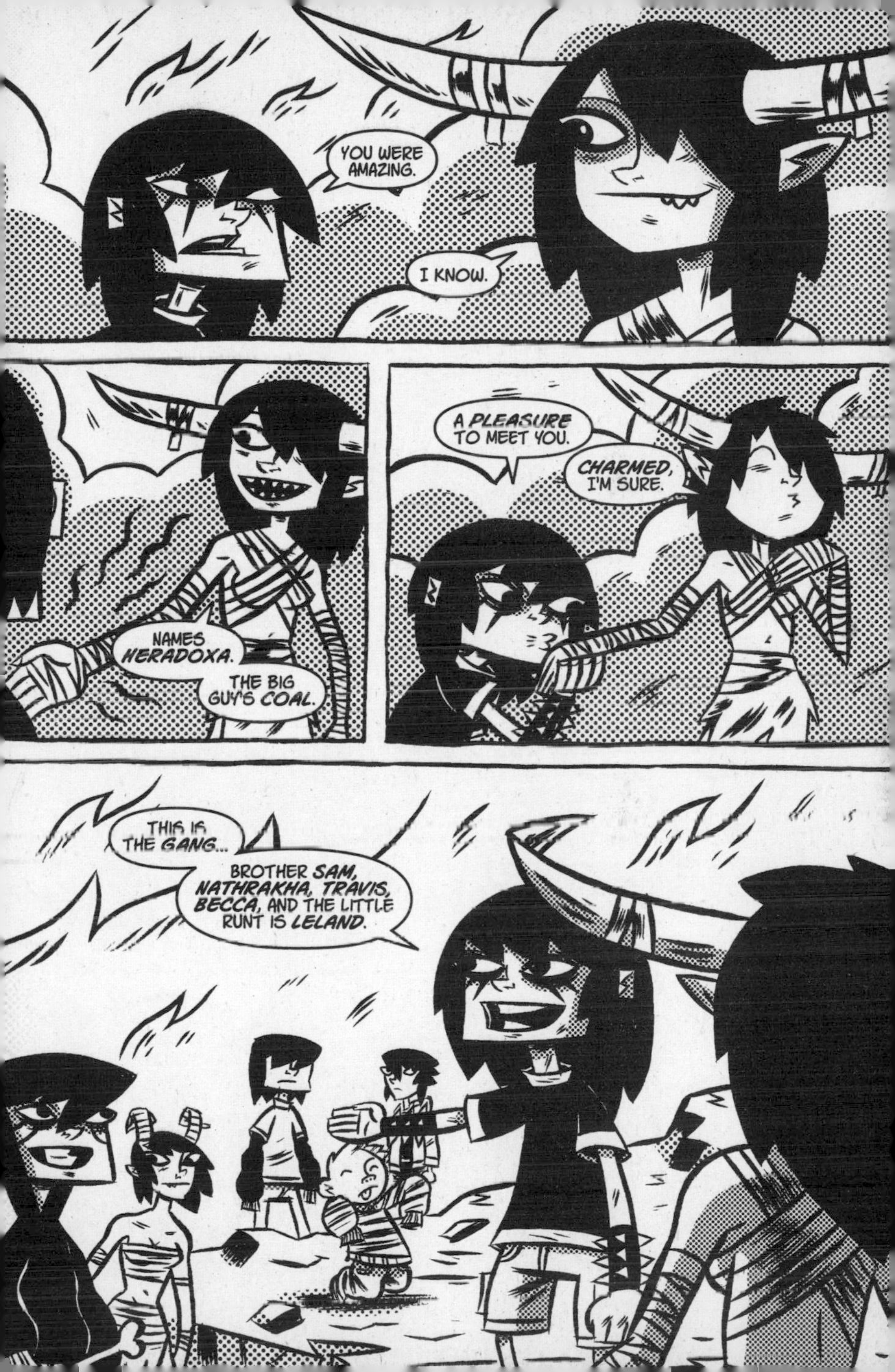
YOU WERE AMAZING.
I KNOW.
NAMES NERADOXA.
THE BIG GUY'S COAL.
A PLEASURE TO MEET YOU.
CHARMED, I'M SURE.
THIS IS THE GANG...
BROTHER SAM, NATHRAKHA, TRAVIS, BECCA, AND THE LITTLE RUNT IS LELAND.

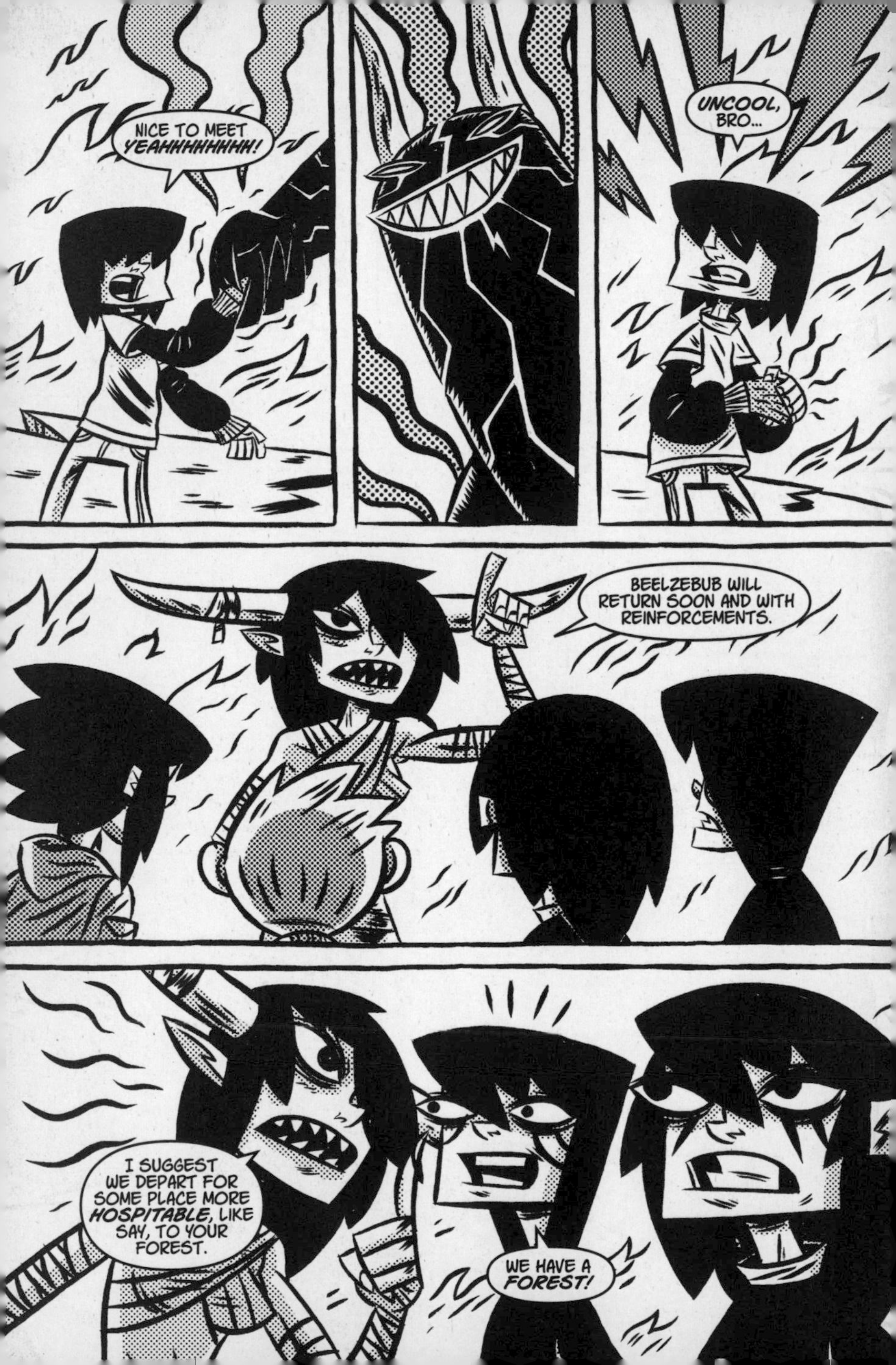
NICE TO MEET YEAHHHHHHHH!
UNCOOL, BRO...
BEELZEBUB WILL RETURN SOON AND WITH REINFORCEMENTS.
I SUGGEST WE DEPART FOR SOME PLACE MORE HOSPITABLE, LIKE SAY, TO YOUR FOREST.
WE HAVE A FOREST!

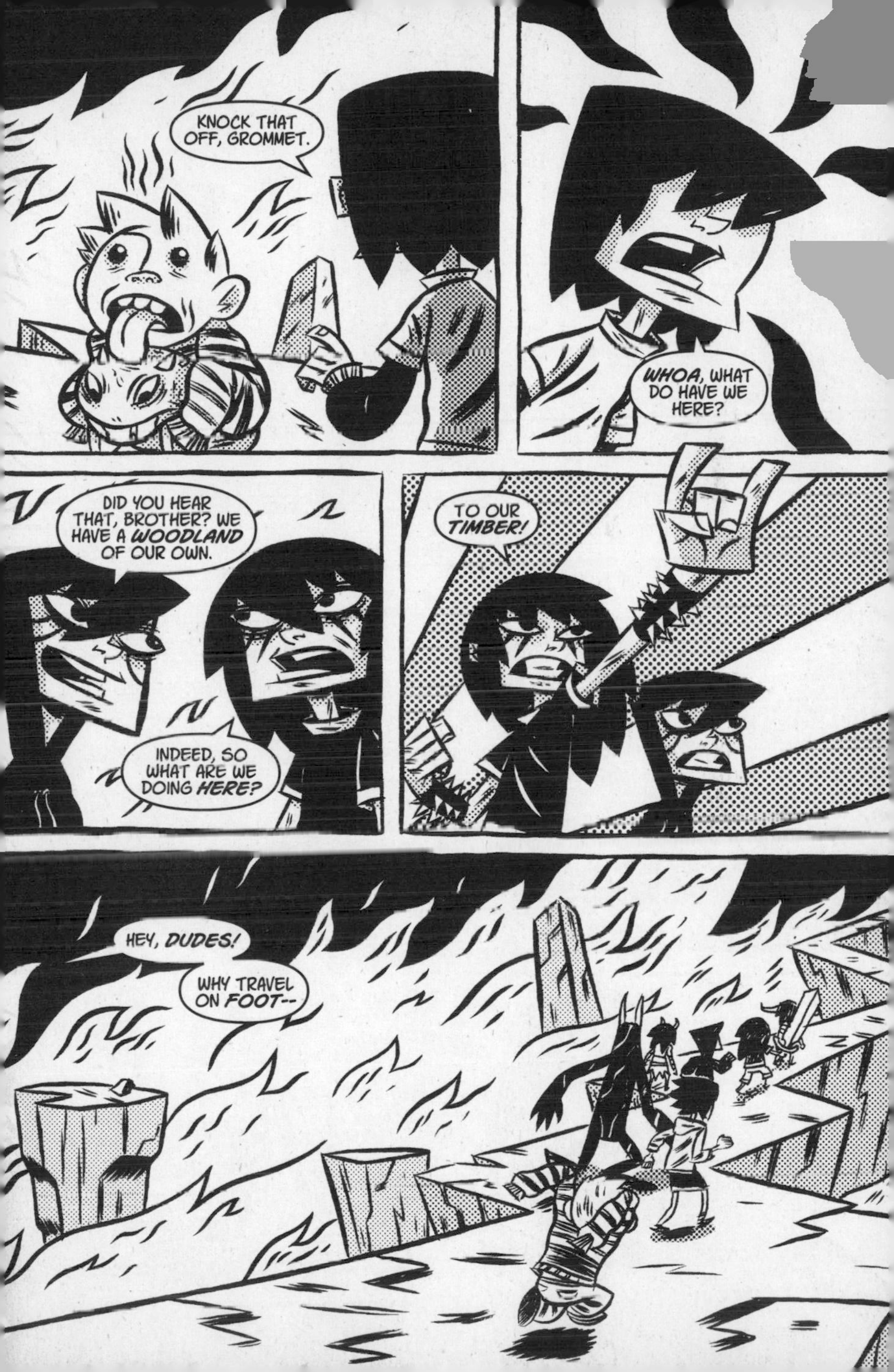
KNOCK THAT OFF, GROMMET.
WHOA, WHAT DO HAVE WE HERE?
DID YOU HEAR THAT, BROTHER? WE HAVE A WOODLAND OF OUR OWN.
INDEED, SO WHAT ARE WE DOING HERE?
TO OUR TIMBER!
HEY, DUDES!
WHY TRAVEL ON FOOT--

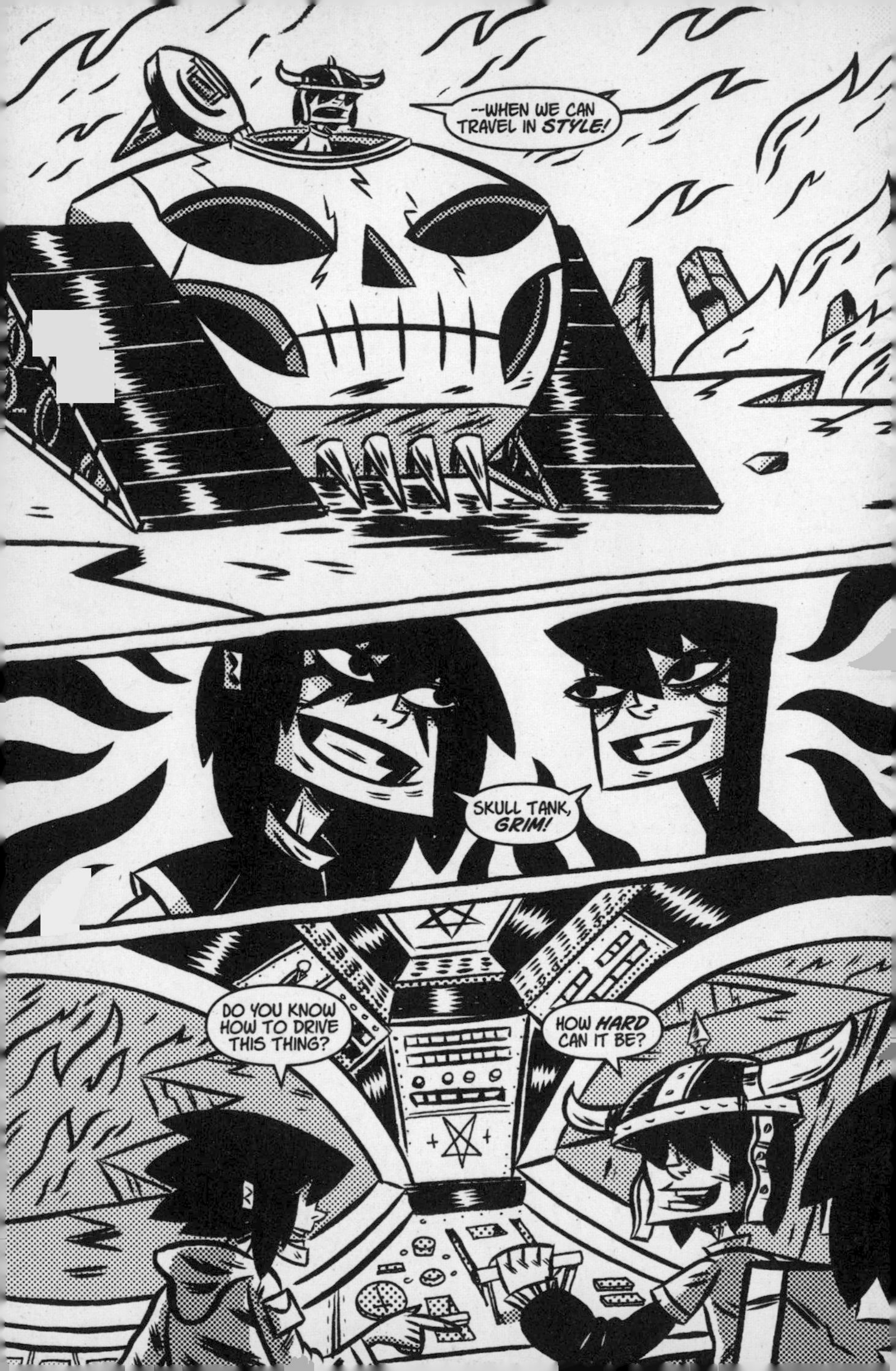
--WHEN WE CAN TRAVEL IN STYLE!
SKULL TANK, GRIM!
DO YOU KNOW HOW TO DRIVE THIS THING?
HOW HARD CAN IT BE?

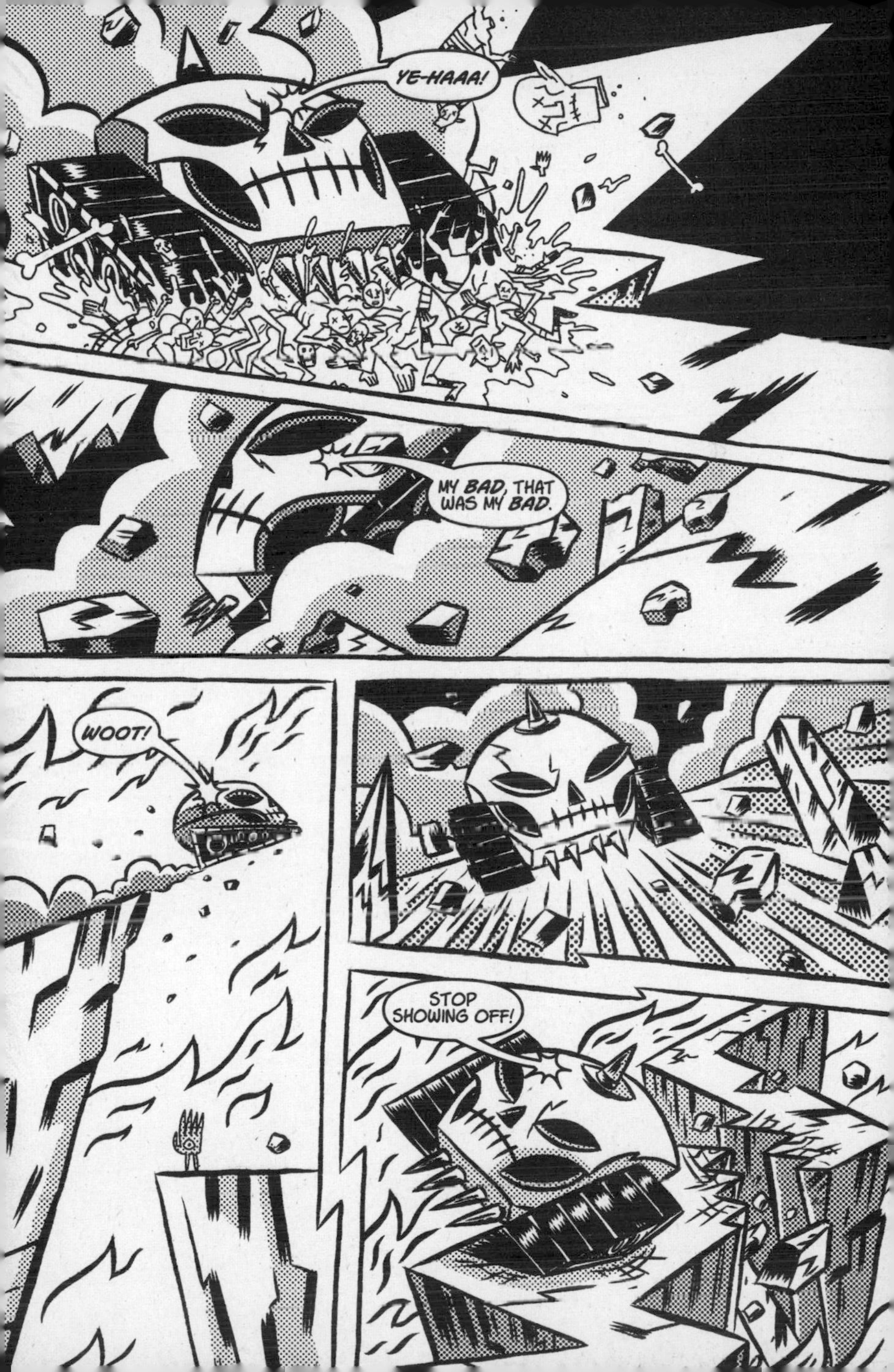
YE-HAAA!
MY BAD, THAT WAS MY BAD.
WOOT!
STOP SHOWING OFF!

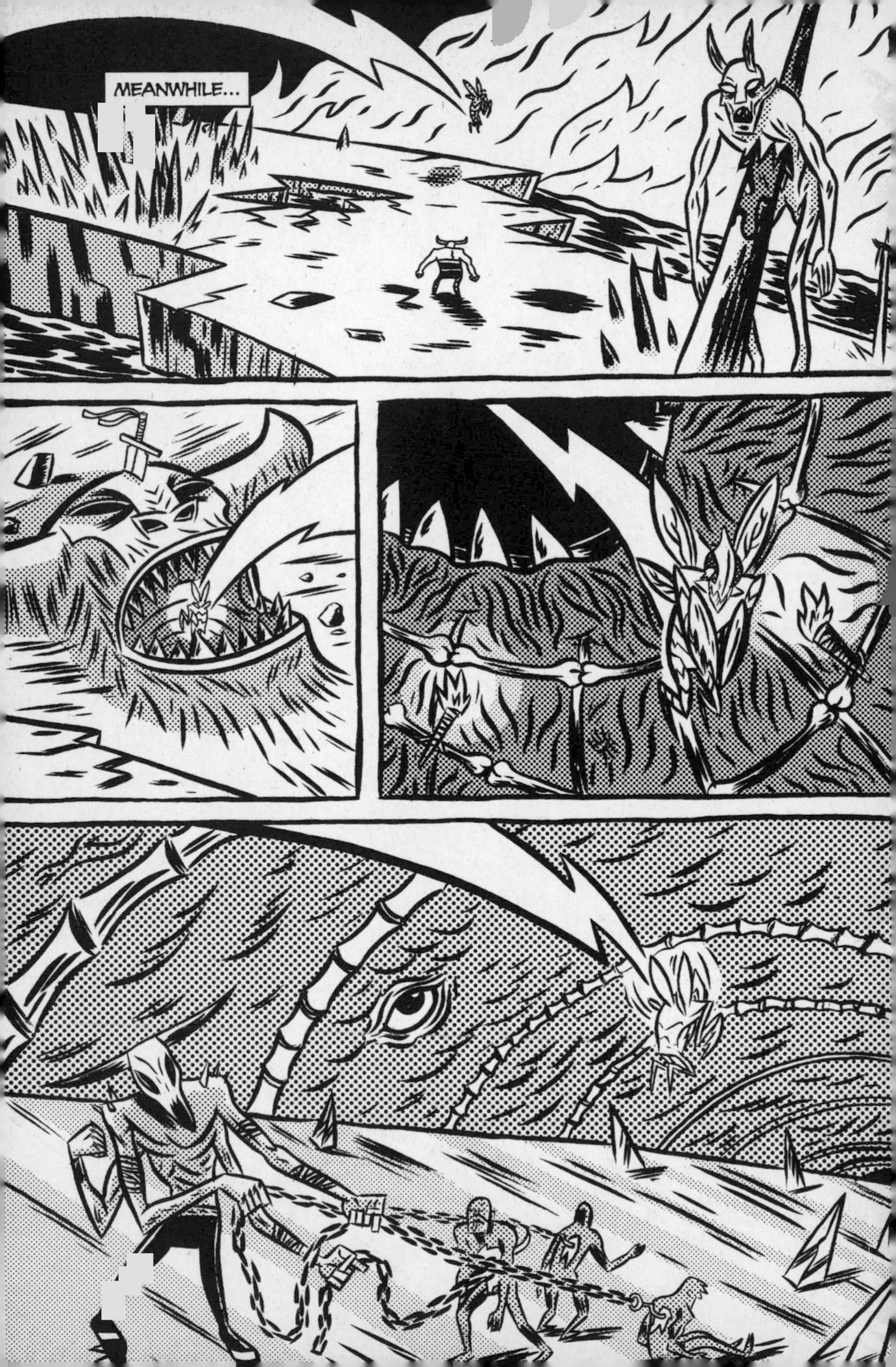
MEANWHILE...

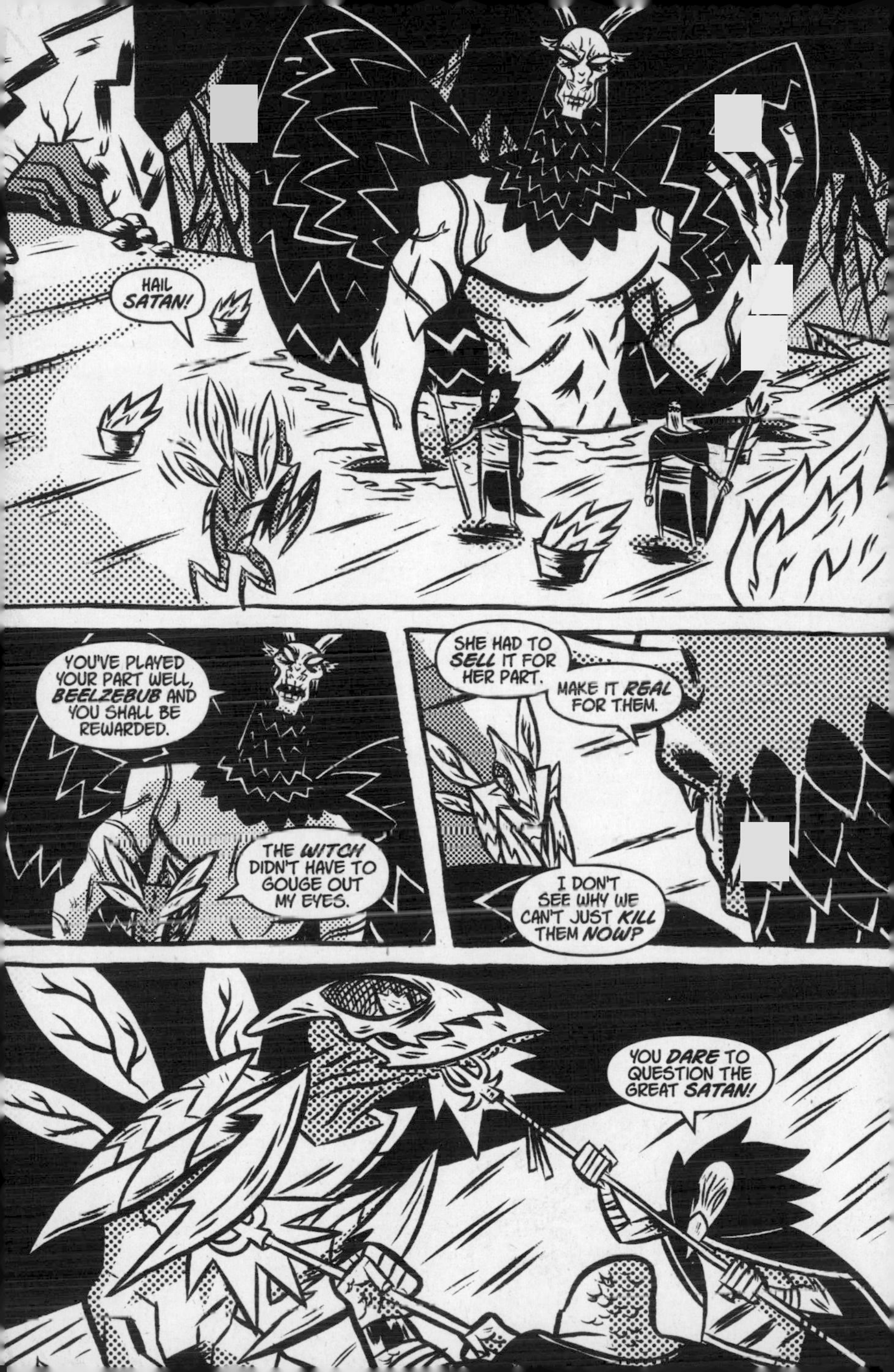
HAIL SATAN!
YOU'VE PLAYED YOUR PART WELL, BEELZEBUB AND YOU SHALL BE REWARDED.
THE WITCH DIDN'T HAVE TO GOUGE OUT MY EYES.
SHE HAD TO SELL IT FOR HER PART.
MAKE IT REAL FOR THEM.
I DON'T SEE WHY WE CAN'T JUST KILL THEM NOW?
YOU DARE TO QUESTION THE GREAT SATAN!

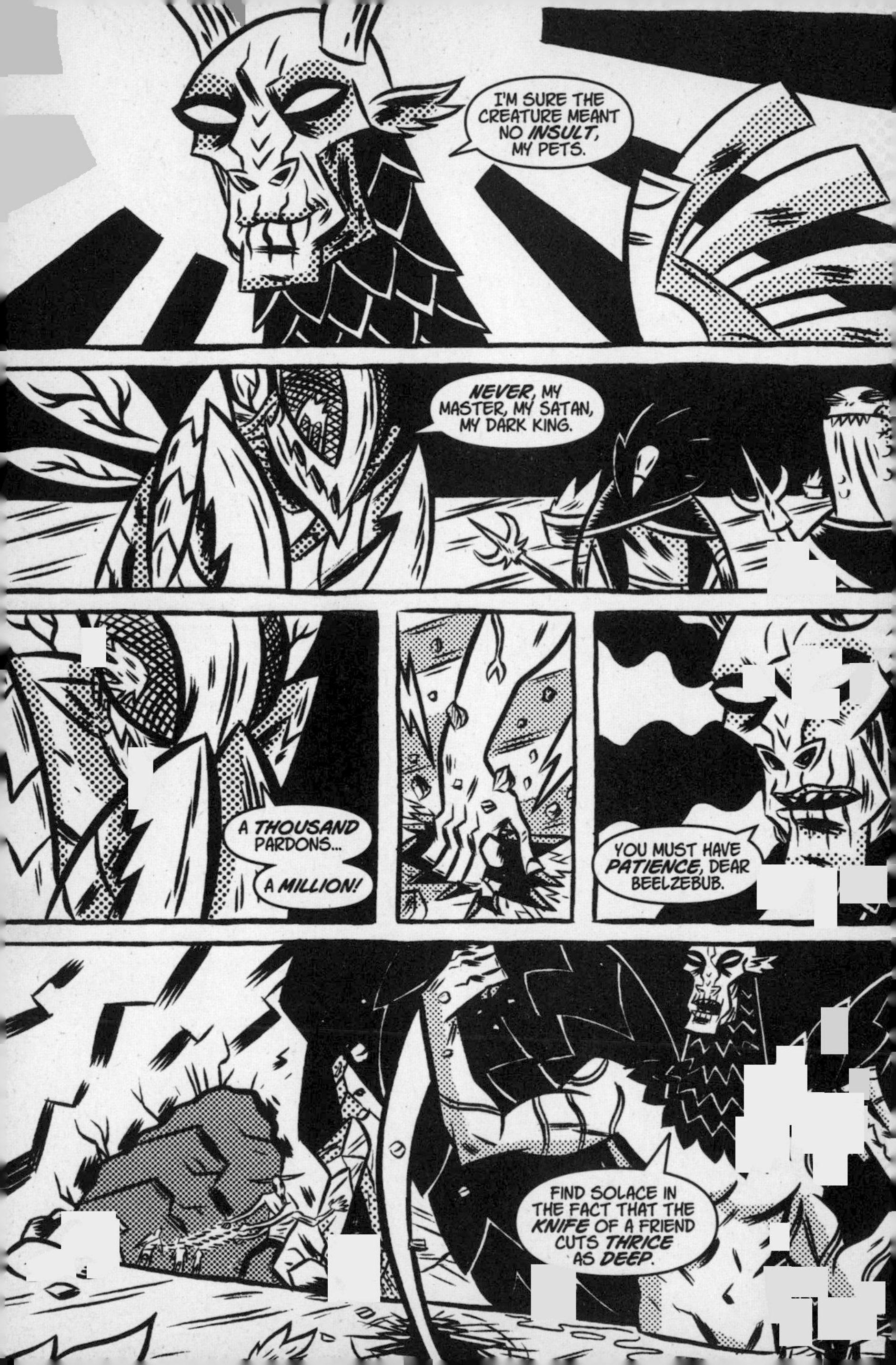
I'M SURE THE CREATURE MEANT NO *INSULT*, MY PETS.
NEVER, MY MASTER, MY SATAN, MY DARK KING.
A *THOUSAND* PARDONS...
A *MILLION!*
YOU MUST HAVE *PATIENCE*, DEAR BEELZEBUB.
FIND SOLACE IN THE FACT THAT THE *KNIFE* OF A FRIEND CUTS *THRICE* AS *DEEP*.

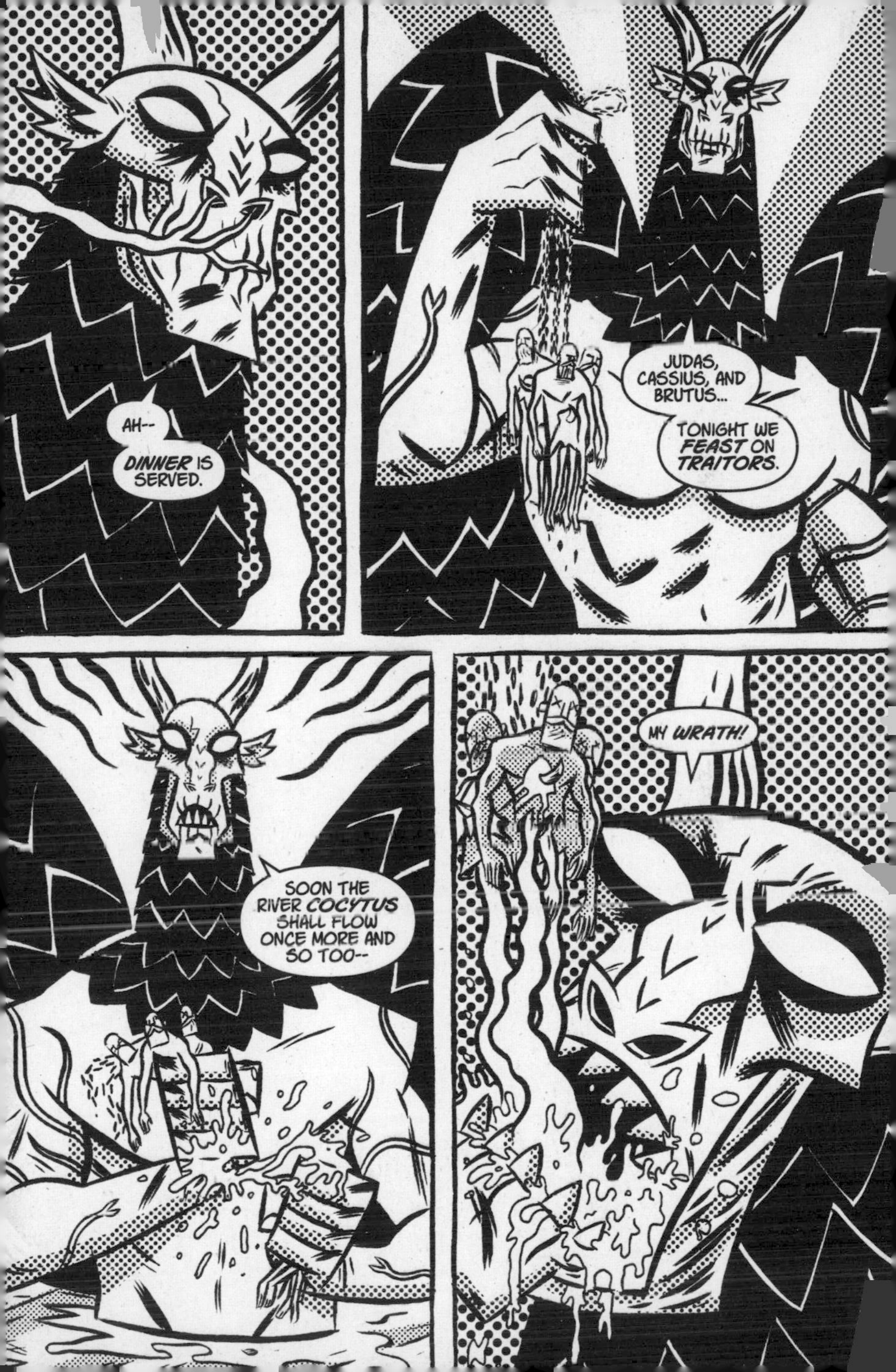
AH--
DINNER IS SERVED.
JUDAS, CASSIUS, AND BRUTUS...
TONIGHT WE FEAST ON TRAITORS.
SOON THE RIVER COCYTUS SHALL FLOW ONCE MORE AND SO TOO--
MY WRATH!

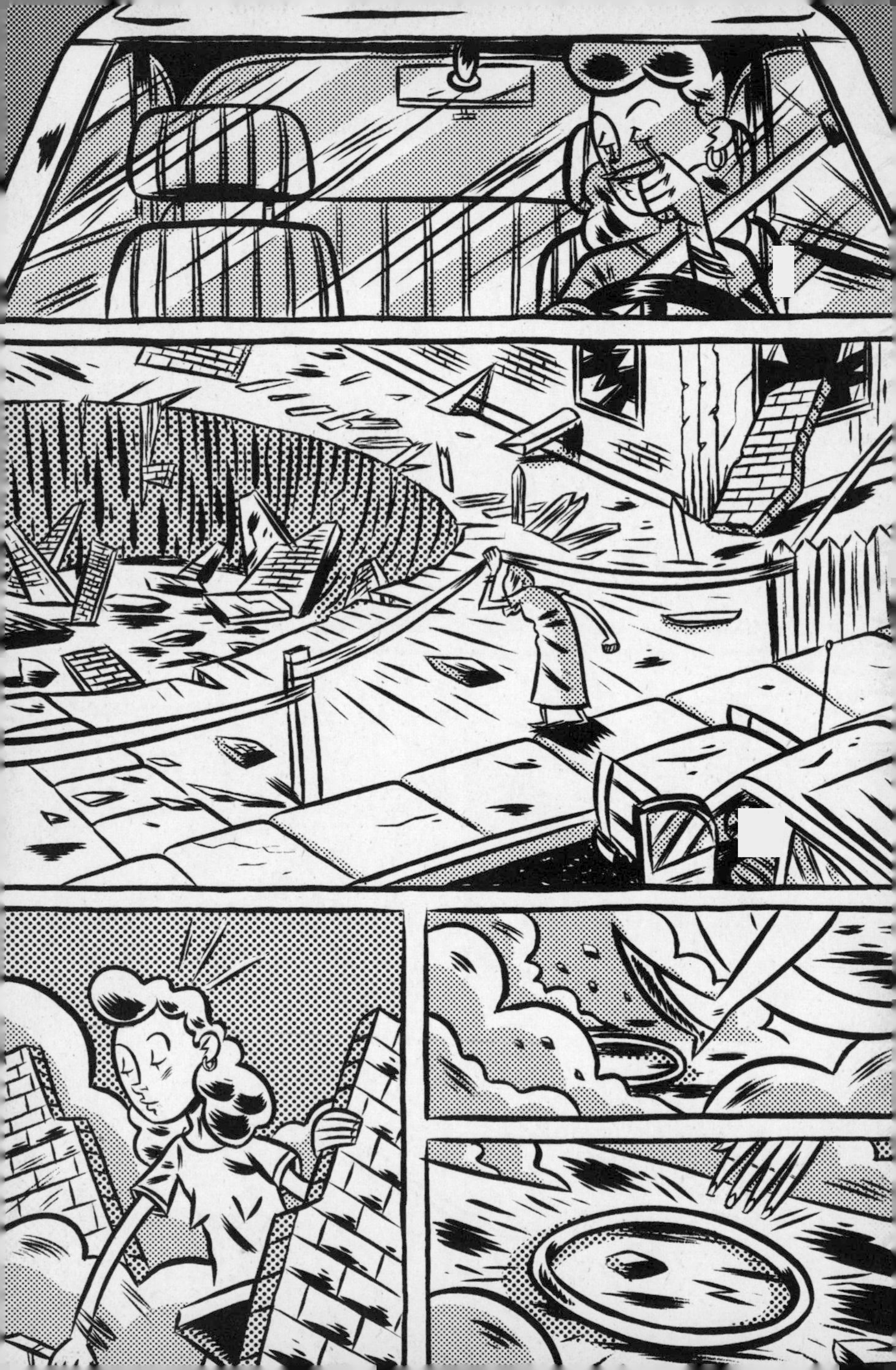

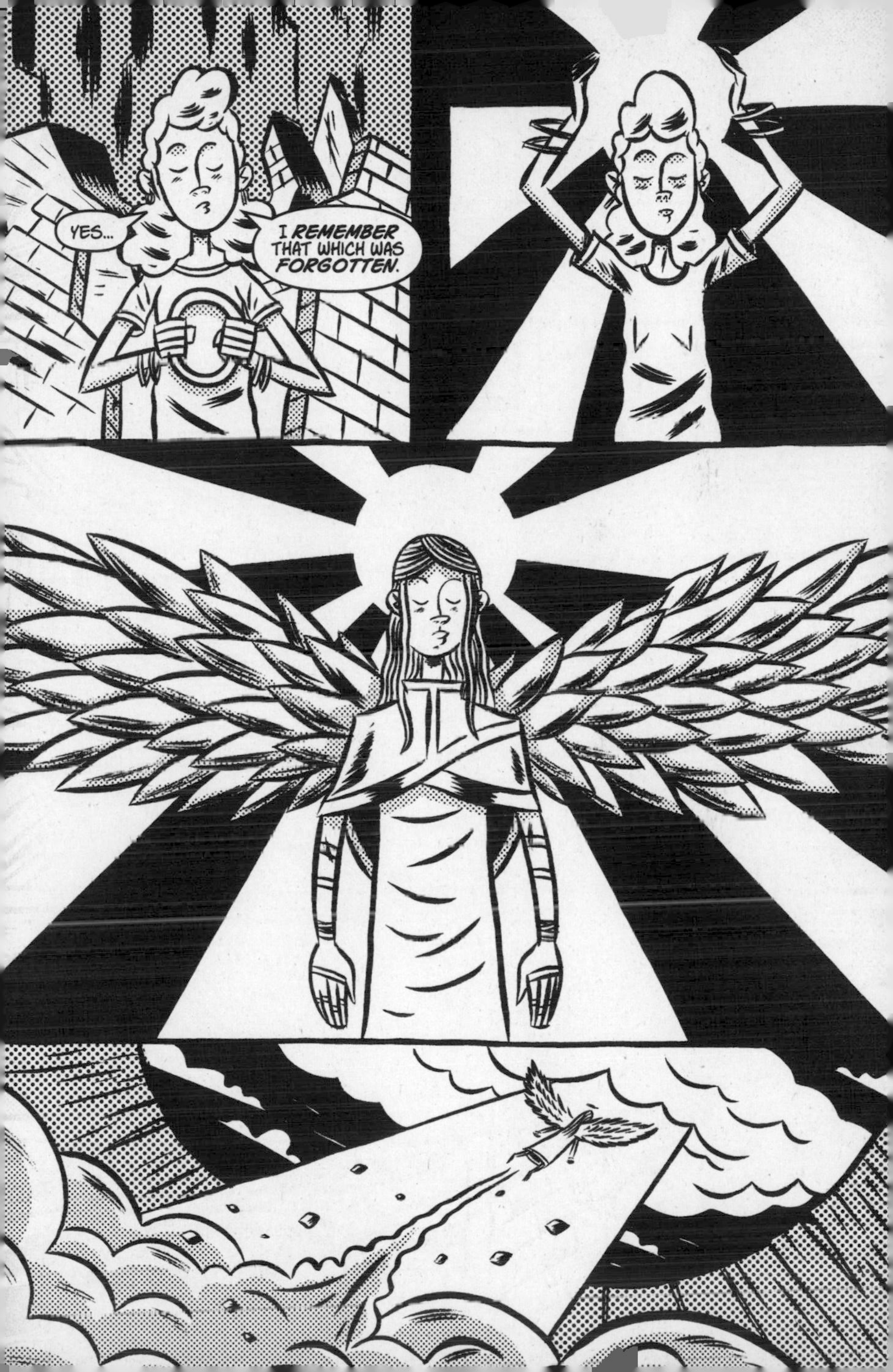
YES...
I *REMEMBER* THAT WHICH WAS *FORGOTTEN.*

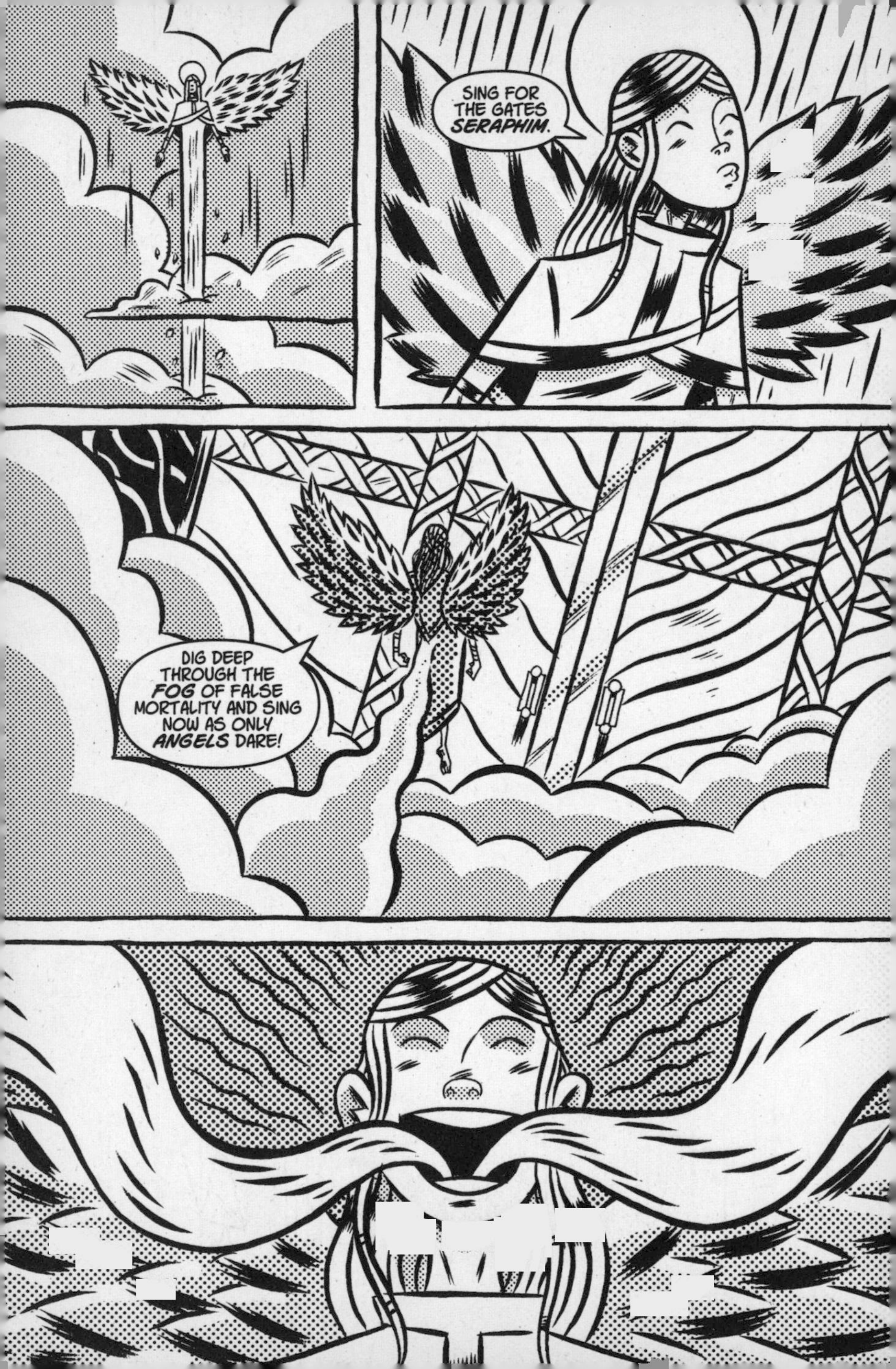
SING FOR THE GATES SERAPHIM.
DIG DEEP THROUGH THE FOG OF FALSE MORTALITY AND SING NOW AS ONLY ANGELS DARE!

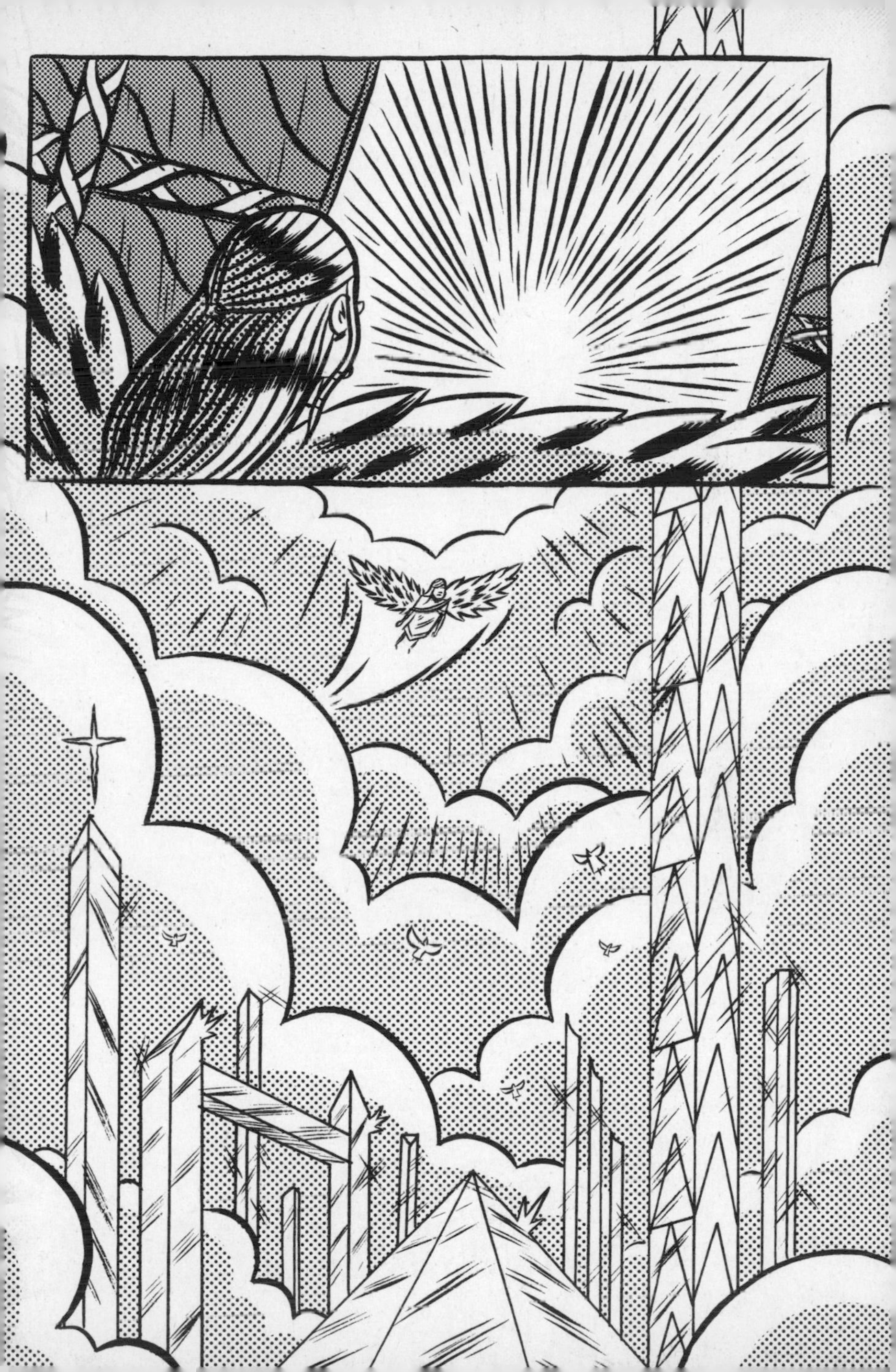

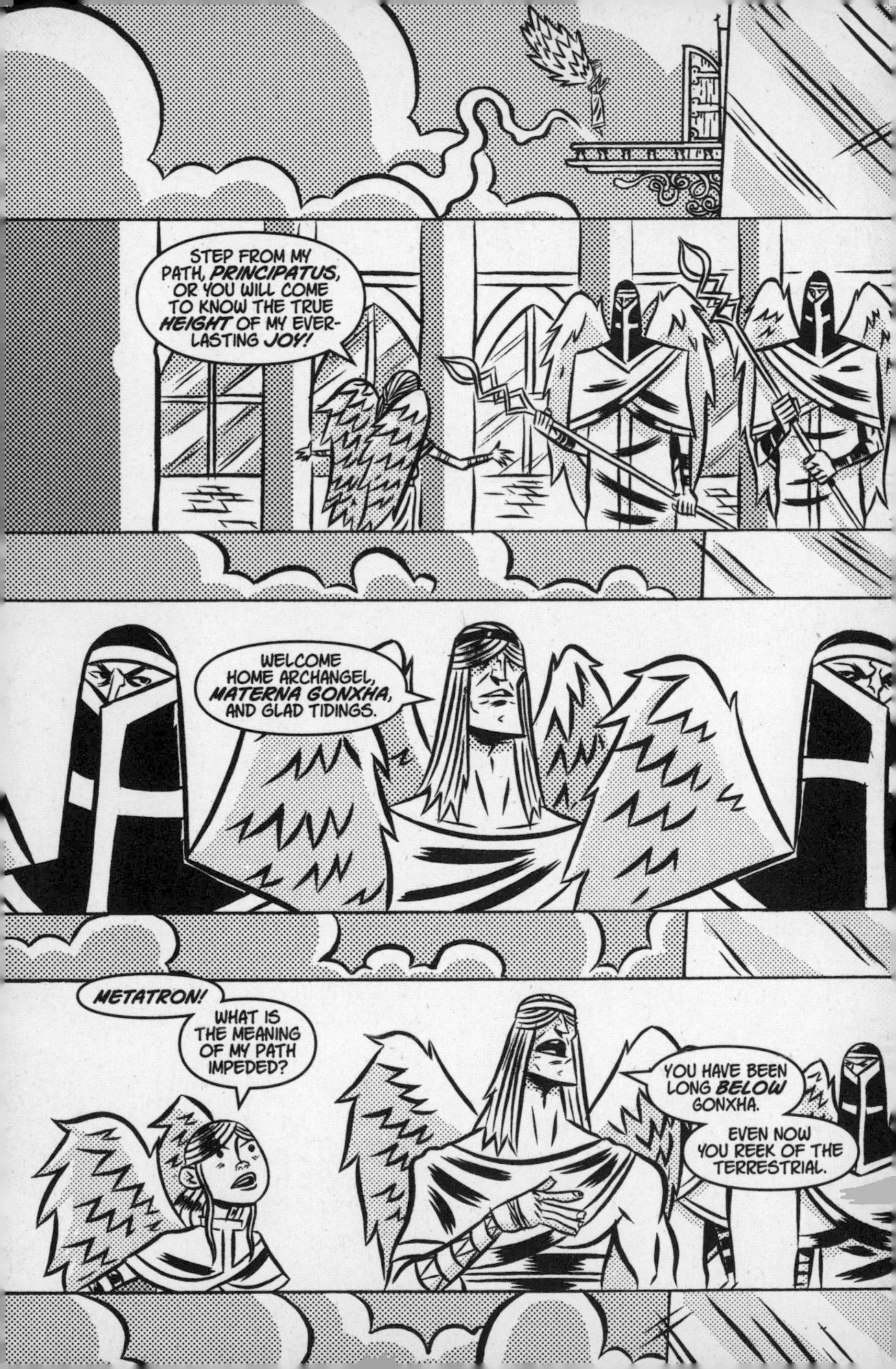
STEP FROM MY PATH, PRINCIPATUS, OR YOU WILL COME TO KNOW THE TRUE HEIGHT OF MY EVER-LASTING JOY!
WELCOME HOME ARCHANGEL, MATERNA GONXHA, AND GLAD TIDINGS.
METATRON!
WHAT IS THE MEANING OF MY PATH IMPEDED?
YOU HAVE BEEN LONG BELOW GONXHA.
EVEN NOW YOU REEK OF THE TERRESTRIAL.

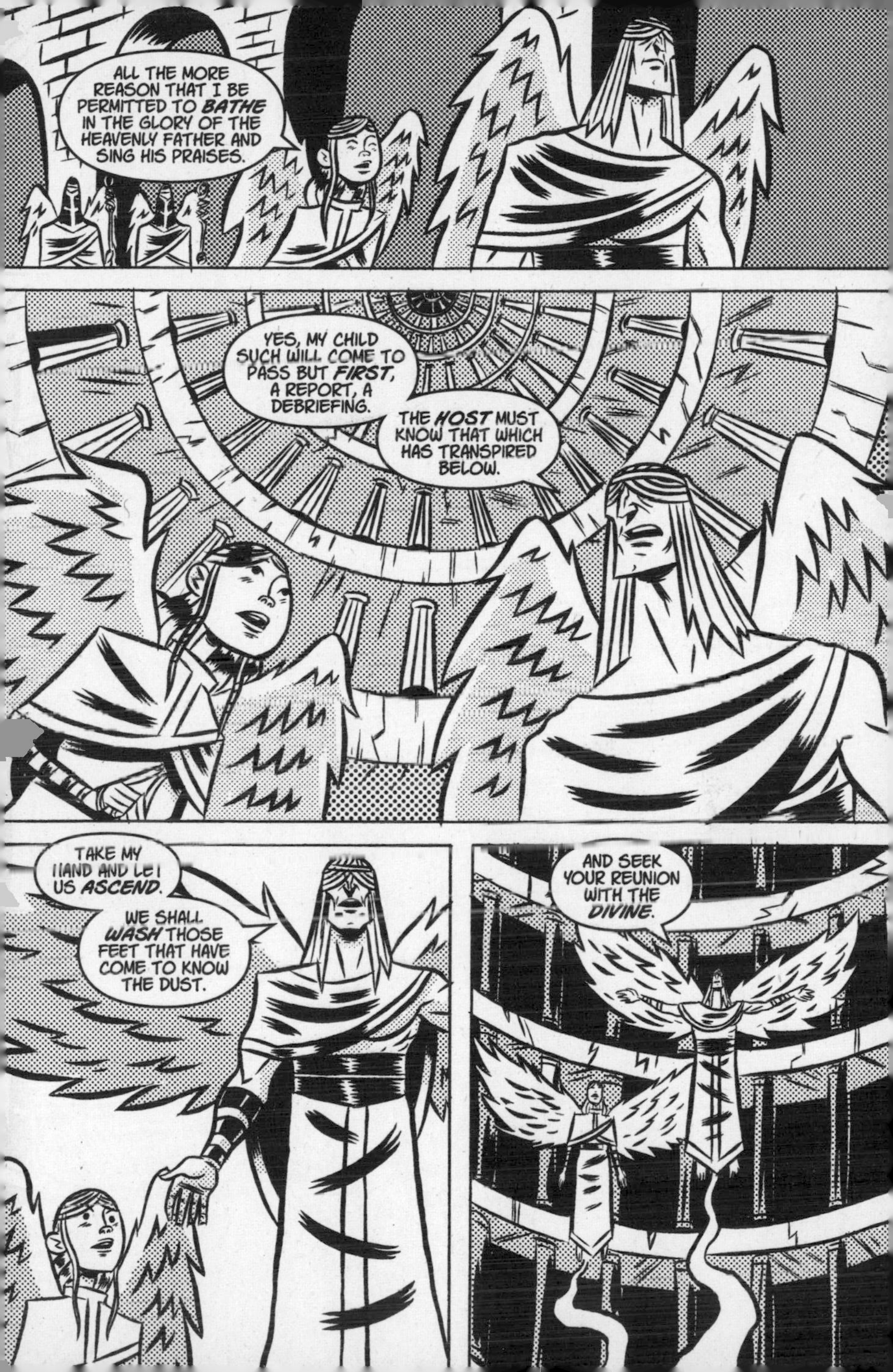
ALL THE MORE REASON THAT I BE PERMITTED TO *BATHE* IN THE GLORY OF THE HEAVENLY FATHER AND SING HIS PRAISES.
YES, MY CHILD SUCH WILL COME TO PASS BUT *FIRST*, A REPORT, A DEBRIEFING.
THE *HOST* MUST KNOW THAT WHICH HAS TRANSPIRED BELOW.
TAKE MY HAND AND LET US *ASCEND*.
WE SHALL *WASH* THOSE FEET THAT HAVE COME TO KNOW THE DUST.
AND SEEK YOUR REUNION WITH THE *DIVINE*.

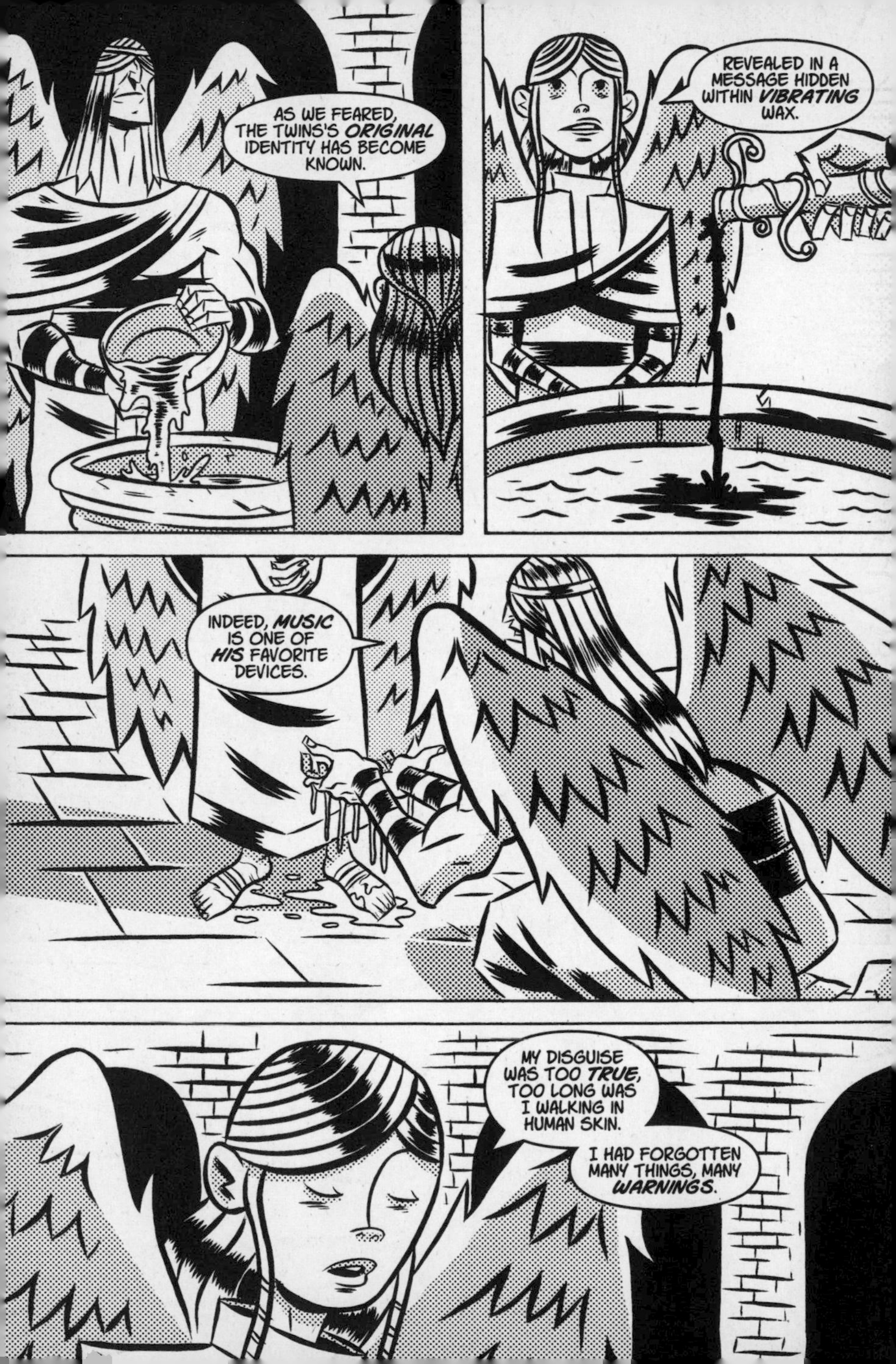
AS WE FEARED, THE TWINS'S *ORIGINAL* IDENTITY HAS BECOME KNOWN.
REVEALED IN A MESSAGE HIDDEN WITHIN *VIBRATING* WAX.
INDEED, *MUSIC* IS ONE OF *HIS* FAVORITE DEVICES.
MY DISGUISE WAS TOO *TRUE*, TOO LONG WAS I WALKING IN HUMAN SKIN.
I HAD FORGOTTEN MANY THINGS, MANY *WARNINGS*.

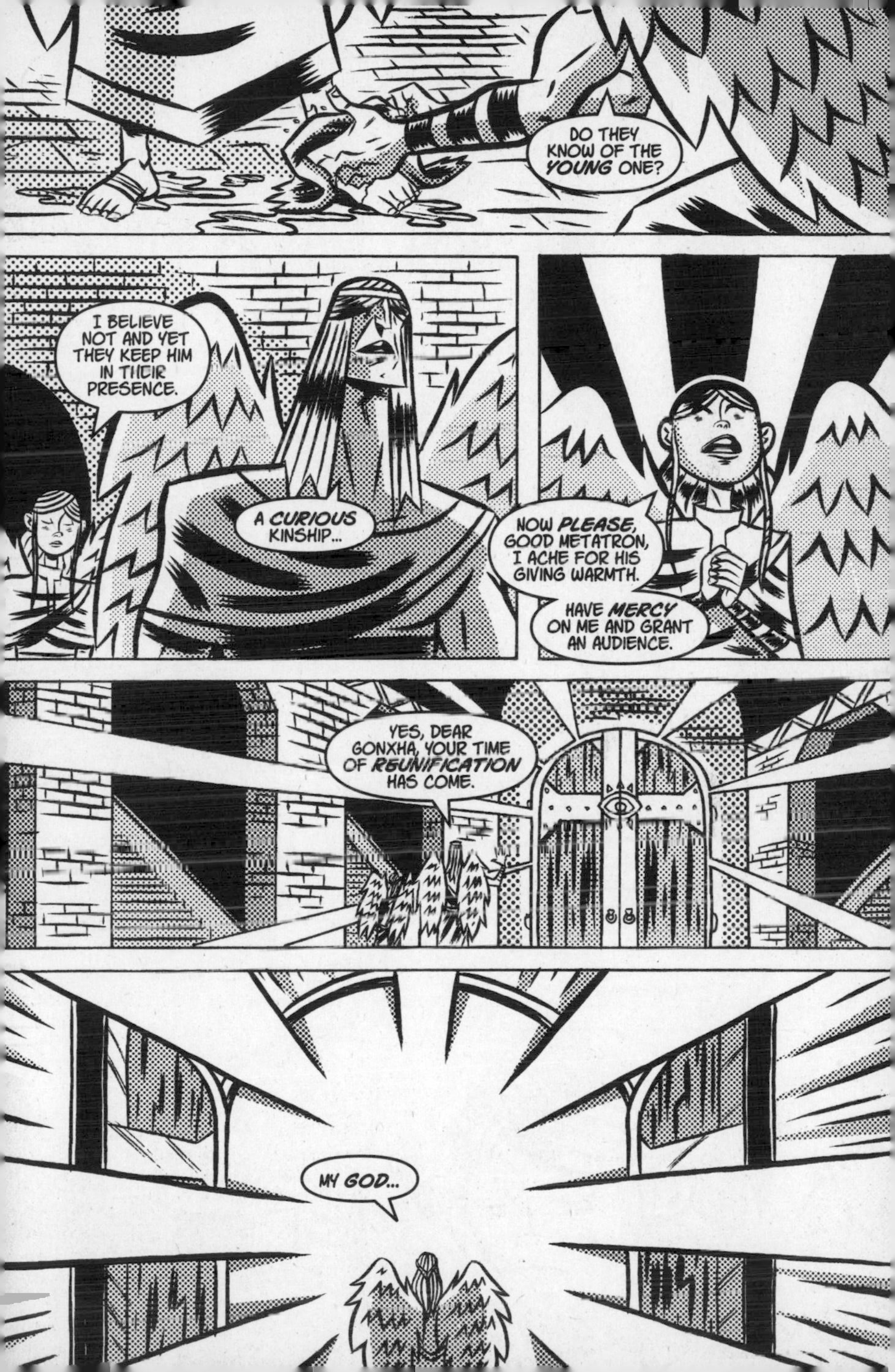
DO THEY KNOW OF THE *YOUNG* ONE?
I BELIEVE NOT AND YET THEY KEEP HIM IN THEIR PRESENCE.
A *CURIOUS* KINSHIP...
NOW *PLEASE*, GOOD METATRON, I ACHE FOR HIS GIVING WARMTH.
HAVE *MERCY* ON ME AND GRANT AN AUDIENCE.
YES, DEAR GONXHA, YOUR TIME OF *REUNIFICATION* HAS COME.
MY *GOD*...

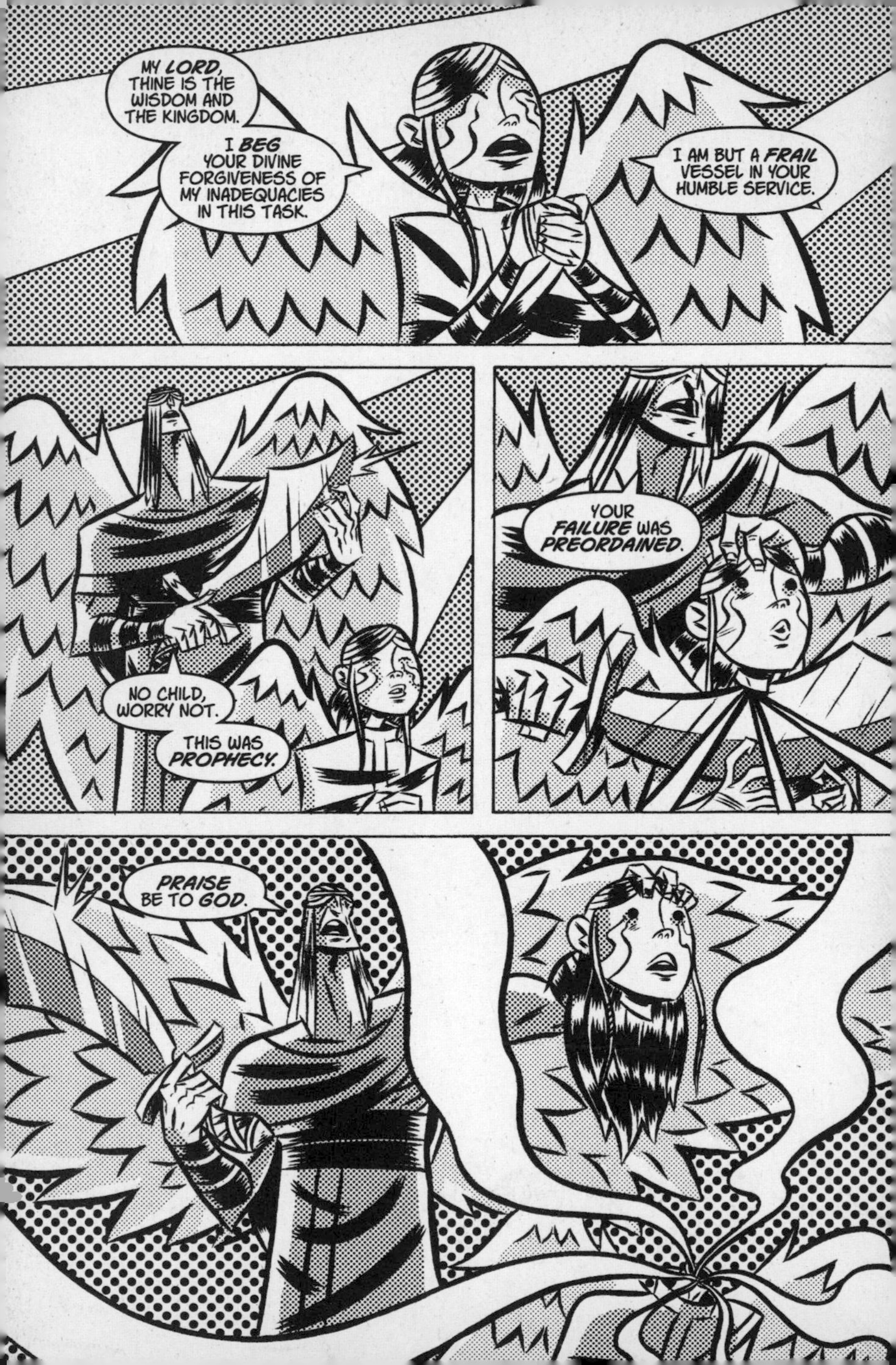
MY LORD, THINE IS THE WISDOM AND THE KINGDOM.
I BEG YOUR DIVINE FORGIVENESS OF MY INADEQUACIES IN THIS TASK.
I AM BUT A FRAIL VESSEL IN YOUR HUMBLE SERVICE.
NO CHILD, WORRY NOT.
THIS WAS PROPHECY.
YOUR FAILURE WAS PREORDAINED.
PRAISE BE TO GOD.

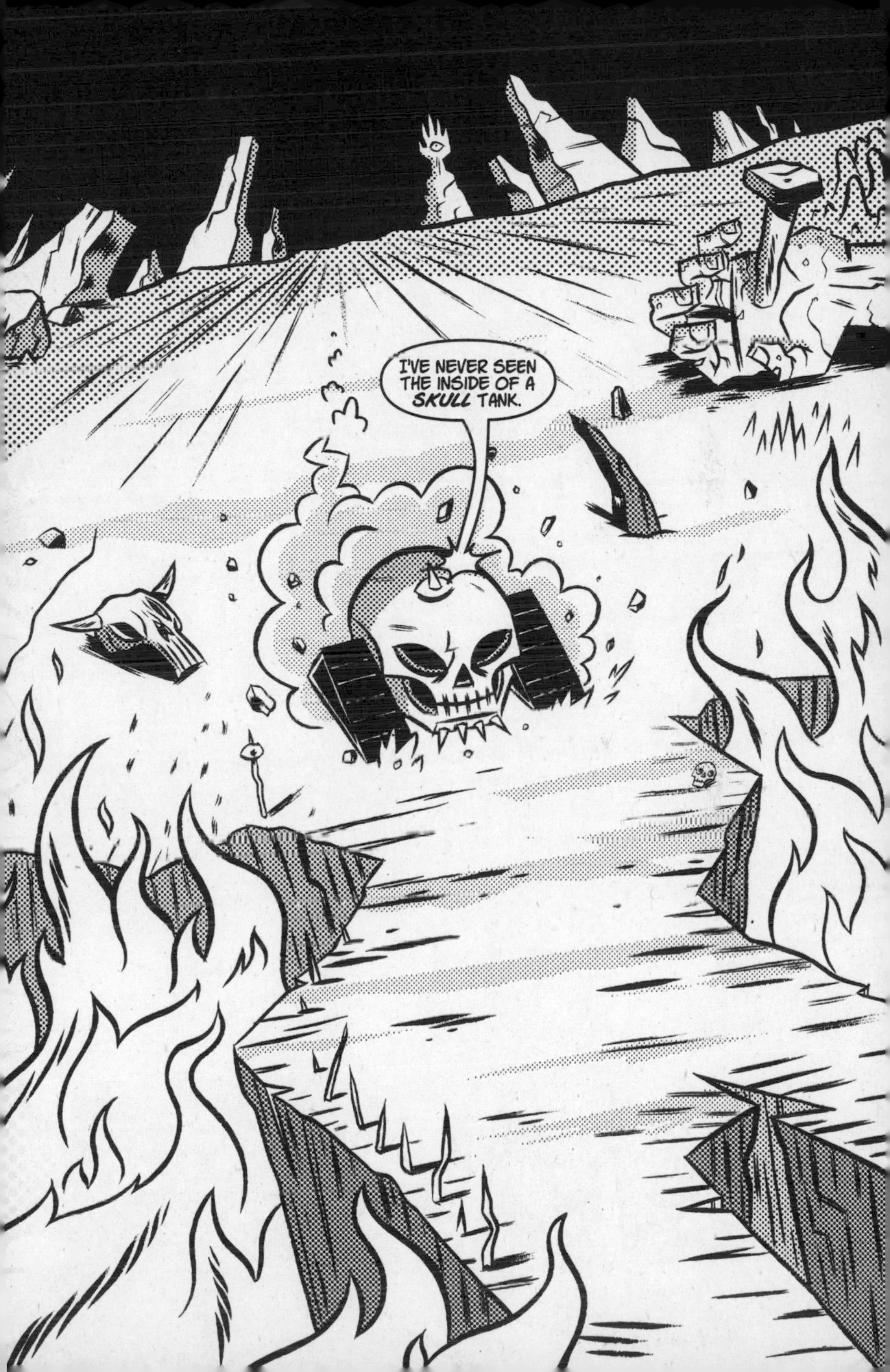
I'VE NEVER SEEN THE INSIDE OF A SKULL TANK.

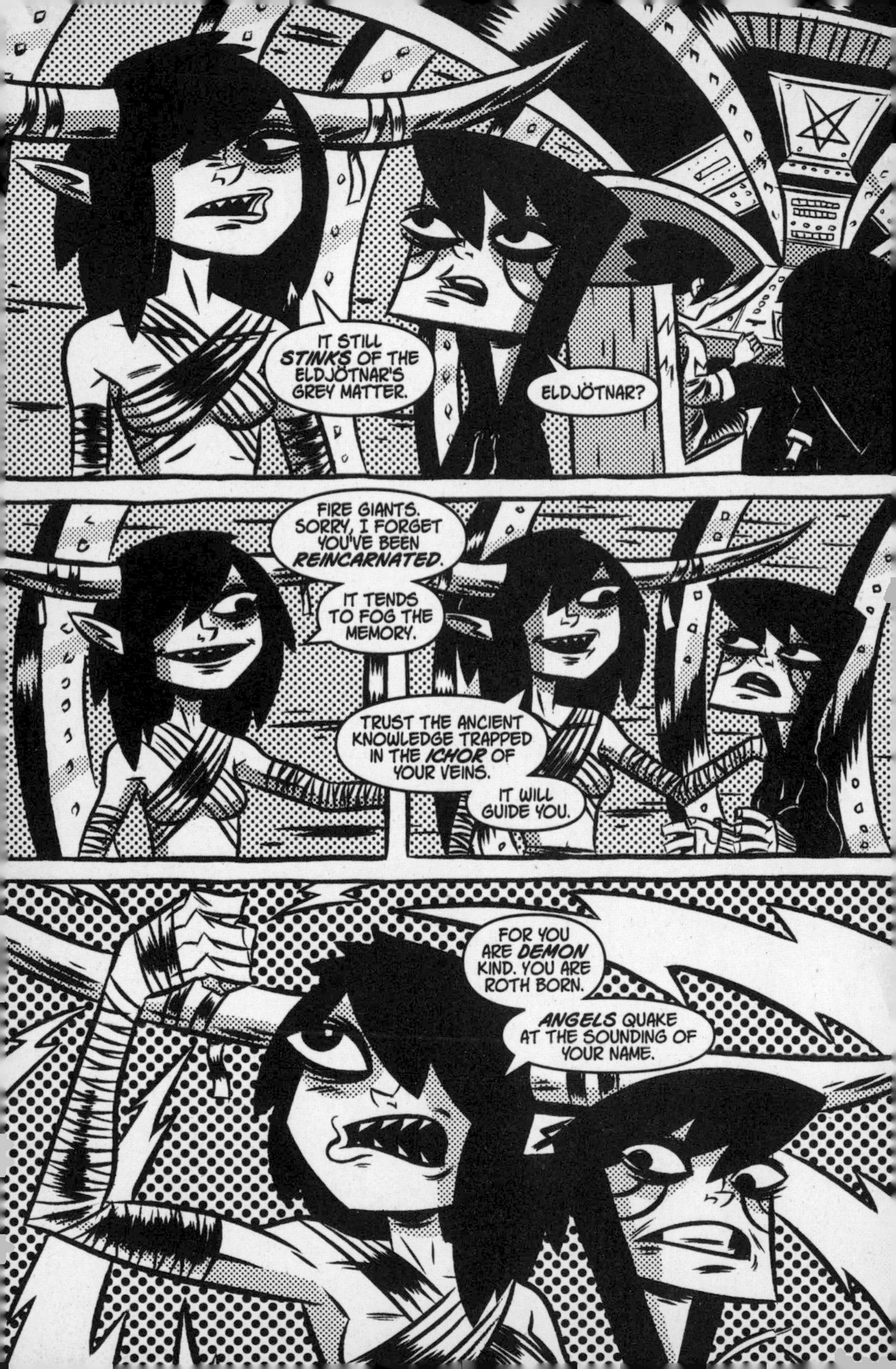
IT STILL STINKS OF THE ELDJÖTNAR'S GREY MATTER.
ELDJÖTNAR?
FIRE GIANTS. SORRY, I FORGET YOU'VE BEEN REINCARNATED.
IT TENDS TO FOG THE MEMORY.
TRUST THE ANCIENT KNOWLEDGE TRAPPED IN THE ICHOR OF YOUR VEINS.
IT WILL GUIDE YOU.
FOR YOU ARE DEMON KIND. YOU ARE ROTH BORN.
ANGELS QUAKE AT THE SOUNDING OF YOUR NAME.

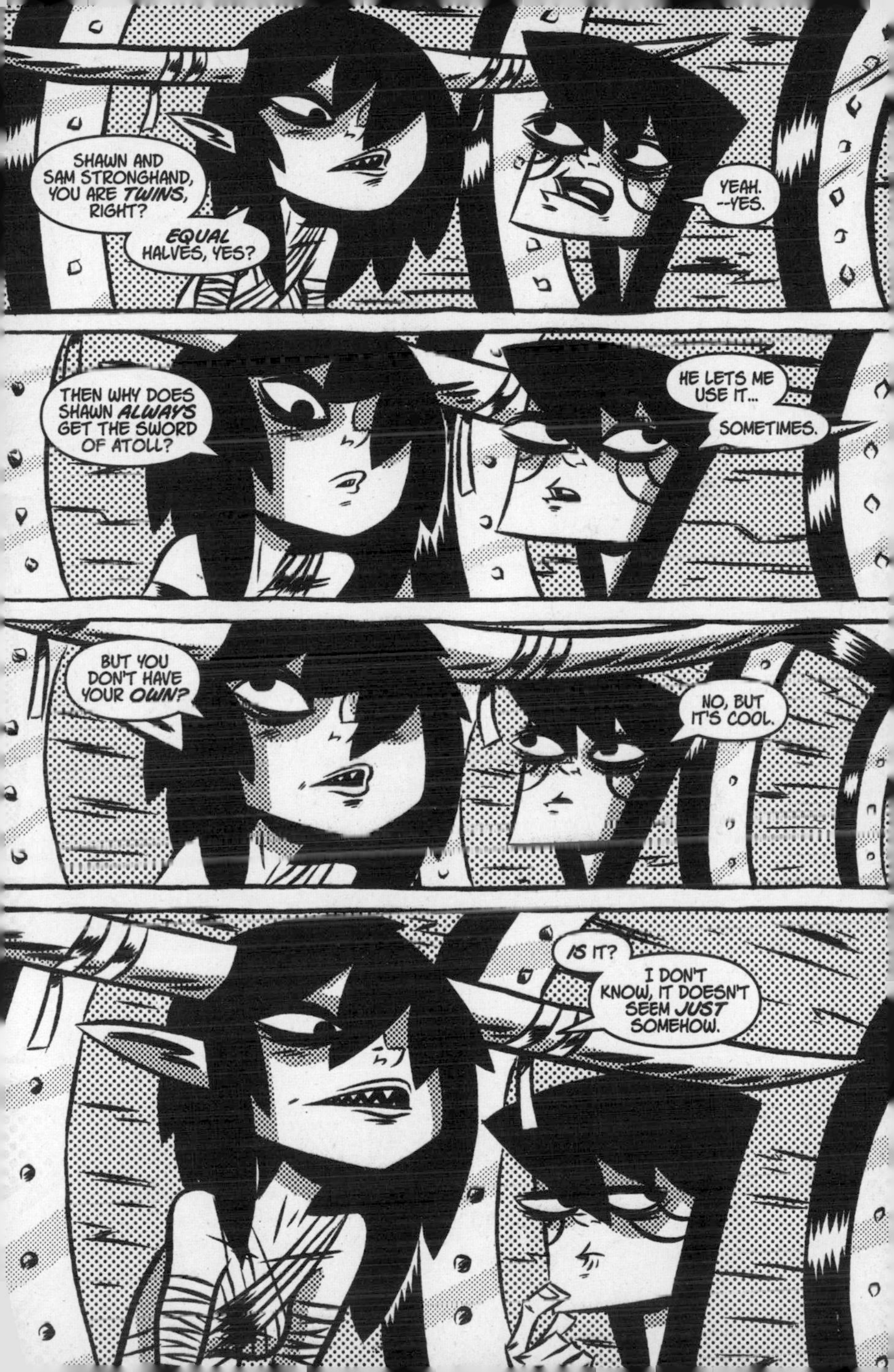
SHAWN AND SAM STRONGHAND, YOU ARE *TWINS*, RIGHT?
EQUAL HALVES, YES?
YEAH. --YES.
THEN WHY DOES SHAWN *ALWAYS* GET THE SWORD OF ATOLL?
HE LETS ME USE IT...
SOMETIMES.
BUT YOU DON'T HAVE YOUR *OWN*?
NO, BUT IT'S COOL.
IS IT?
I DON'T KNOW, IT DOESN'T SEEM *JUST* SOMEHOW.

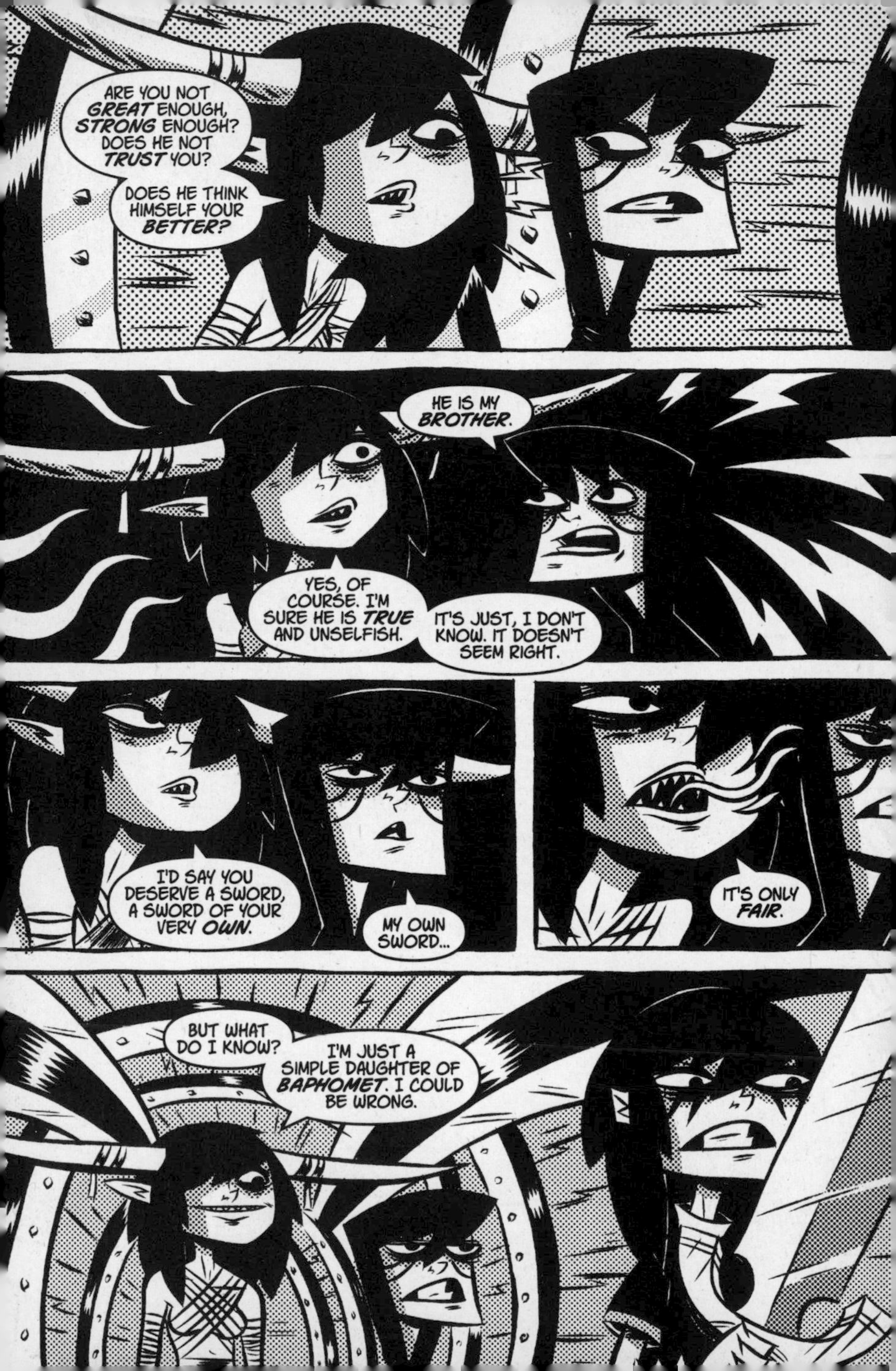
ARE YOU NOT GREAT ENOUGH, STRONG ENOUGH? DOES HE NOT TRUST YOU?
DOES HE THINK HIMSELF YOUR BETTER?
HE IS MY BROTHER.
YES, OF COURSE. I'M SURE HE IS TRUE AND UNSELFISH.
IT'S JUST, I DON'T KNOW. IT DOESN'T SEEM RIGHT.
I'D SAY YOU DESERVE A SWORD, A SWORD OF YOUR VERY OWN.
MY OWN SWORD...
IT'S ONLY FAIR.
BUT WHAT DO I KNOW?
I'M JUST A SIMPLE DAUGHTER OF BAPHOMET. I COULD BE WRONG.

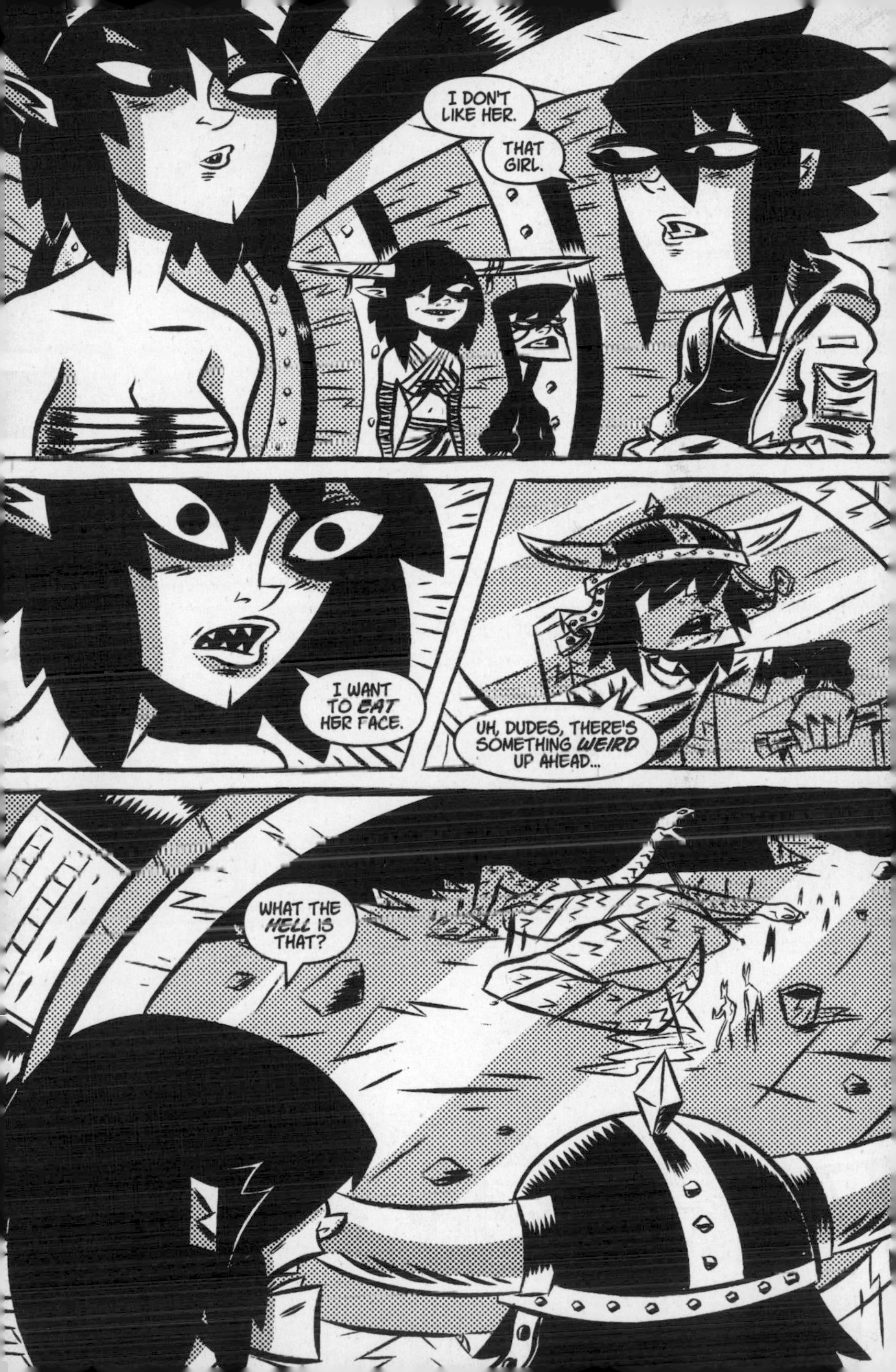
I DON'T LIKE HER.
THAT GIRL.
I WANT TO *EAT* HER FACE.
UH, DUDES, THERE'S SOMETHING *WEIRD* UP AHEAD...
WHAT THE *HELL* IS THAT?

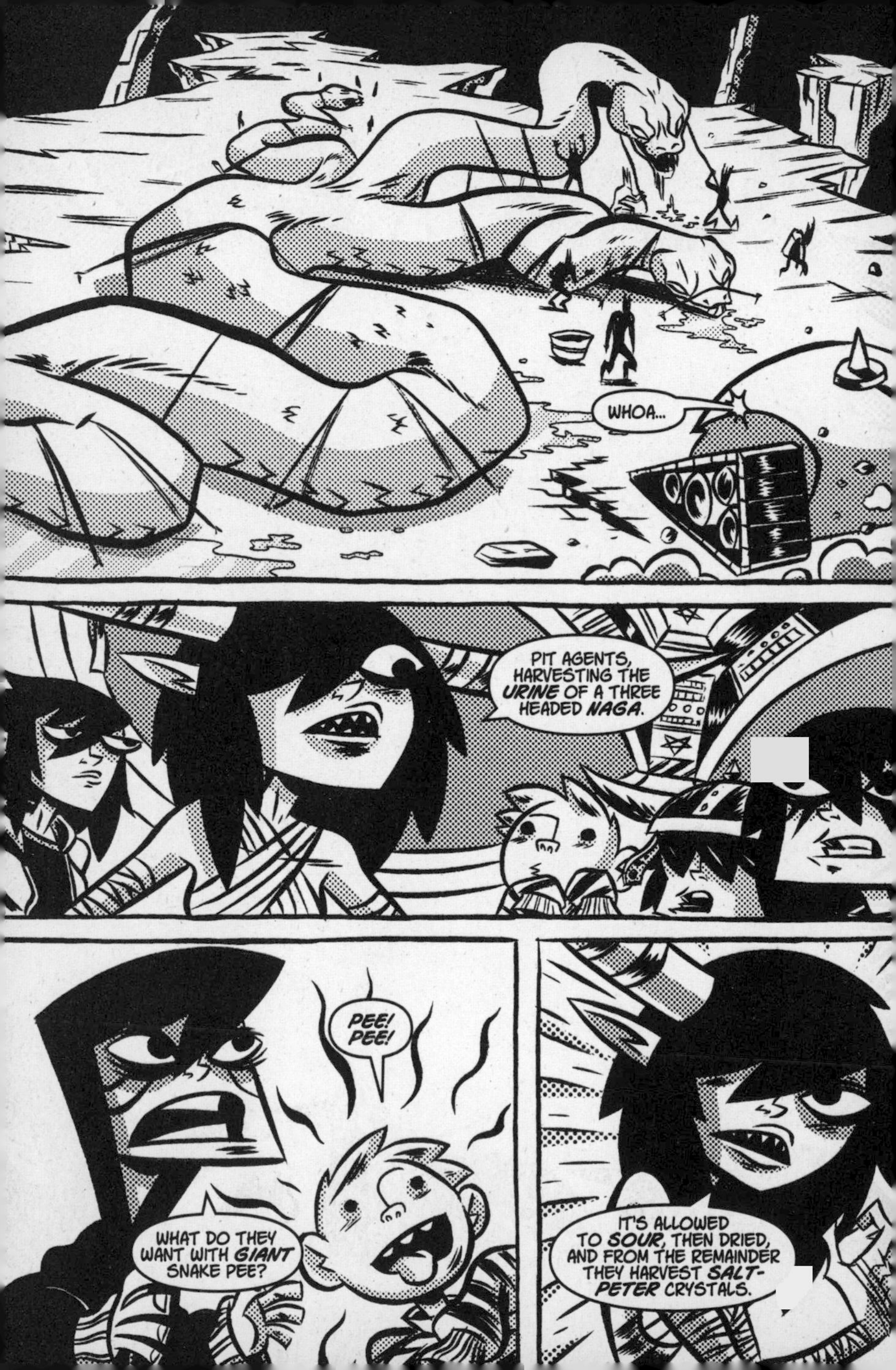
WHOA...
PIT AGENTS, HARVESTING THE URINE OF A THREE HEADED NAGA.
PEE! PEE!
WHAT DO THEY WANT WITH GIANT SNAKE PEE?
IT'S ALLOWED TO SOUR, THEN DRIED, AND FROM THE REMAINDER THEY HARVEST SALT-PETER CRYSTALS.

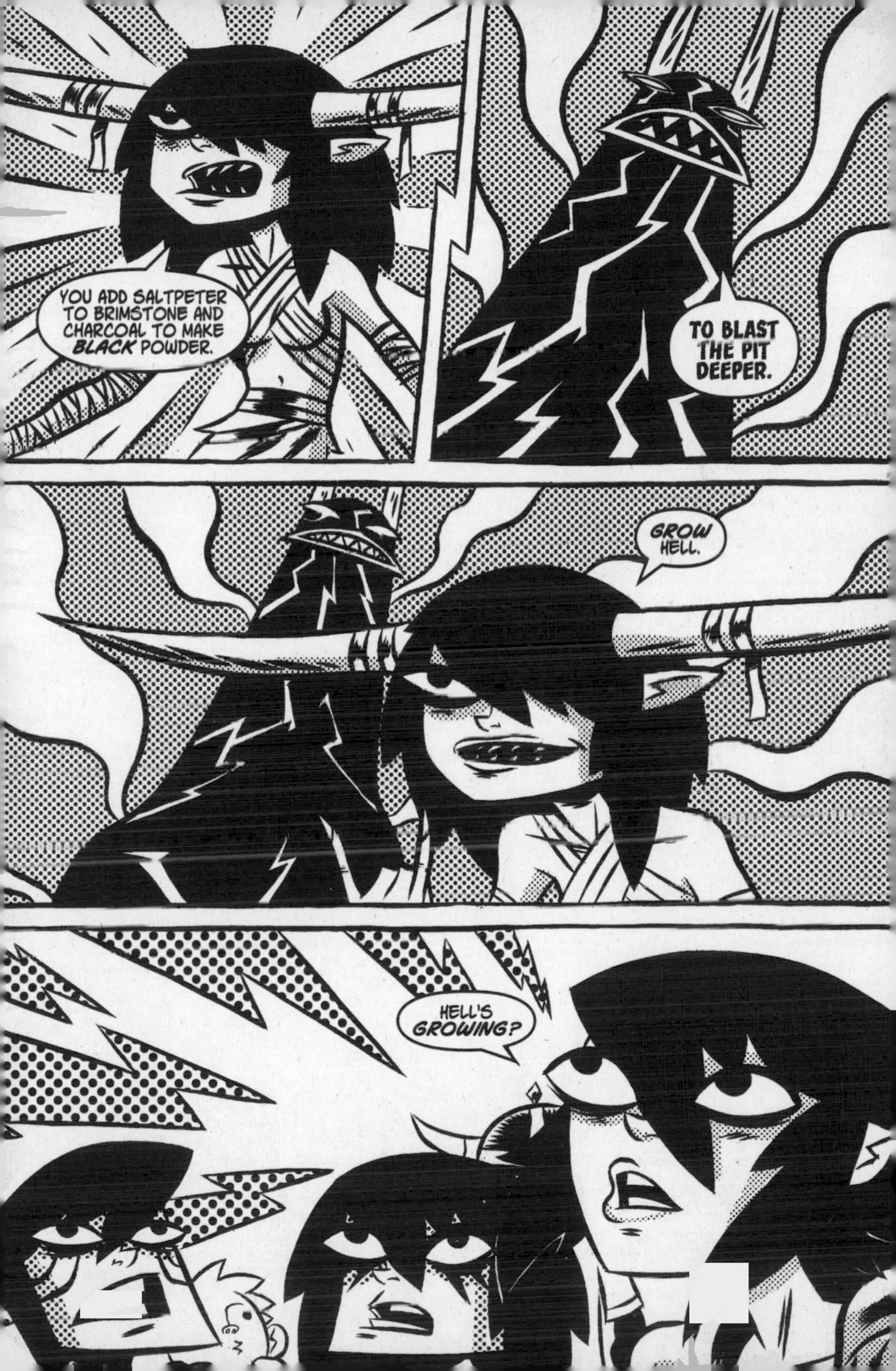
YOU ADD SALTPETER TO BRIMSTONE AND CHARCOAL TO MAKE *BLACK* POWDER.
TO BLAST THE PIT DEEPER.
GROW HELL.
HELL'S *GROWING?*

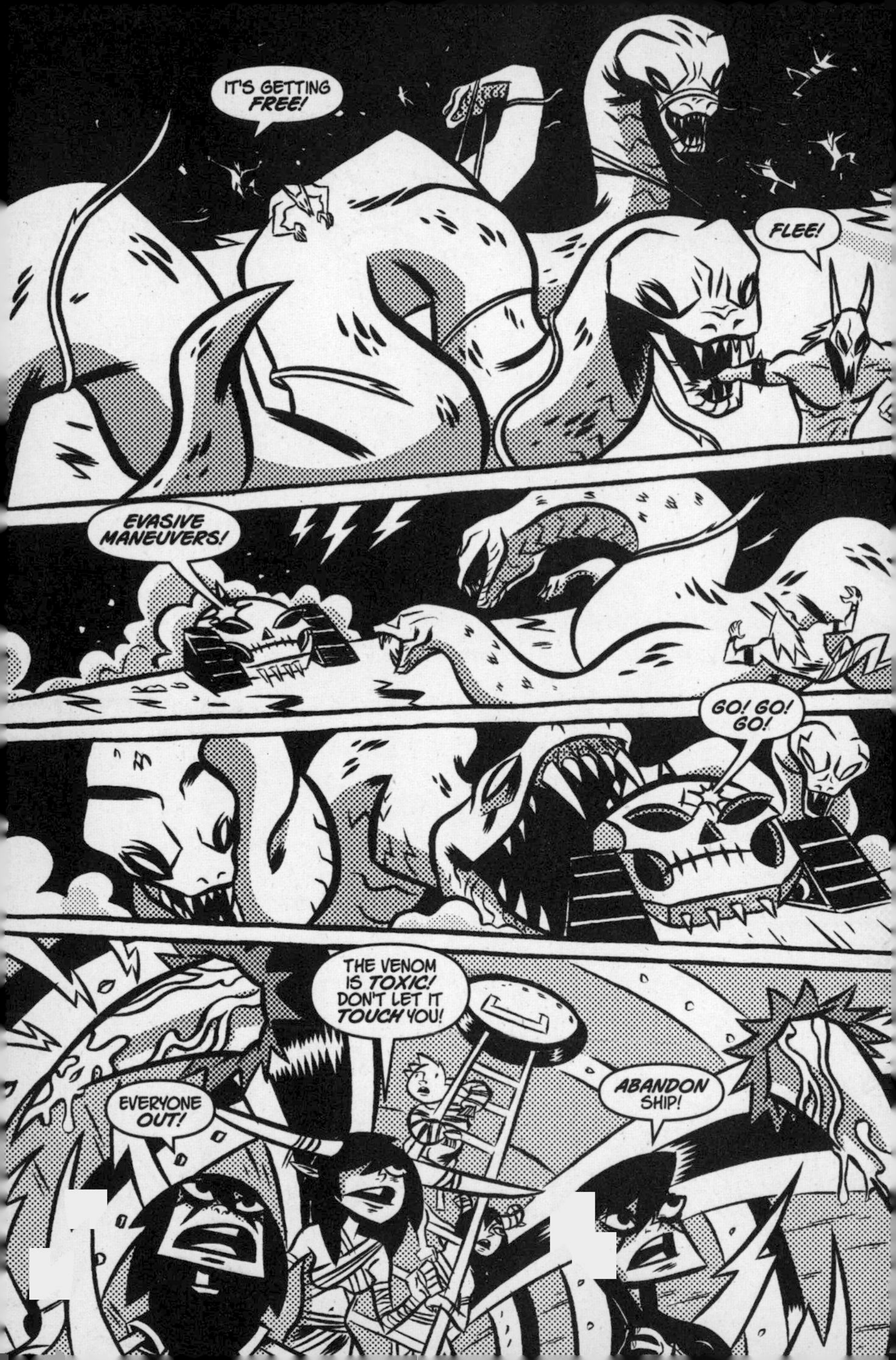
IT'S GETTING FREE!
FLEE!
EVASIVE MANEUVERS!
GO! GO! GO!
THE VENOM IS TOXIC! DON'T LET IT TOUCH YOU!
EVERYONE OUT!
ABANDON SHIP!

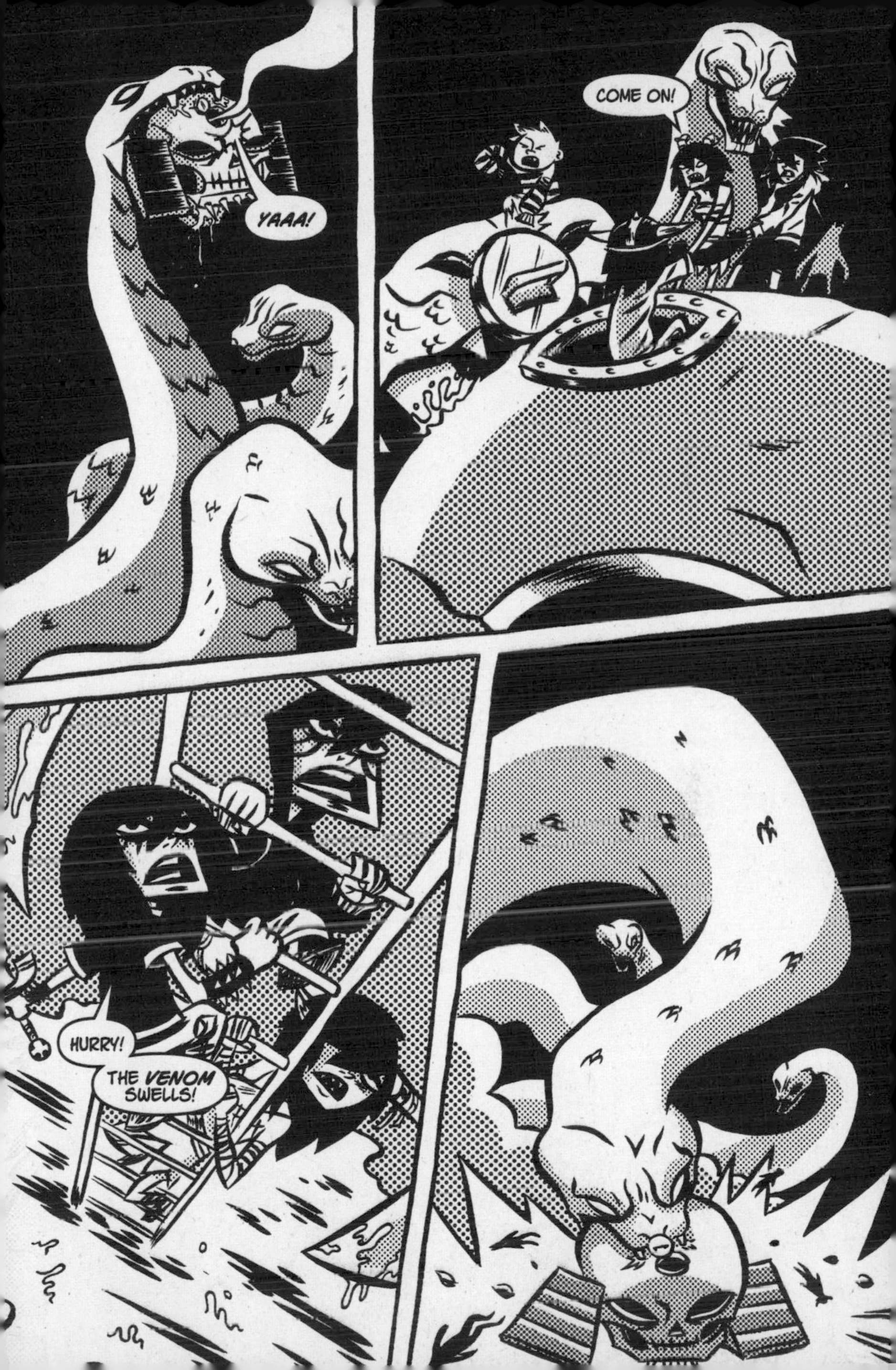
YAAA!
COME ON!
HURRY!
THE VENOM SWELLS!

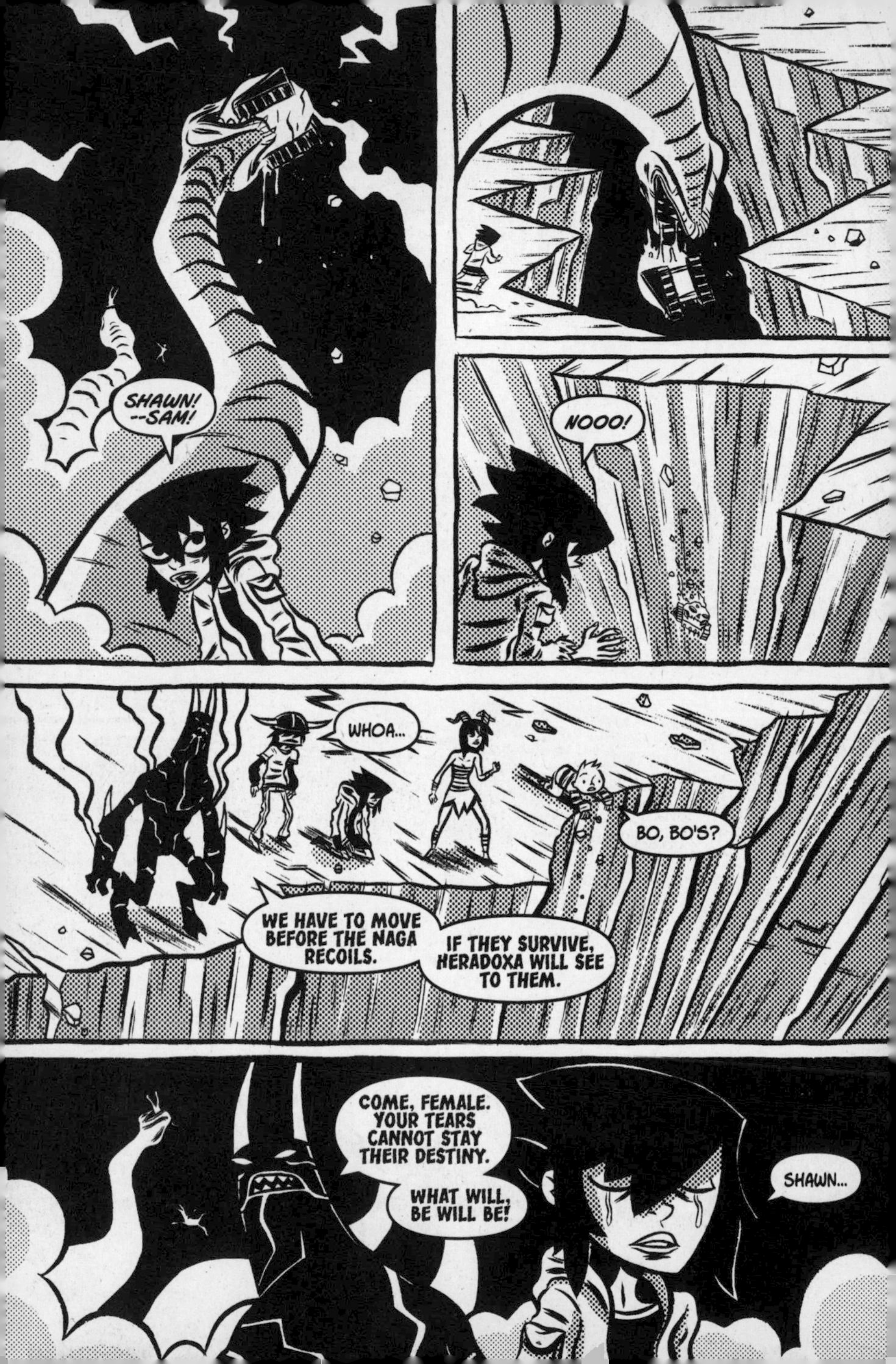
SHAWN! --SAM!
NOOO!
WHOA...
BO, BO'S?
WE HAVE TO MOVE BEFORE THE NAGA RECOILS.
IF THEY SURVIVE, HERADOXA WILL SEE TO THEM.
COME, FEMALE. YOUR TEARS CANNOT STAY THEIR DESTINY.
WHAT WILL, BE WILL BE!
SHAWN...

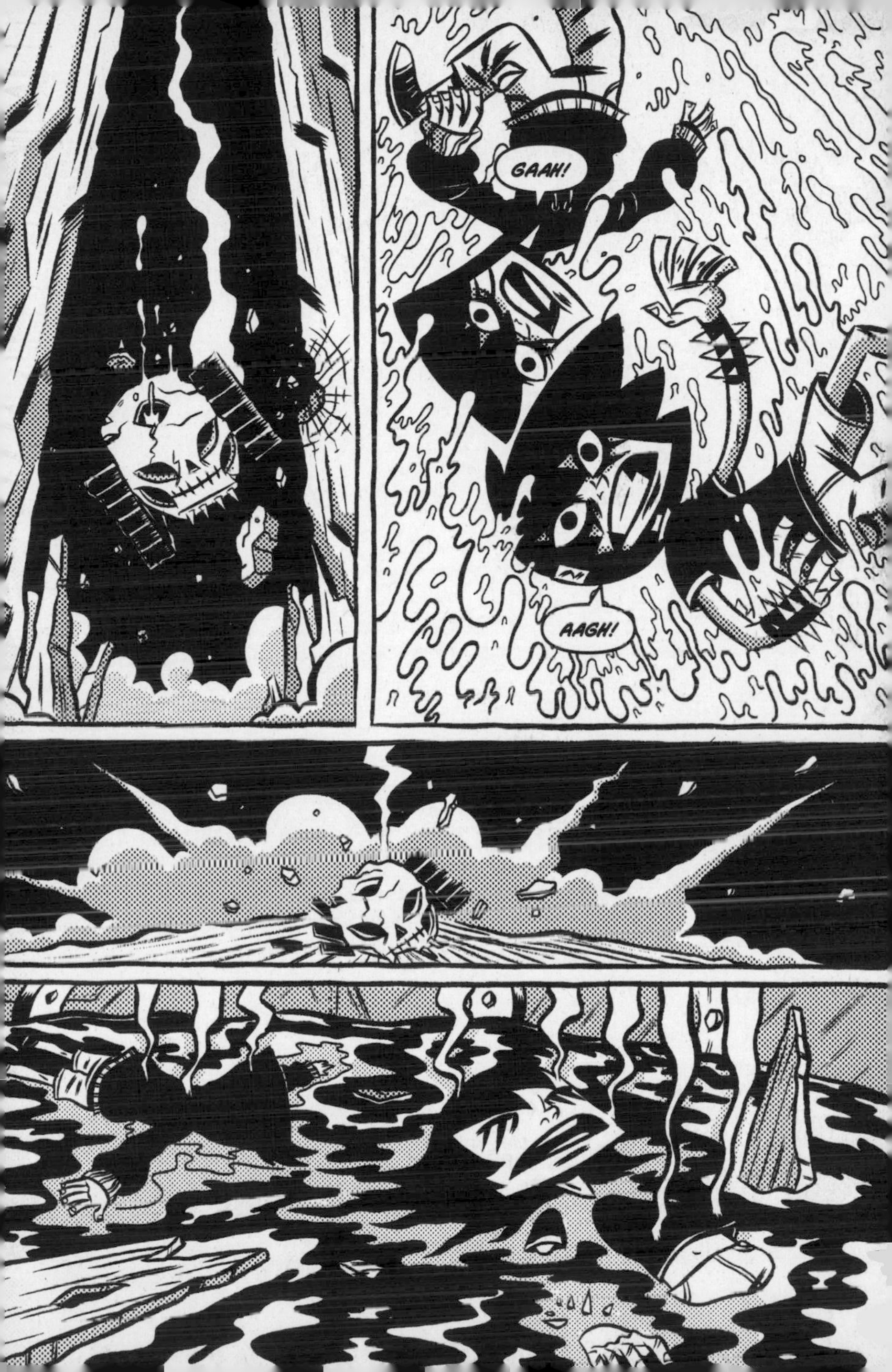
GAAH!
AAGH!

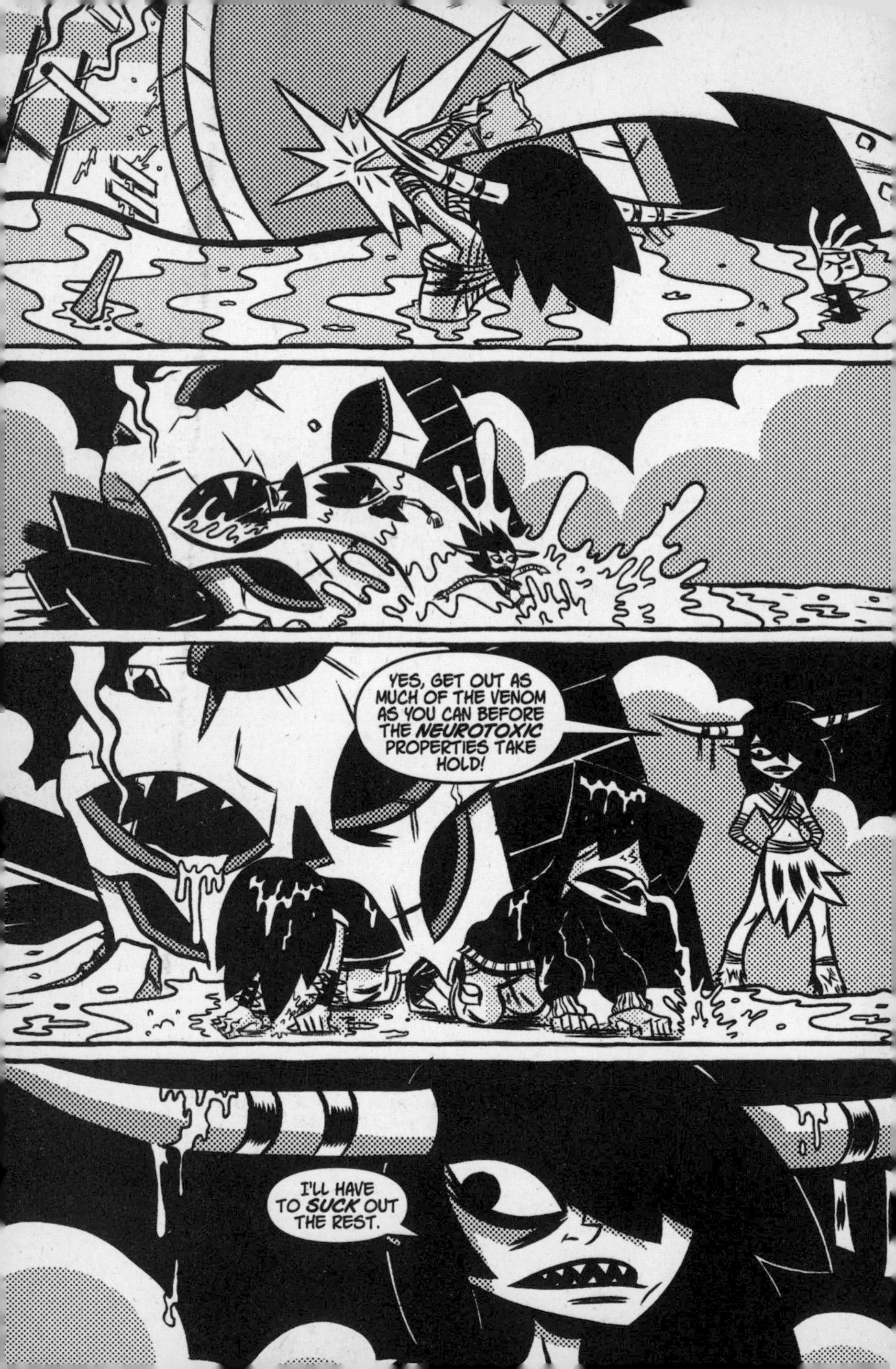
YES, GET OUT AS MUCH OF THE VENOM AS YOU CAN BEFORE THE NEUROTOXIC PROPERTIES TAKE HOLD!
I'LL HAVE TO SUCK OUT THE REST.

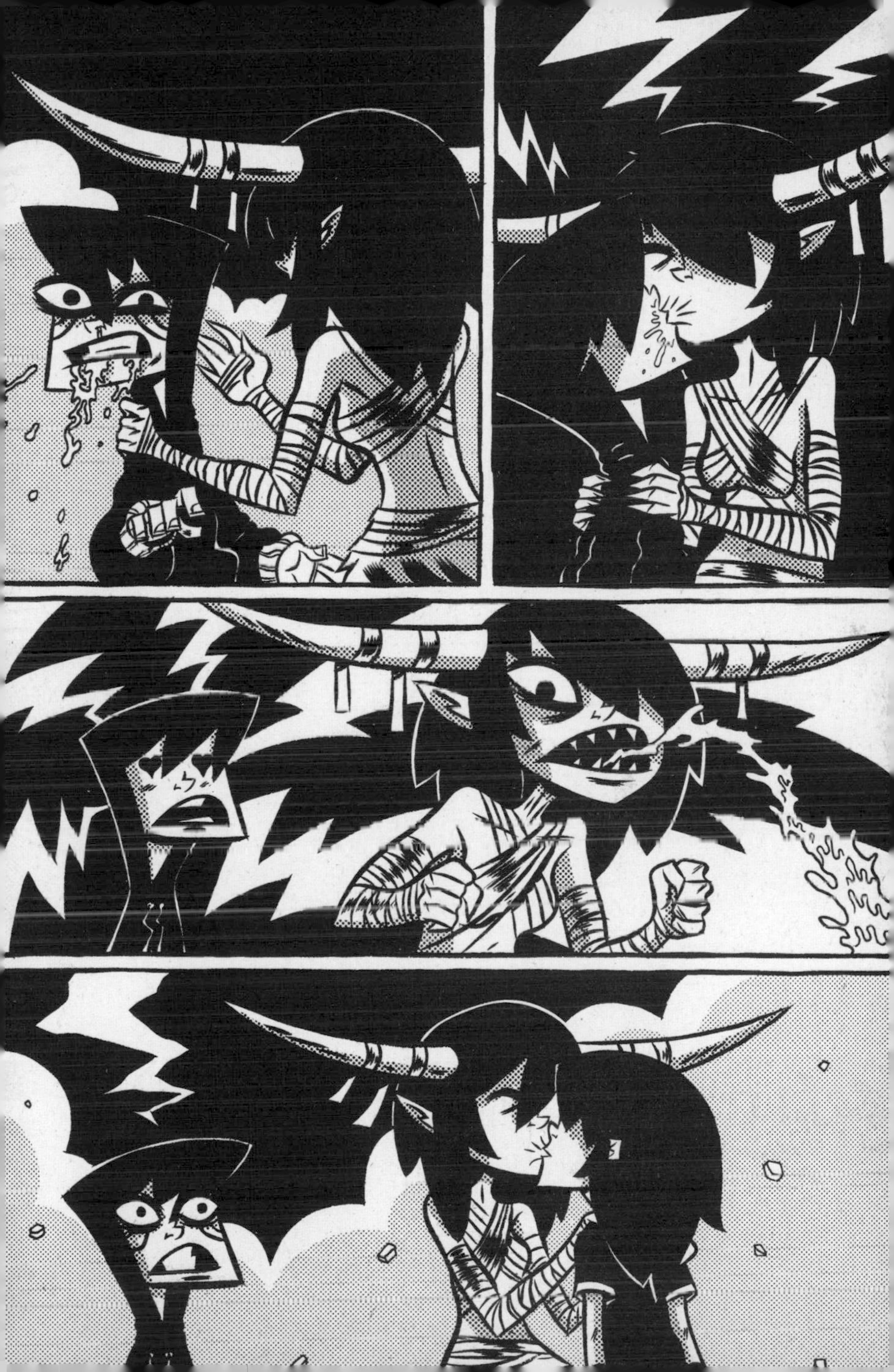

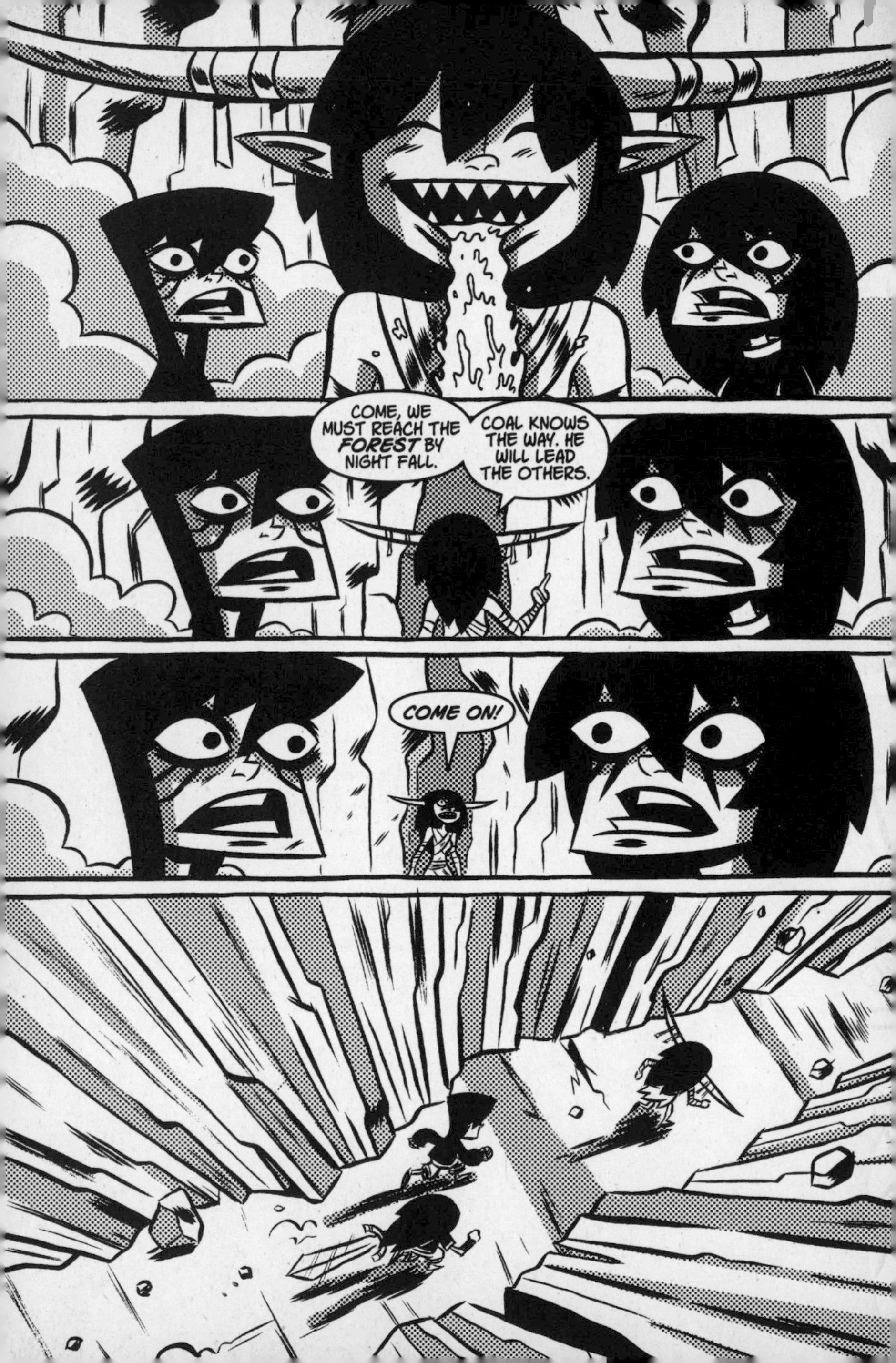
COME, WE MUST REACH THE FOREST BY NIGHT FALL.
COAL KNOWS THE WAY. HE WILL LEAD THE OTHERS.
COME ON!

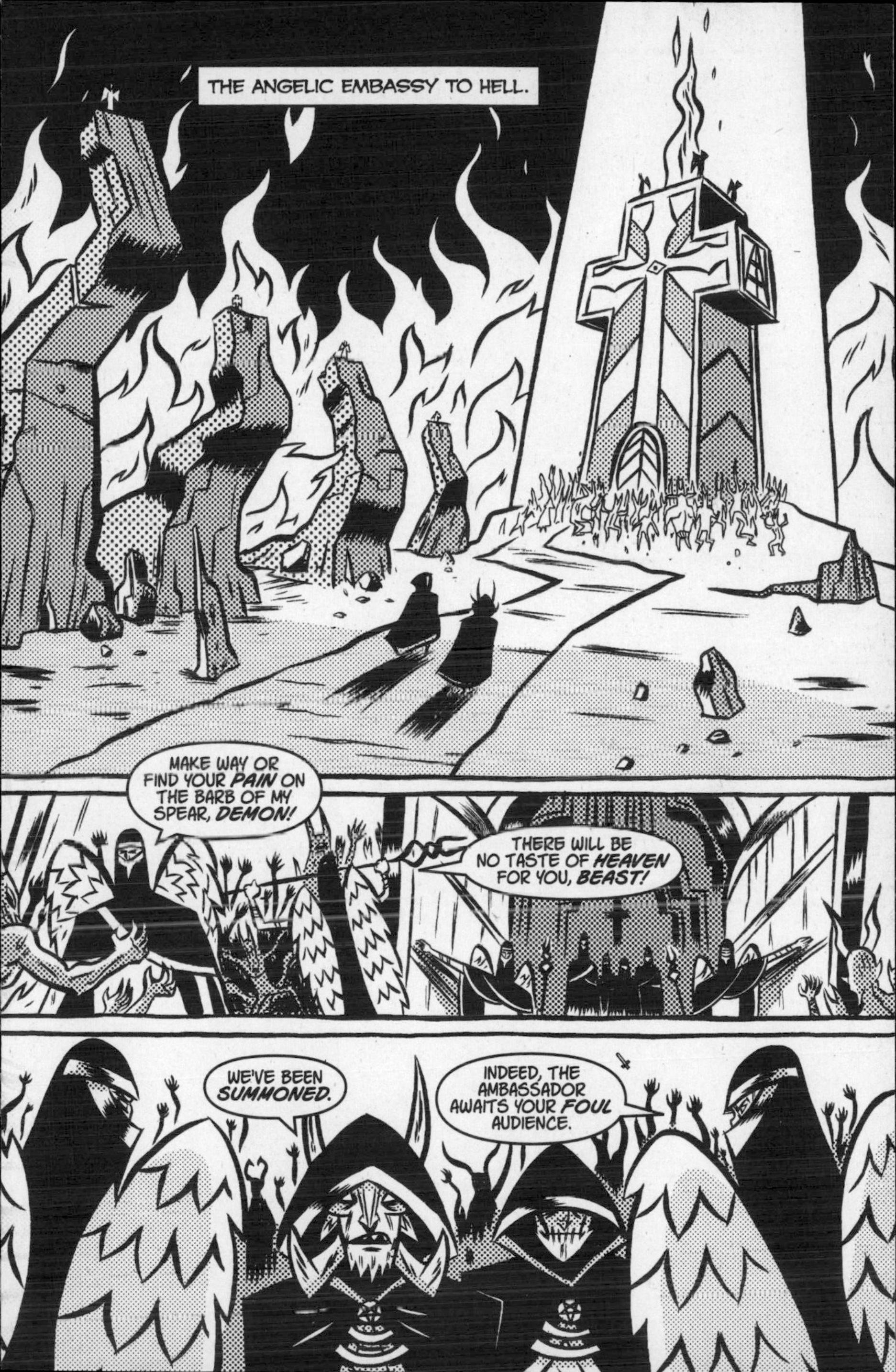
THE ANGELIC EMBASSY TO HELL.
MAKE WAY OR FIND YOUR *PAIN* ON THE BARB OF MY SPEAR, *DEMON!*
THERE WILL BE NO TASTE OF *HEAVEN* FOR YOU, *BEAST!*
WE'VE BEEN *SUMMONED.*
INDEED, THE AMBASSADOR AWAITS YOUR *FOUL* AUDIENCE.

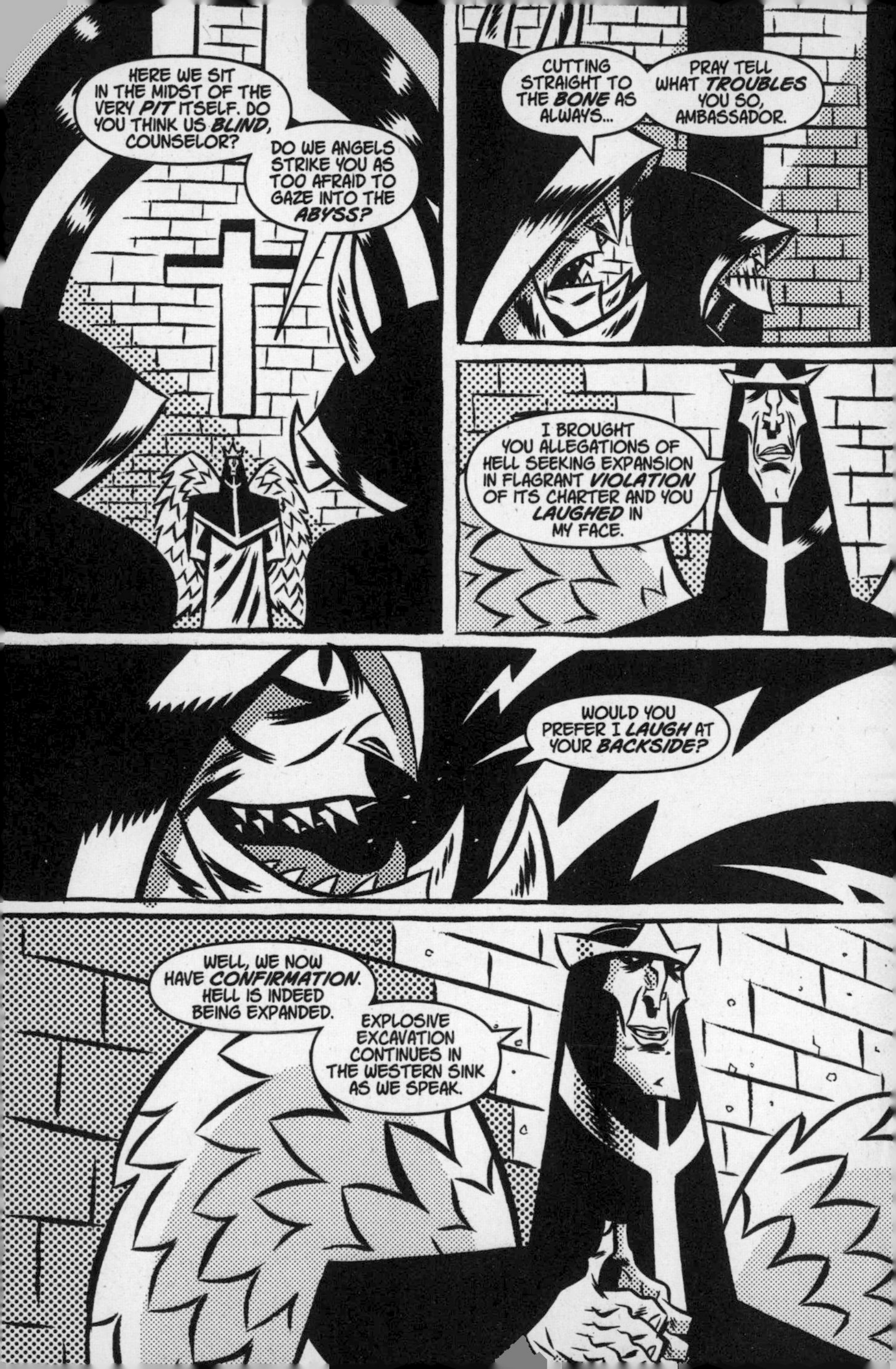
HERE WE SIT IN THE MIDST OF THE VERY PIT ITSELF. DO YOU THINK US BLIND, COUNSELOR?
DO WE ANGELS STRIKE YOU AS TOO AFRAID TO GAZE INTO THE ABYSS?
CUTTING STRAIGHT TO THE BONE AS ALWAYS...
PRAY TELL WHAT TROUBLES YOU SO, AMBASSADOR.
I BROUGHT YOU ALLEGATIONS OF HELL SEEKING EXPANSION IN FLAGRANT VIOLATION OF ITS CHARTER AND YOU LAUGHED IN MY FACE.
WOULD YOU PREFER I LAUGH AT YOUR BACKSIDE?
WELL, WE NOW HAVE CONFIRMATION. HELL IS INDEED BEING EXPANDED.
EXPLOSIVE EXCAVATION CONTINUES IN THE WESTERN SINK AS WE SPEAK.

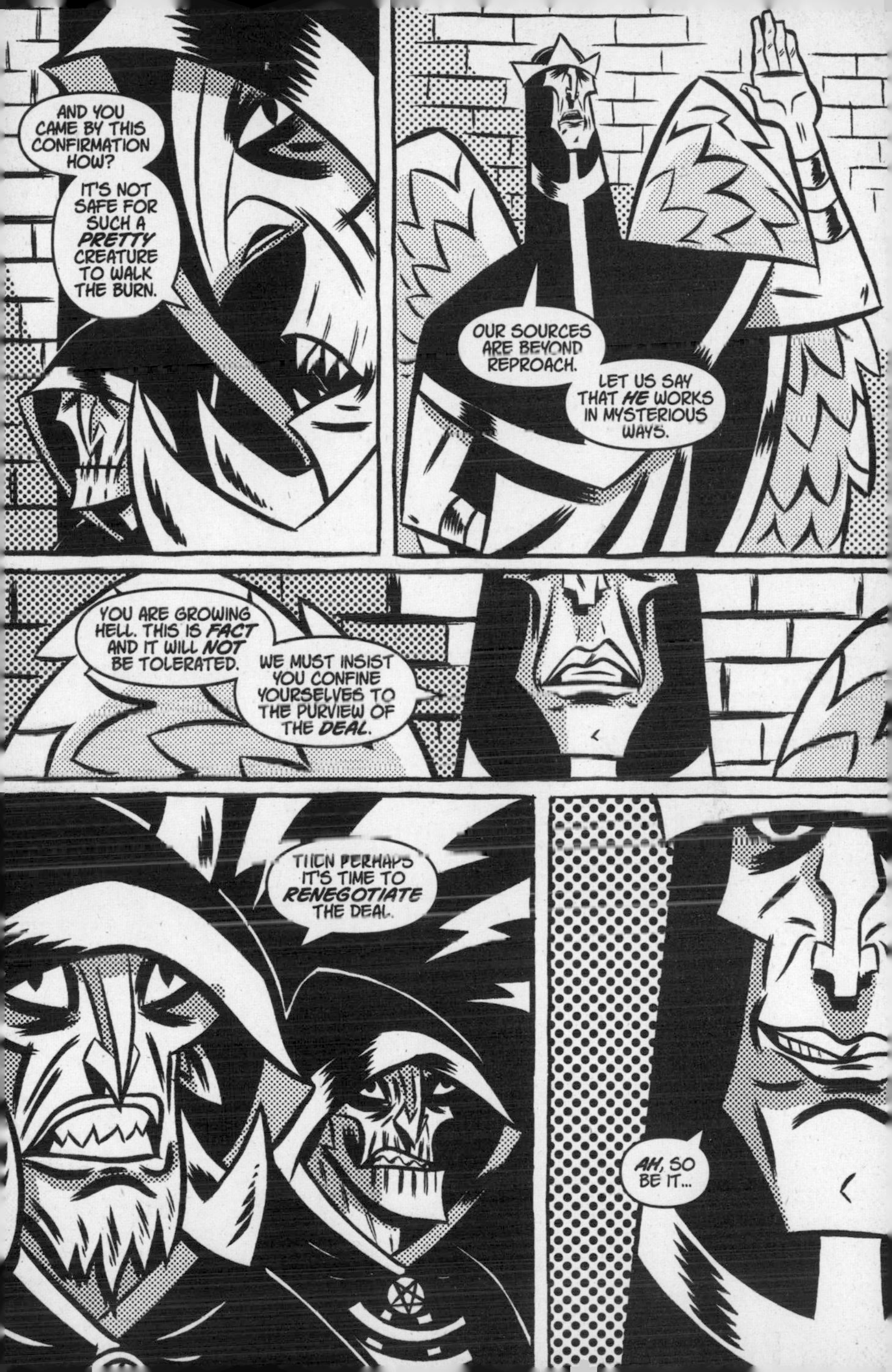
AND YOU CAME BY THIS CONFIRMATION HOW?
IT'S NOT SAFE FOR SUCH A *PRETTY* CREATURE TO WALK THE BURN.
OUR SOURCES ARE BEYOND REPROACH.
LET US SAY THAT *HE* WORKS IN MYSTERIOUS WAYS.
YOU ARE GROWING HELL. THIS IS *FACT* AND IT WILL *NOT* BE TOLERATED.
WE MUST INSIST YOU CONFINE YOURSELVES TO THE PURVIEW OF THE *DEAL*.
THEN PERHAPS IT'S TIME TO *RENEGOTIATE* THE DEAL.
AH, SO BE IT...

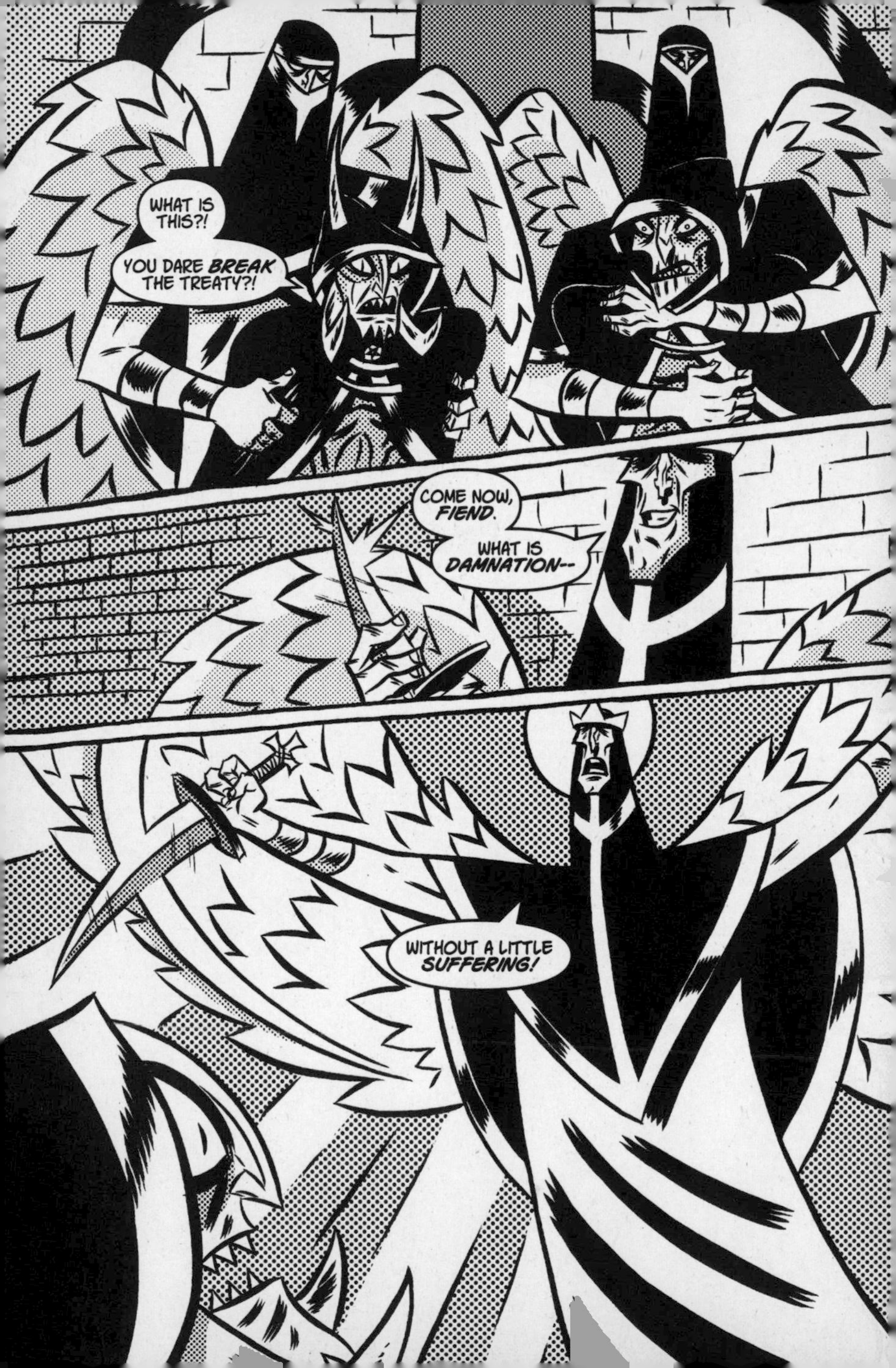
WHAT IS THIS?!
YOU DARE *BREAK* THE TREATY?!
COME NOW, *FIEND*.
WHAT IS *DAMNATION*--
WITHOUT A LITTLE *SUFFERING*!

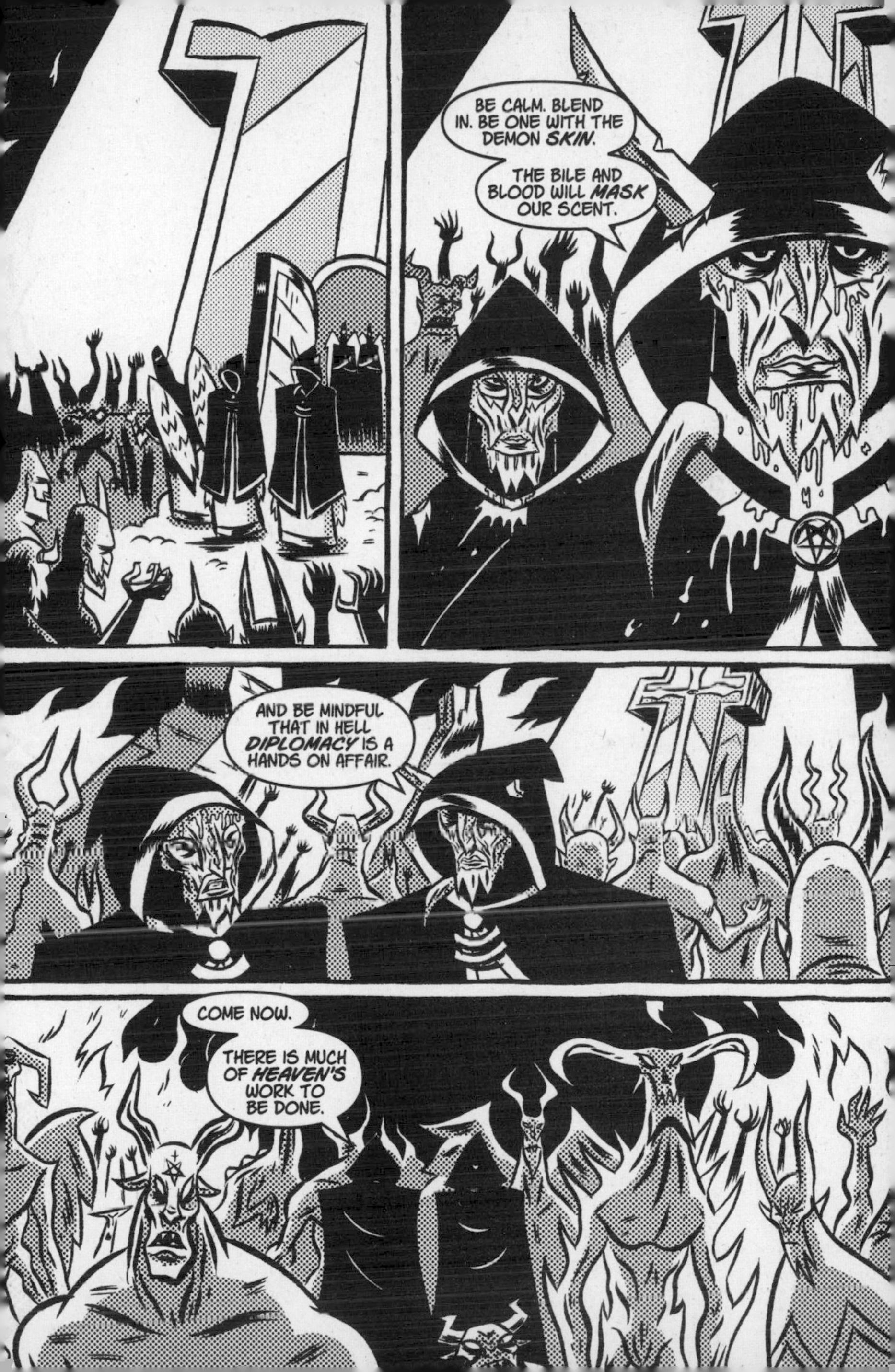
BE CALM. BLEND IN. BE ONE WITH THE DEMON SKIN.
THE BILE AND BLOOD WILL MASK OUR SCENT.
AND BE MINDFUL THAT IN HELL DIPLOMACY IS A HANDS ON AFFAIR.
COME NOW.
THERE IS MUCH OF HEAVEN'S WORK TO BE DONE.

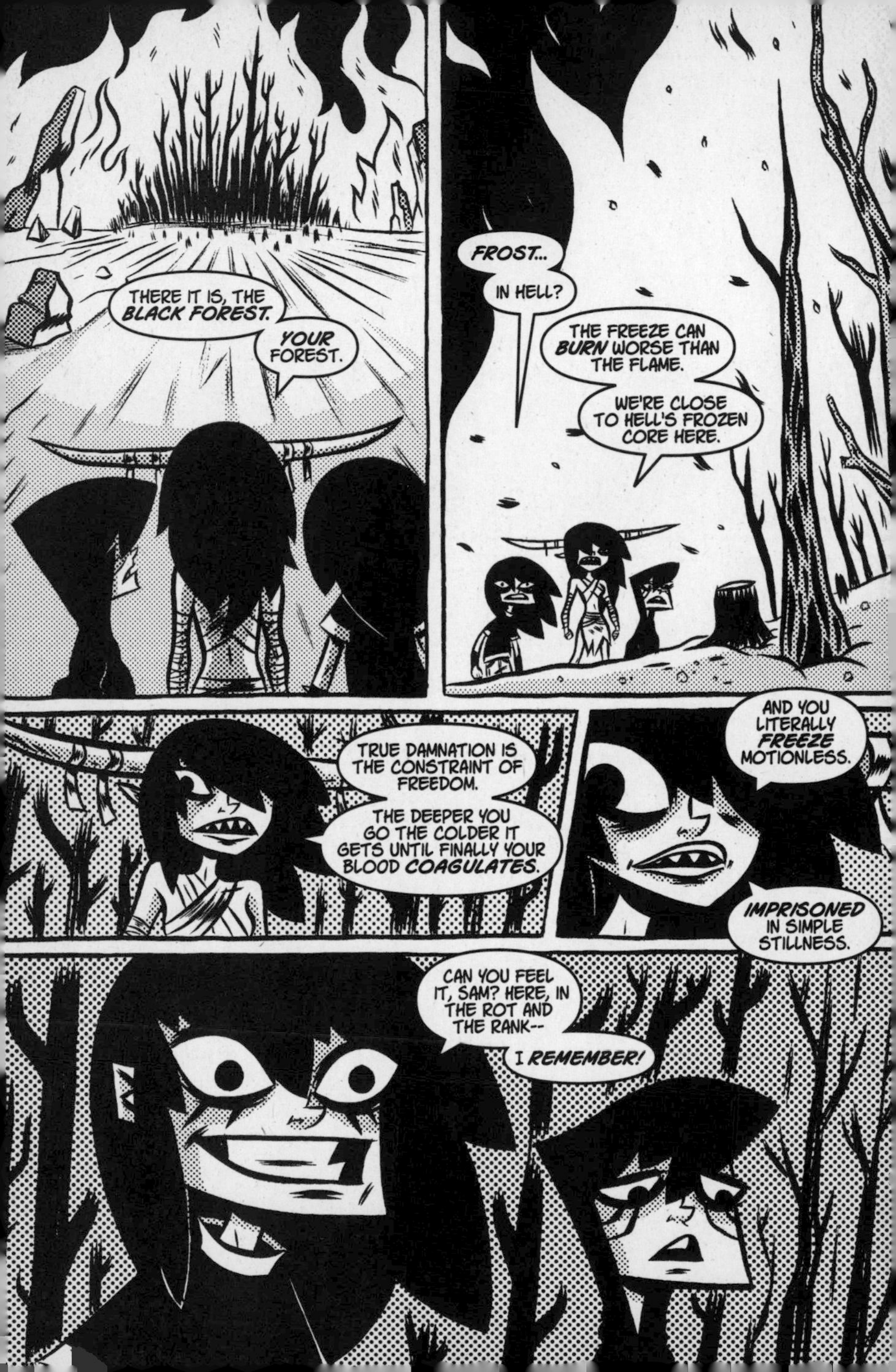

THERE IT IS, THE BLACK FOREST.
YOUR FOREST.
FROST...
IN HELL?
THE FREEZE CAN BURN WORSE THAN THE FLAME.
WE'RE CLOSE TO HELL'S FROZEN CORE HERE.
TRUE DAMNATION IS THE CONSTRAINT OF FREEDOM.
THE DEEPER YOU GO THE COLDER IT GETS UNTIL FINALLY YOUR BLOOD COAGULATES.
AND YOU LITERALLY FREEZE MOTIONLESS.
IMPRISONED IN SIMPLE STILLNESS.
CAN YOU FEEL IT, SAM? HERE, IN THE ROT AND THE RANK--
I REMEMBER!

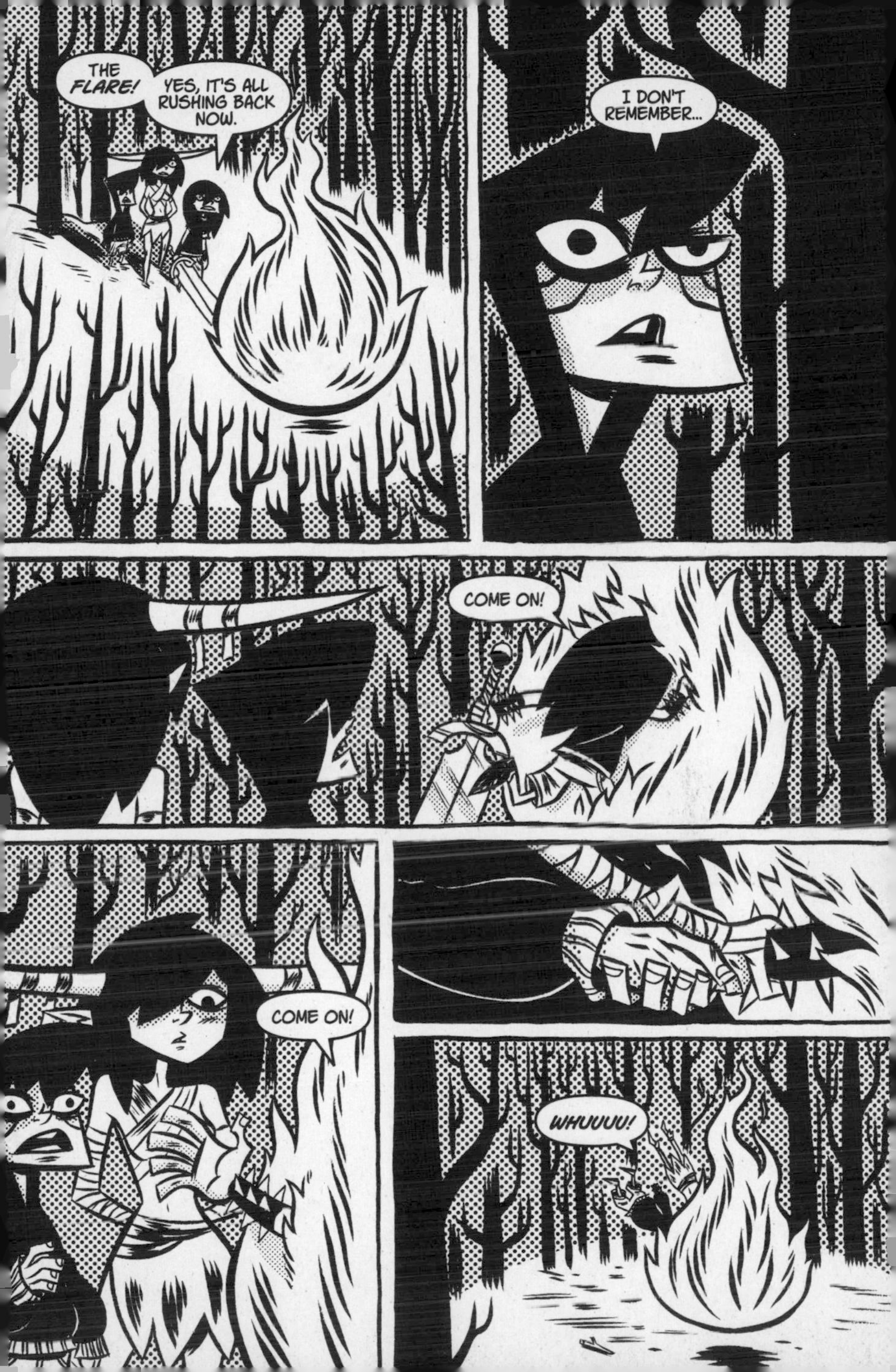
THE *FLARE!*
YES, IT'S ALL RUSHING BACK NOW.
I DON'T REMEMBER...
COME ON!
COME ON!
WHUUUU!

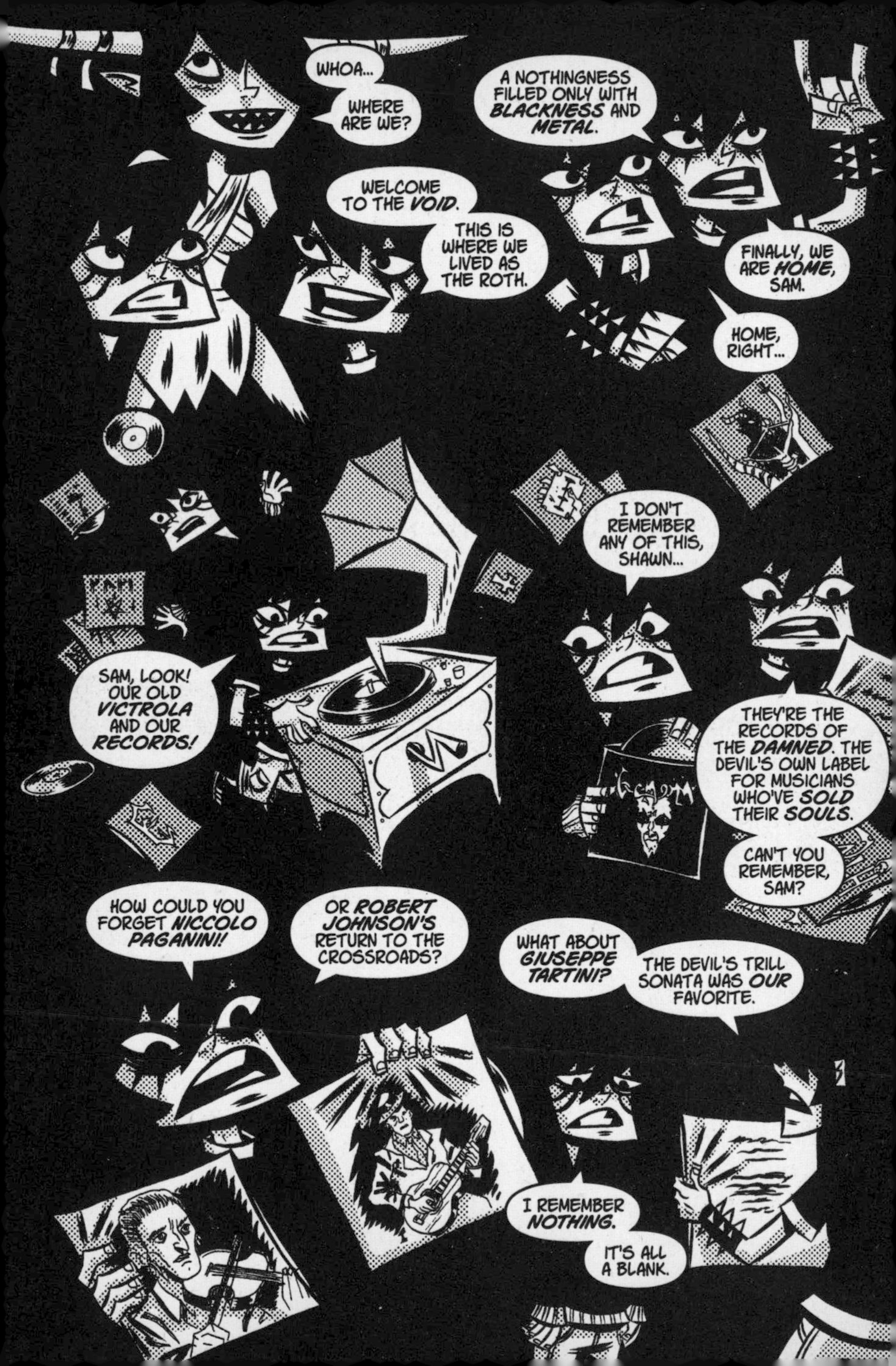
WHOA...
WHERE ARE WE?
A NOTHINGNESS FILLED ONLY WITH BLACKNESS AND METAL.
WELCOME TO THE VOID.
THIS IS WHERE WE LIVED AS THE ROTH.
FINALLY, WE ARE HOME, SAM.
HOME, RIGHT...
I DON'T REMEMBER ANY OF THIS, SHAWN...
SAM, LOOK! OUR OLD VICTROLA AND OUR RECORDS!
THEY'RE THE RECORDS OF THE DAMNED. THE DEVIL'S OWN LABEL FOR MUSICIANS WHO'VE SOLD THEIR SOULS.
CAN'T YOU REMEMBER, SAM?
HOW COULD YOU FORGET NICCOLO PAGANINI!
OR ROBERT JOHNSON'S RETURN TO THE CROSSROADS?
WHAT ABOUT GIUSEPPE TARTINI?
THE DEVIL'S TRILL SONATA WAS OUR FAVORITE.
I REMEMBER NOTHING.
IT'S ALL A BLANK.

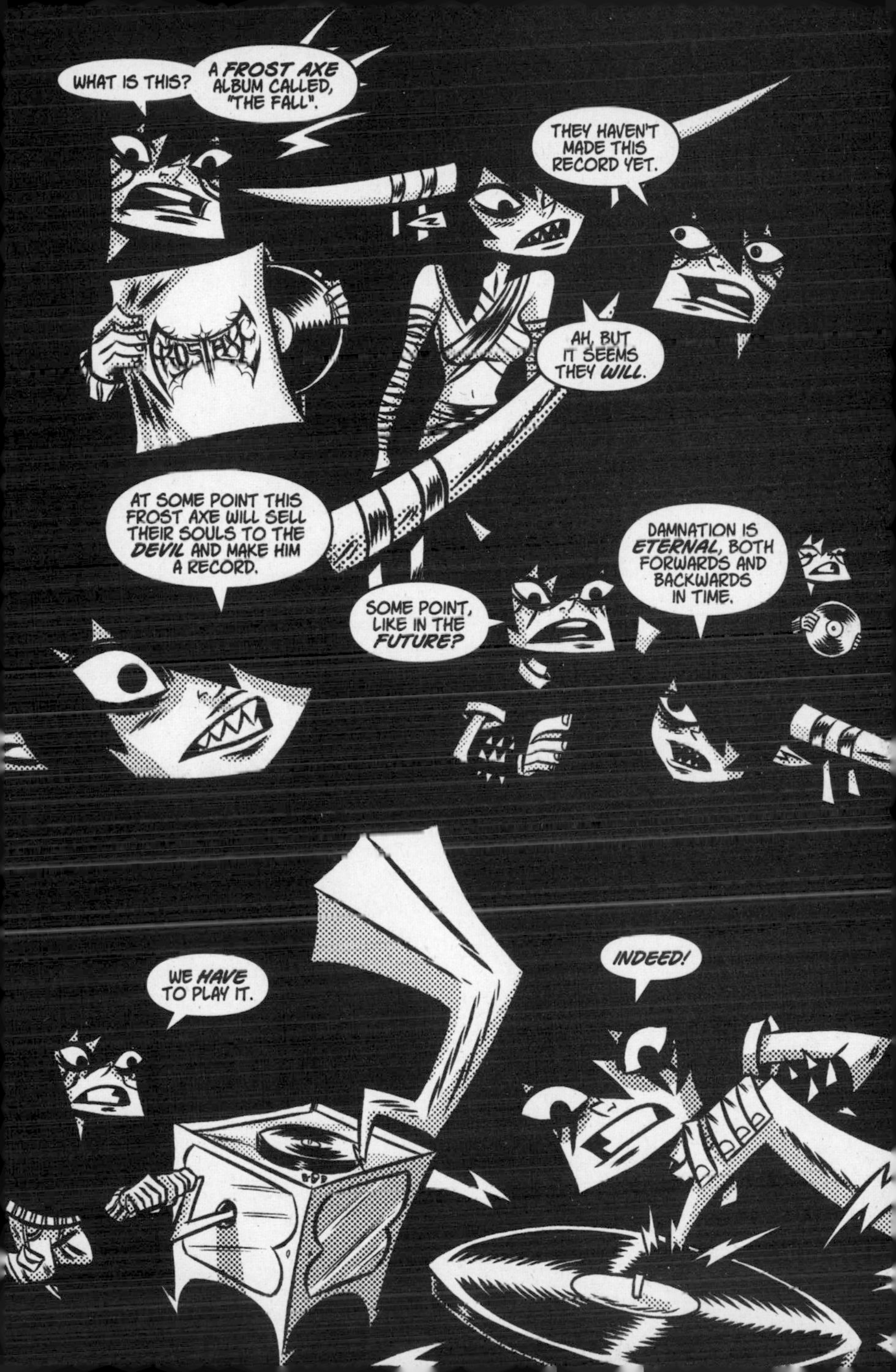
WHAT IS THIS?
A FROST AXE ALBUM CALLED, "THE FALL".
THEY HAVEN'T MADE THIS RECORD YET.
AH, BUT IT SEEMS THEY WILL.
AT SOME POINT THIS FROST AXE WILL SELL THEIR SOULS TO THE DEVIL AND MAKE HIM A RECORD.
SOME POINT, LIKE IN THE FUTURE?
DAMNATION IS ETERNAL, BOTH FORWARDS AND BACKWARDS IN TIME.
WE HAVE TO PLAY IT.
INDEED!

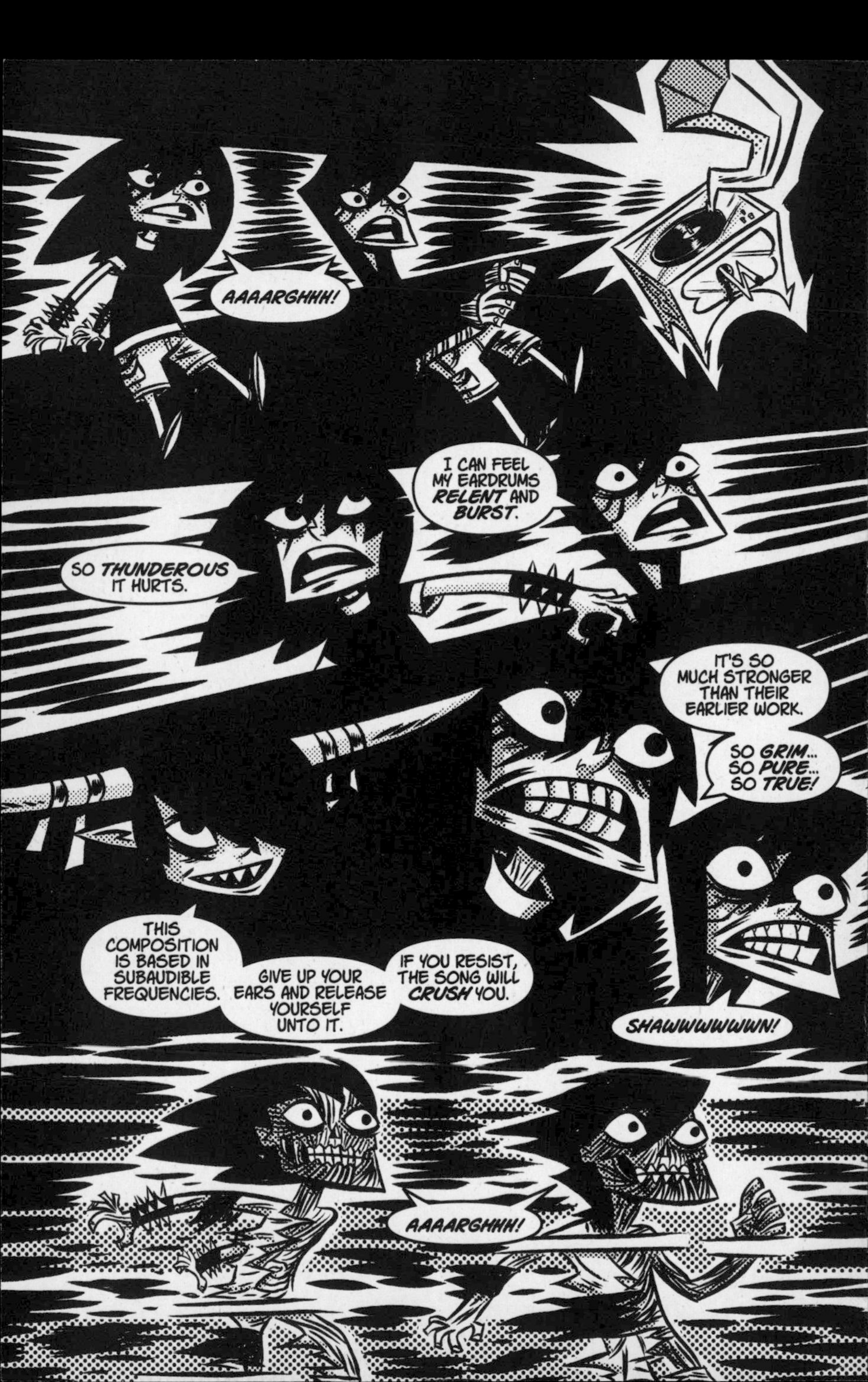
AAAARGHHH!
I CAN FEEL MY EARDRUMS *RELENT* AND *BURST*.
SO *THUNDEROUS* IT HURTS.
IT'S SO MUCH STRONGER THAN THEIR EARLIER WORK.
SO *GRIM*... SO *PURE*... SO *TRUE!*
THIS COMPOSITION IS BASED IN SUBAUDIBLE FREQUENCIES.
GIVE UP YOUR EARS AND RELEASE YOURSELF UNTO IT.
IF YOU RESIST, THE SONG WILL *CRUSH* YOU.
SHAWWWWWWN!
AAAARGHHH!

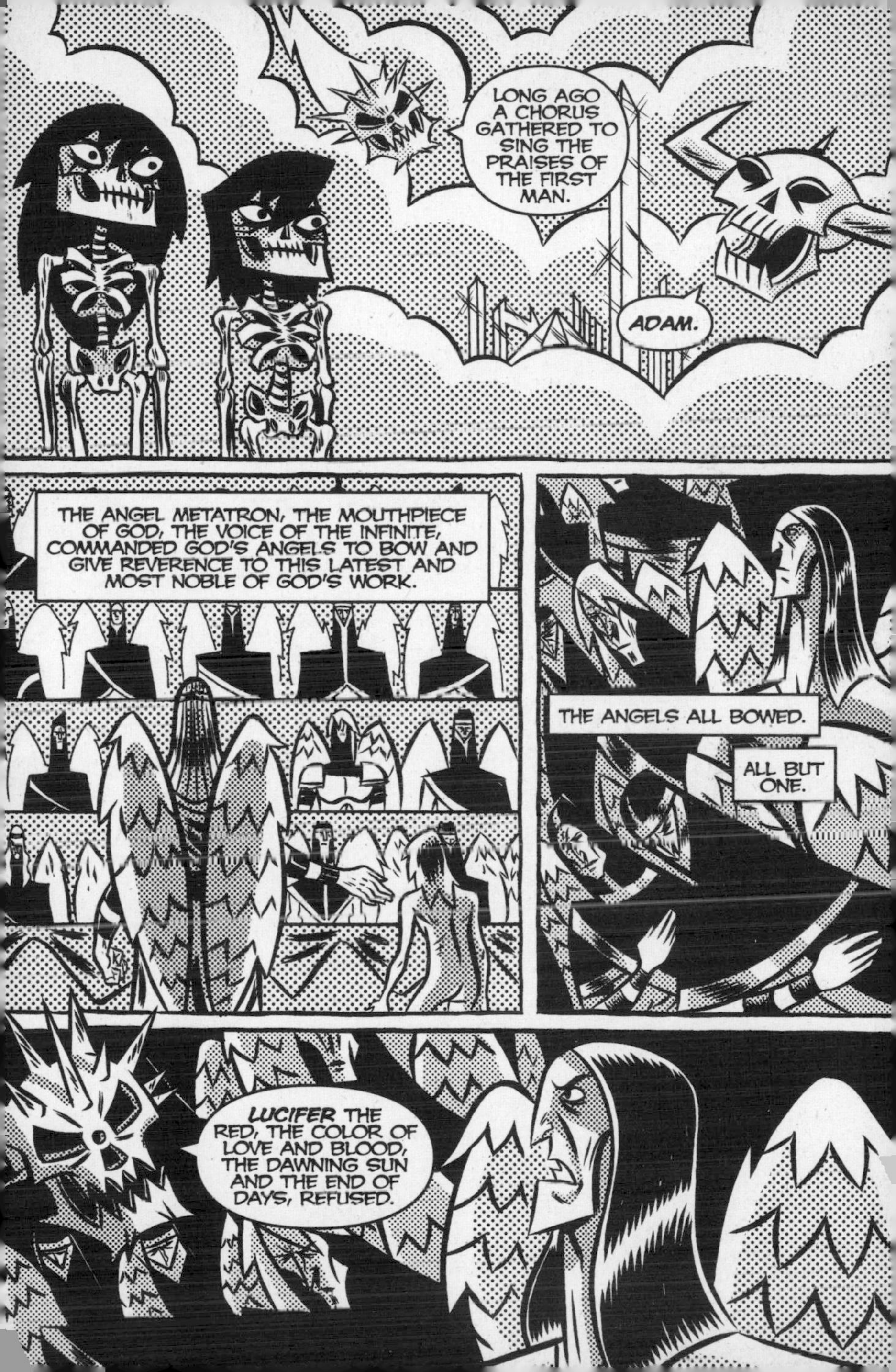
LONG AGO A CHORUS GATHERED TO SING THE PRAISES OF THE FIRST MAN.
ADAM.
THE ANGEL METATRON, THE MOUTHPIECE OF GOD, THE VOICE OF THE INFINITE, COMMANDED GOD'S ANGELS TO BOW AND GIVE REVERENCE TO THIS LATEST AND MOST NOBLE OF GOD'S WORK.
THE ANGELS ALL BOWED.
ALL BUT ONE.
LUCIFER THE RED, THE COLOR OF LOVE AND BLOOD, THE DAWNING SUN AND THE END OF DAYS, REFUSED.

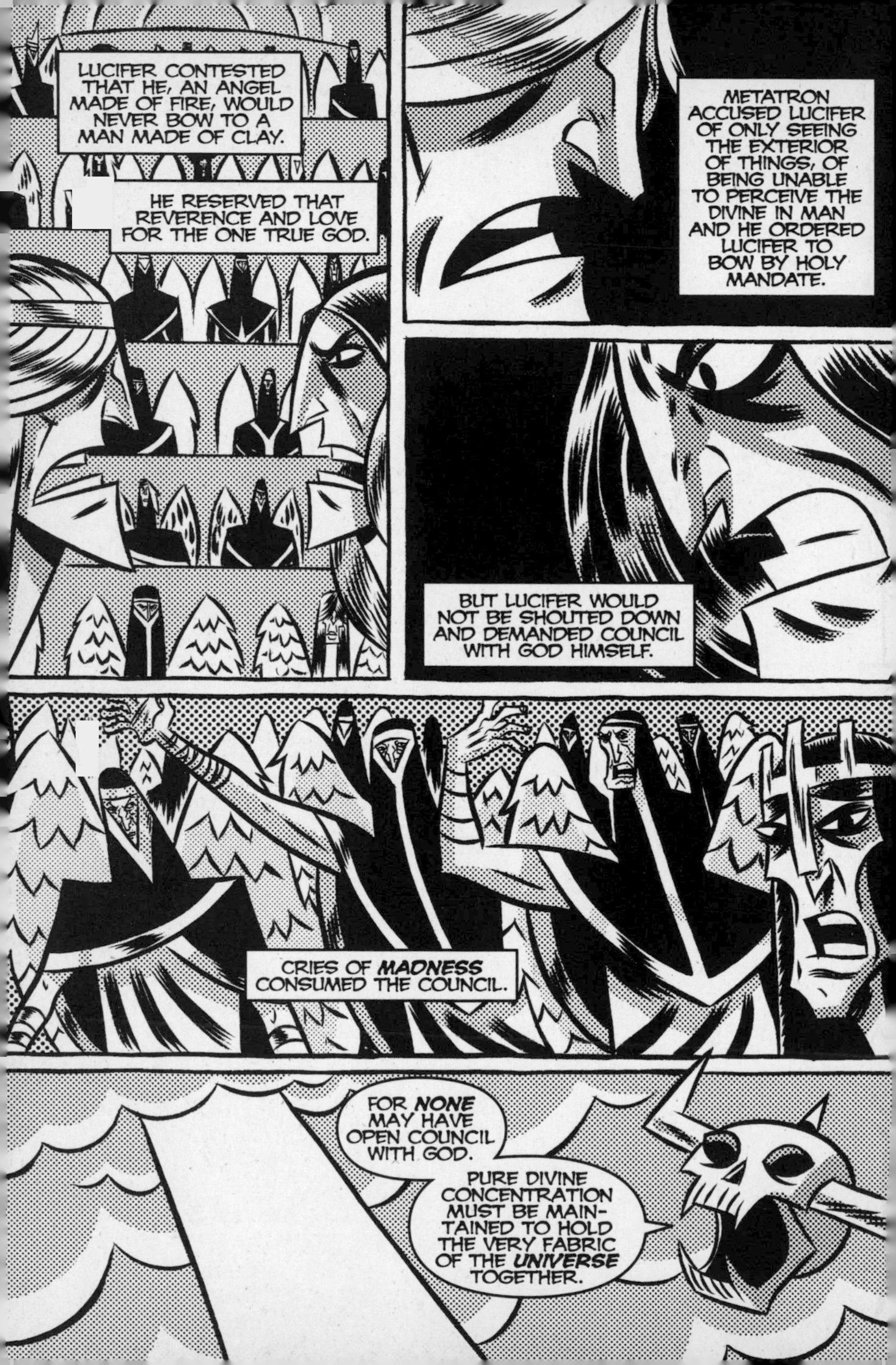
LUCIFER CONTESTED THAT HE, AN ANGEL MADE OF FIRE, WOULD NEVER BOW TO A MAN MADE OF CLAY.
HE RESERVED THAT REVERENCE AND LOVE FOR THE ONE TRUE GOD.
METATRON ACCUSED LUCIFER OF ONLY SEEING THE EXTERIOR OF THINGS, OF BEING UNABLE TO PERCEIVE THE DIVINE IN MAN AND HE ORDERED LUCIFER TO BOW BY HOLY MANDATE.
BUT LUCIFER WOULD NOT BE SHOUTED DOWN AND DEMANDED COUNCIL WITH GOD HIMSELF.
CRIES OF ***MADNESS*** CONSUMED THE COUNCIL.
FOR ***NONE*** MAY HAVE OPEN COUNCIL WITH GOD.
PURE DIVINE CONCENTRATION MUST BE MAIN-TAINED TO HOLD THE VERY FABRIC OF THE ***UNIVERSE*** TOGETHER.

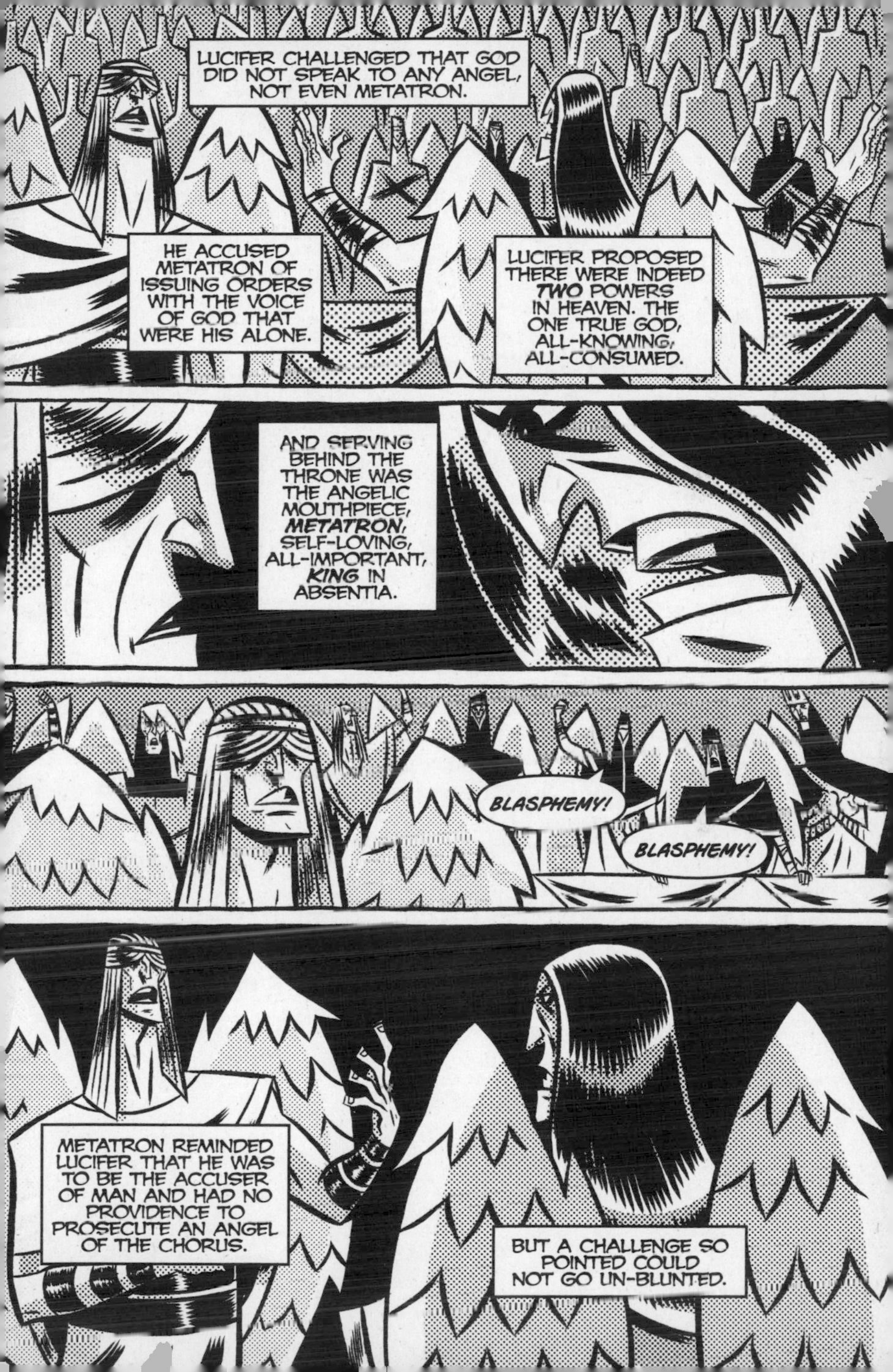

LUCIFER CHALLENGED THAT GOD DID NOT SPEAK TO ANY ANGEL, NOT EVEN METATRON.
HE ACCUSED METATRON OF ISSUING ORDERS WITH THE VOICE OF GOD THAT WERE HIS ALONE.
LUCIFER PROPOSED THERE WERE INDEED TWO POWERS IN HEAVEN. THE ONE TRUE GOD, ALL-KNOWING, ALL-CONSUMED.
AND SERVING BEHIND THE THRONE WAS THE ANGELIC MOUTHPIECE, METATRON, SELF-LOVING, ALL-IMPORTANT, KING IN ABSENTIA.
BLASPHEMY!
BLASPHEMY!
METATRON REMINDED LUCIFER THAT HE WAS TO BE THE ACCUSER OF MAN AND HAD NO PROVIDENCE TO PROSECUTE AN ANGEL OF THE CHORUS.
BUT A CHALLENGE SO POINTED COULD NOT GO UN-BLUNTED.

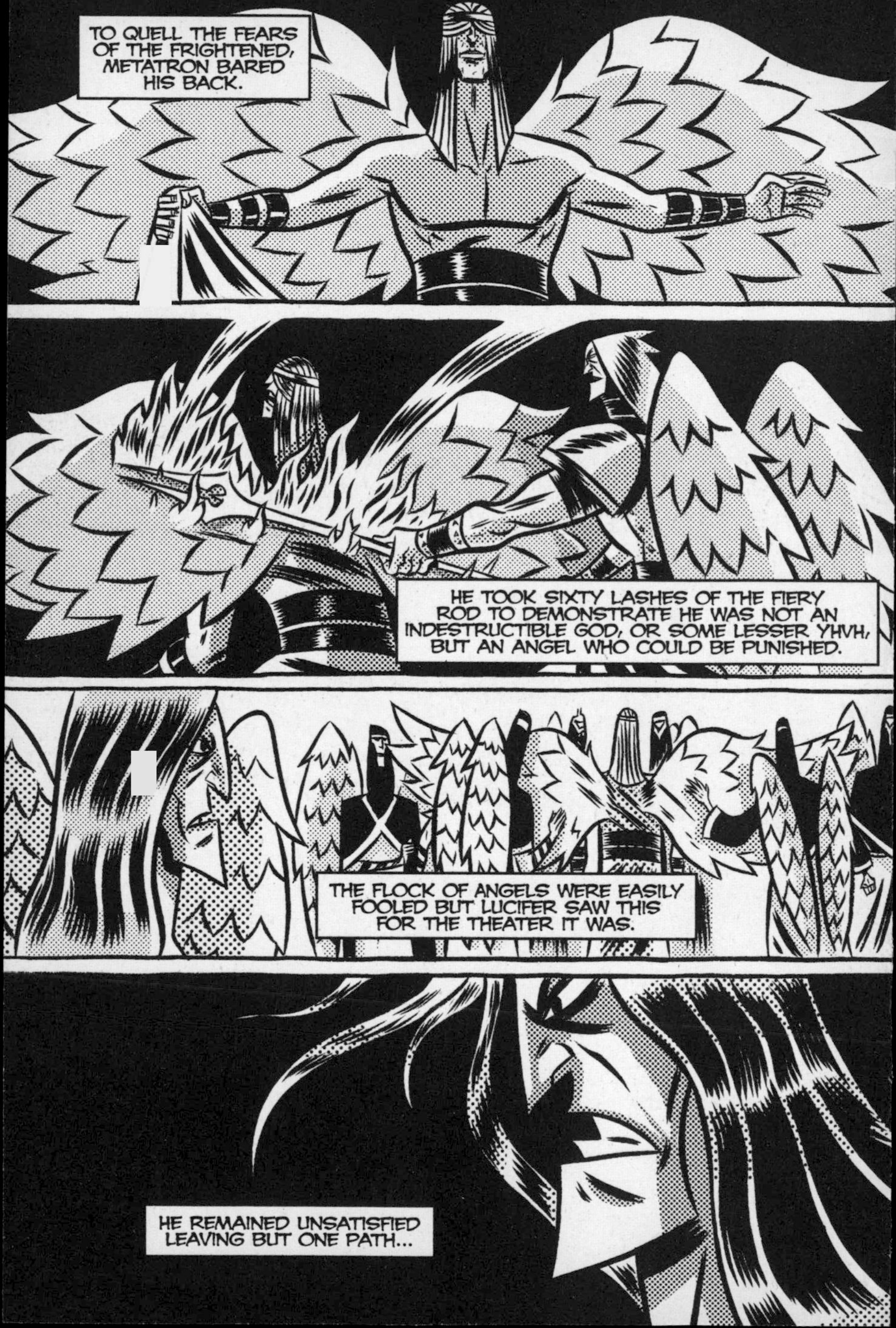
TO QUELL THE FEARS OF THE FRIGHTENED, METATRON BARED HIS BACK.
HE TOOK SIXTY LASHES OF THE FIERY ROD TO DEMONSTRATE HE WAS NOT AN INDESTRUCTIBLE GOD, OR SOME LESSER YHVH, BUT AN ANGEL WHO COULD BE PUNISHED.
THE FLOCK OF ANGELS WERE EASILY FOOLED BUT LUCIFER SAW THIS FOR THE THEATER IT WAS.
HE REMAINED UNSATISFIED LEAVING BUT ONE PATH...

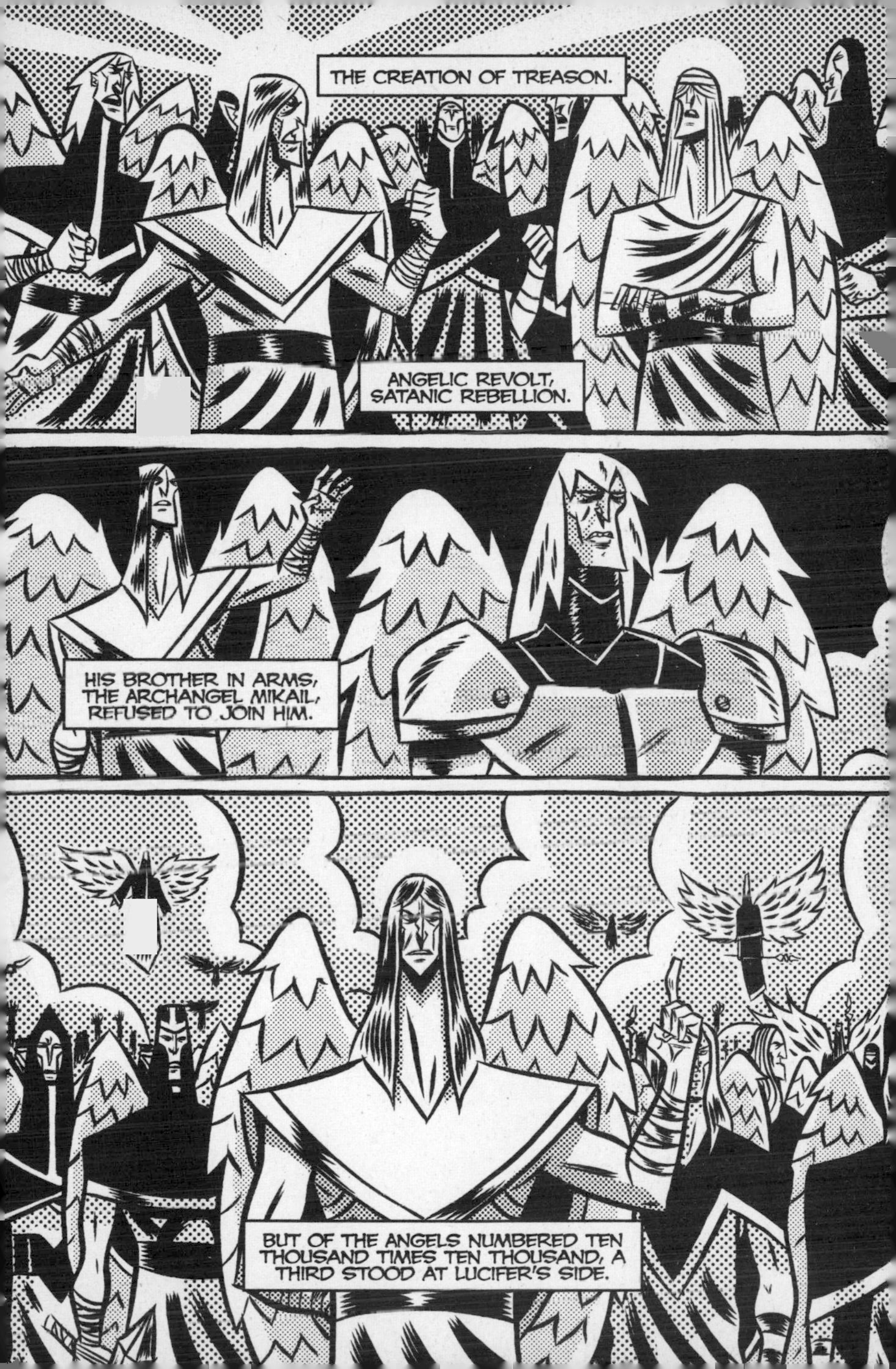
THE CREATION OF TREASON.
ANGELIC REVOLT, SATANIC REBELLION.
HIS BROTHER IN ARMS, THE ARCHANGEL MIKAIL, REFUSED TO JOIN HIM.
BUT OF THE ANGELS NUMBERED TEN THOUSAND TIMES TEN THOUSAND, A THIRD STOOD AT LUCIFER'S SIDE.

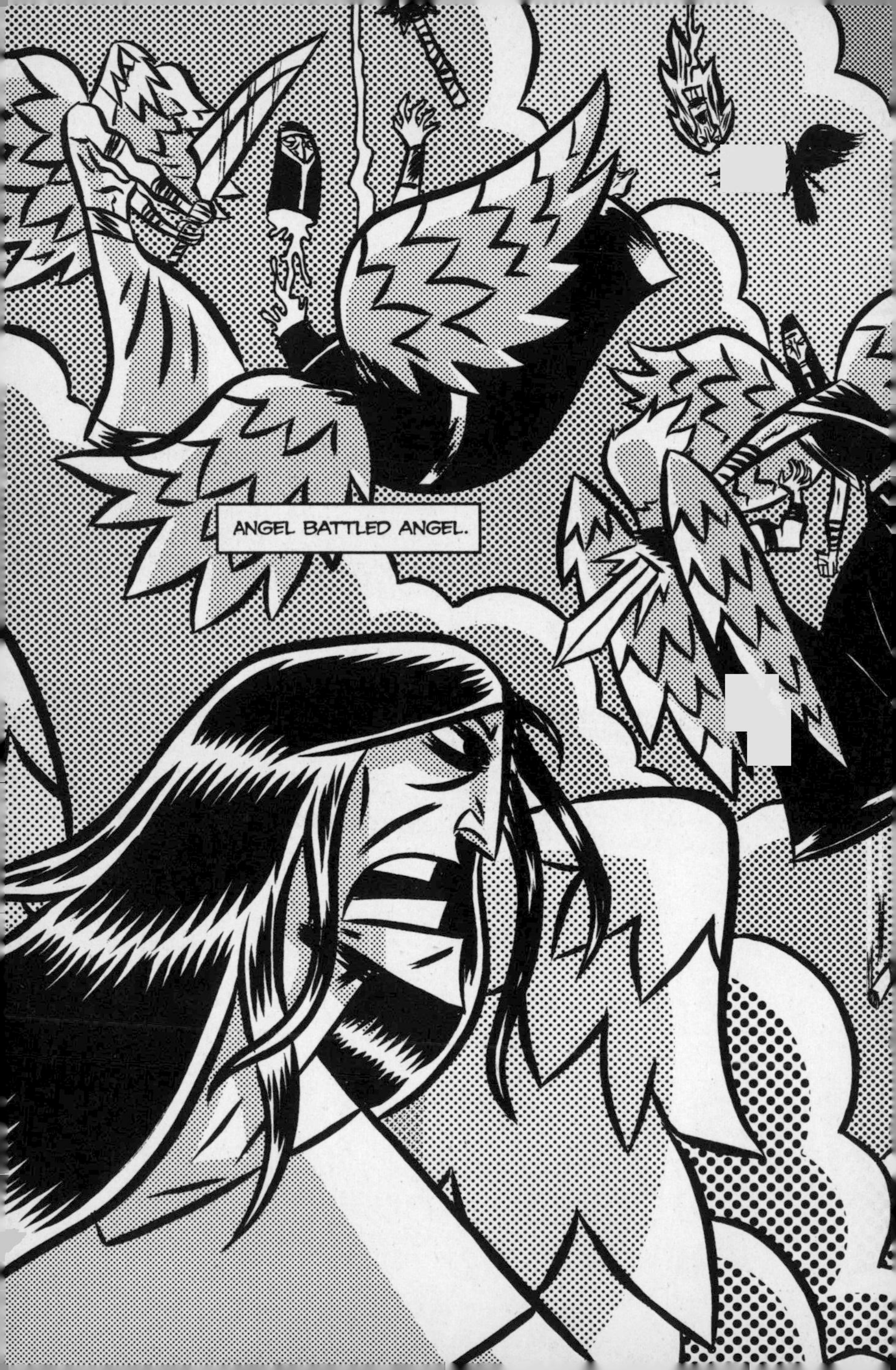
ANGEL BATTLED ANGEL.

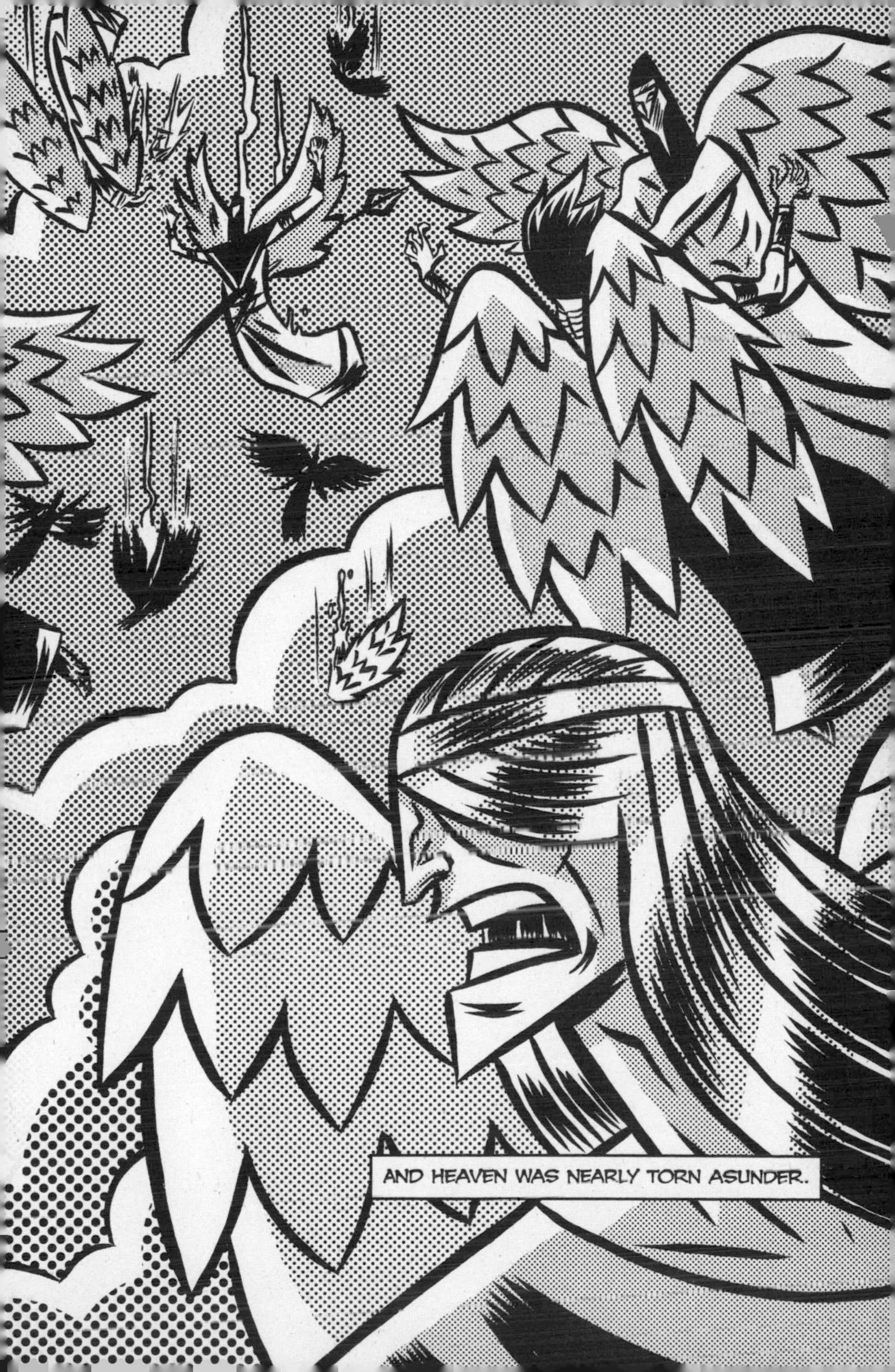
AND HEAVEN WAS NEARLY TORN ASUNDER.

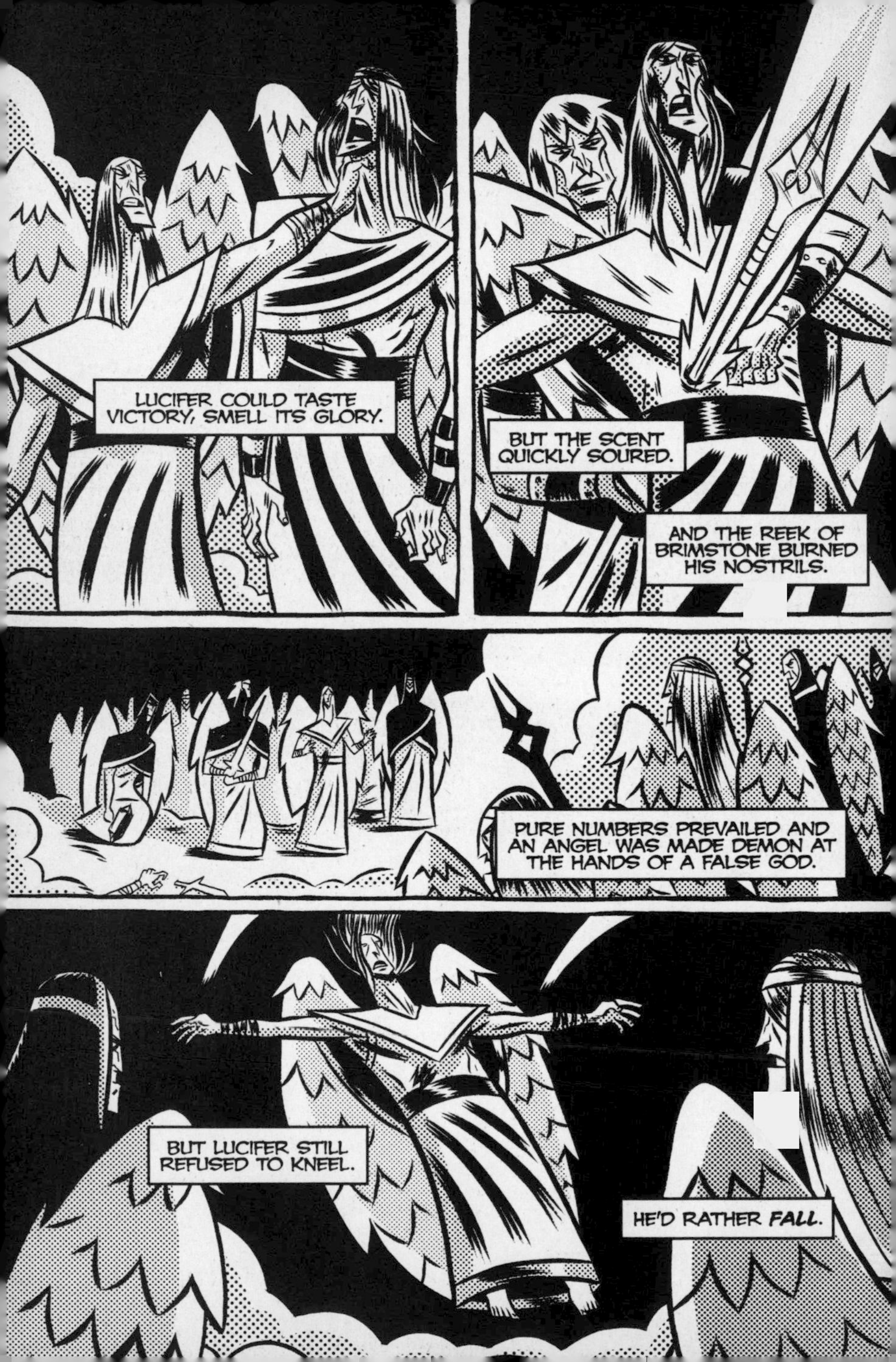
LUCIFER COULD TASTE VICTORY, SMELL ITS GLORY.
BUT THE SCENT QUICKLY SOURED.
AND THE REEK OF BRIMSTONE BURNED HIS NOSTRILS.
PURE NUMBERS PREVAILED AND AN ANGEL WAS MADE DEMON AT THE HANDS OF A FALSE GOD.
BUT LUCIFER STILL REFUSED TO KNEEL.
HE'D RATHER *FALL*.

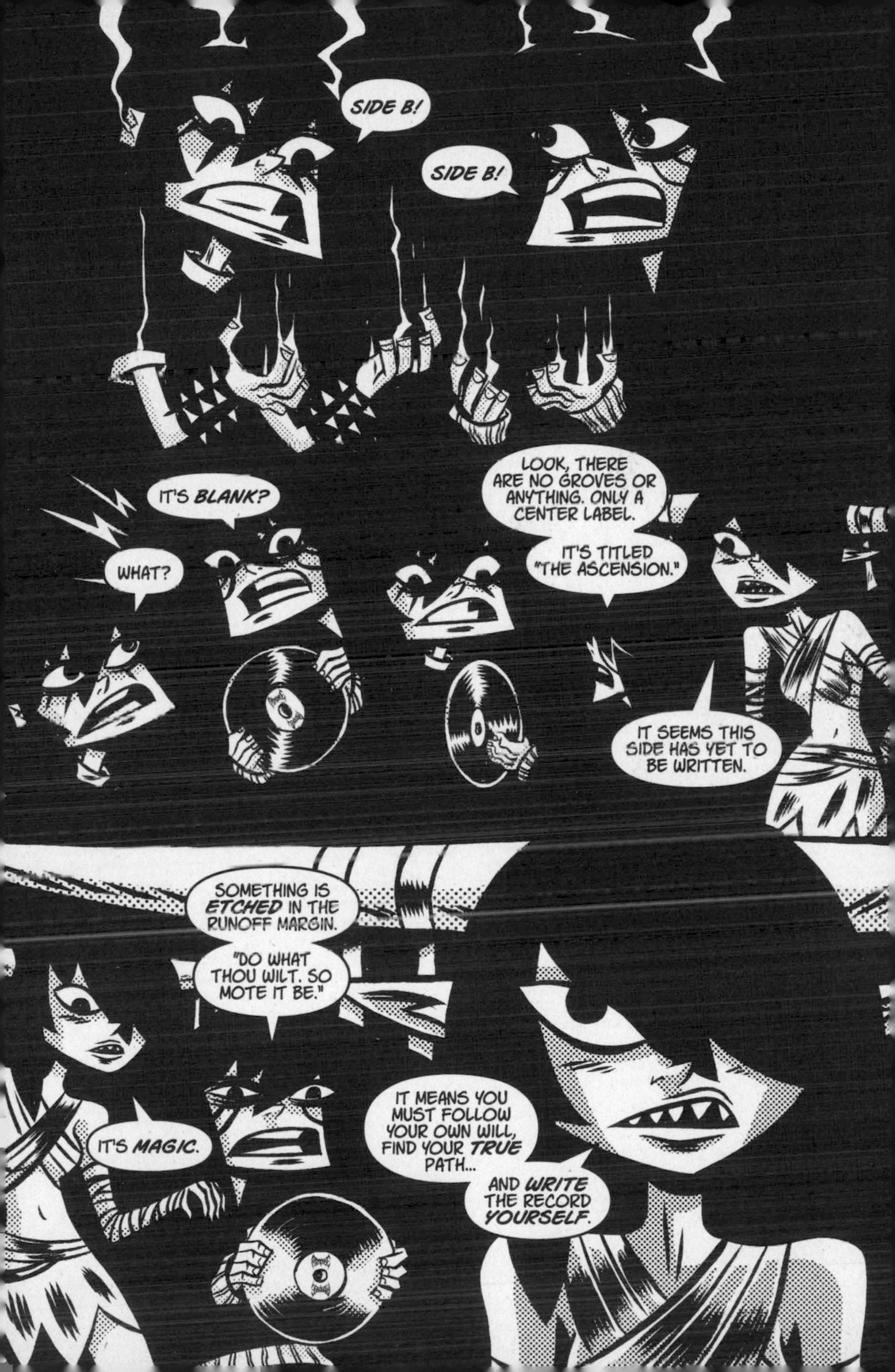
SIDE B!
SIDE B!
IT'S BLANK?
WHAT?
LOOK, THERE ARE NO GROVES OR ANYTHING. ONLY A CENTER LABEL.
IT'S TITLED "THE ASCENSION."
IT SEEMS THIS SIDE HAS YET TO BE WRITTEN.
SOMETHING IS ETCHED IN THE RUNOFF MARGIN.
"DO WHAT THOU WILT. SO MOTE IT BE."
IT'S MAGIC.
IT MEANS YOU MUST FOLLOW YOUR OWN WILL, FIND YOUR TRUE PATH...
AND WRITE THE RECORD YOURSELF.

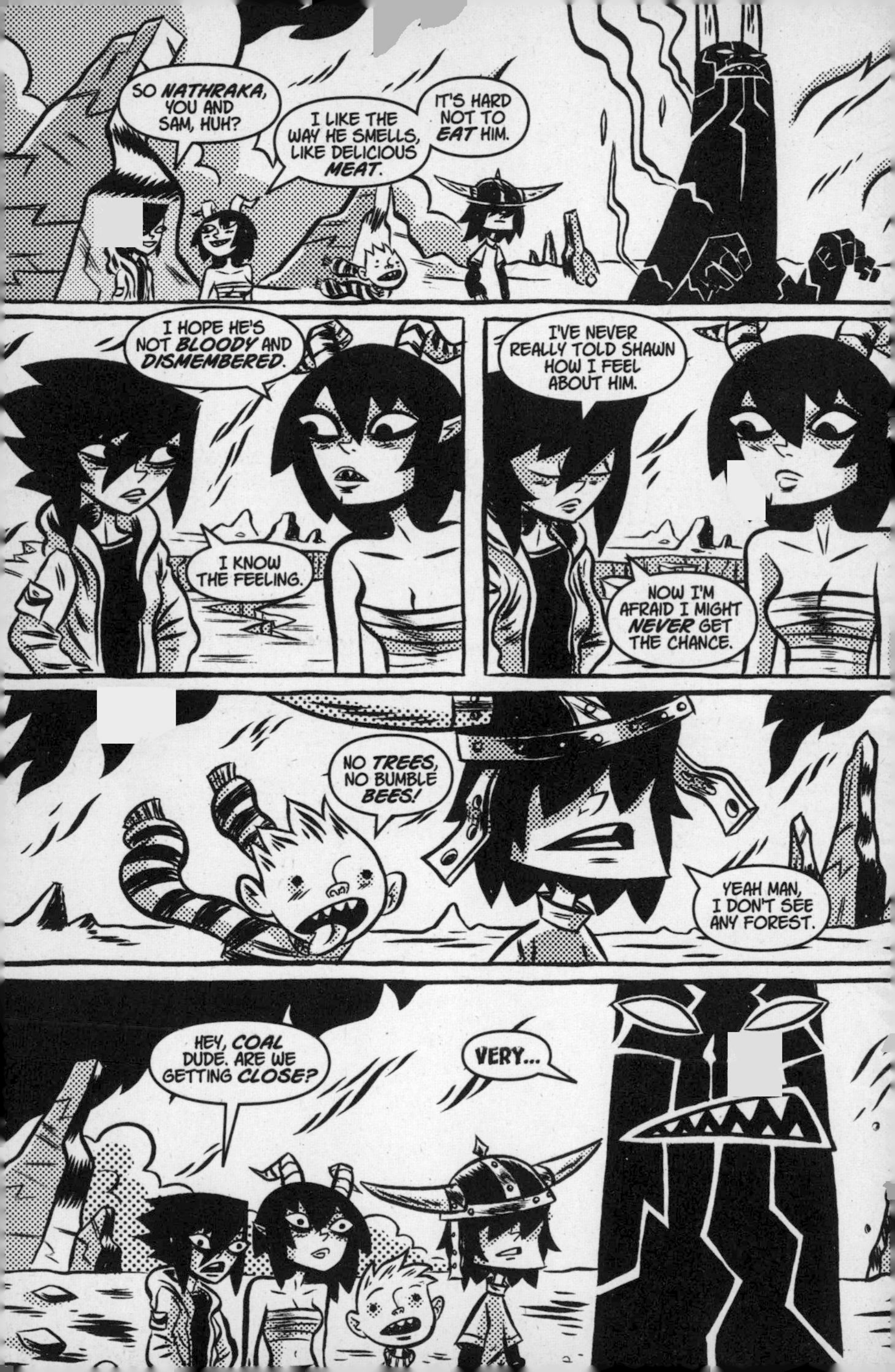
SO NATHRAKA, YOU AND SAM, HUH?
I LIKE THE WAY HE SMELLS, LIKE DELICIOUS MEAT.
IT'S HARD NOT TO EAT HIM.
I HOPE HE'S NOT BLOODY AND DISMEMBERED.
I KNOW THE FEELING.
I'VE NEVER REALLY TOLD SHAWN HOW I FEEL ABOUT HIM.
NOW I'M AFRAID I MIGHT NEVER GET THE CHANCE.
NO TREES, NO BUMBLE BEES!
YEAH MAN, I DON'T SEE ANY FOREST.
HEY, COAL DUDE. ARE WE GETTING CLOSE?
VERY...

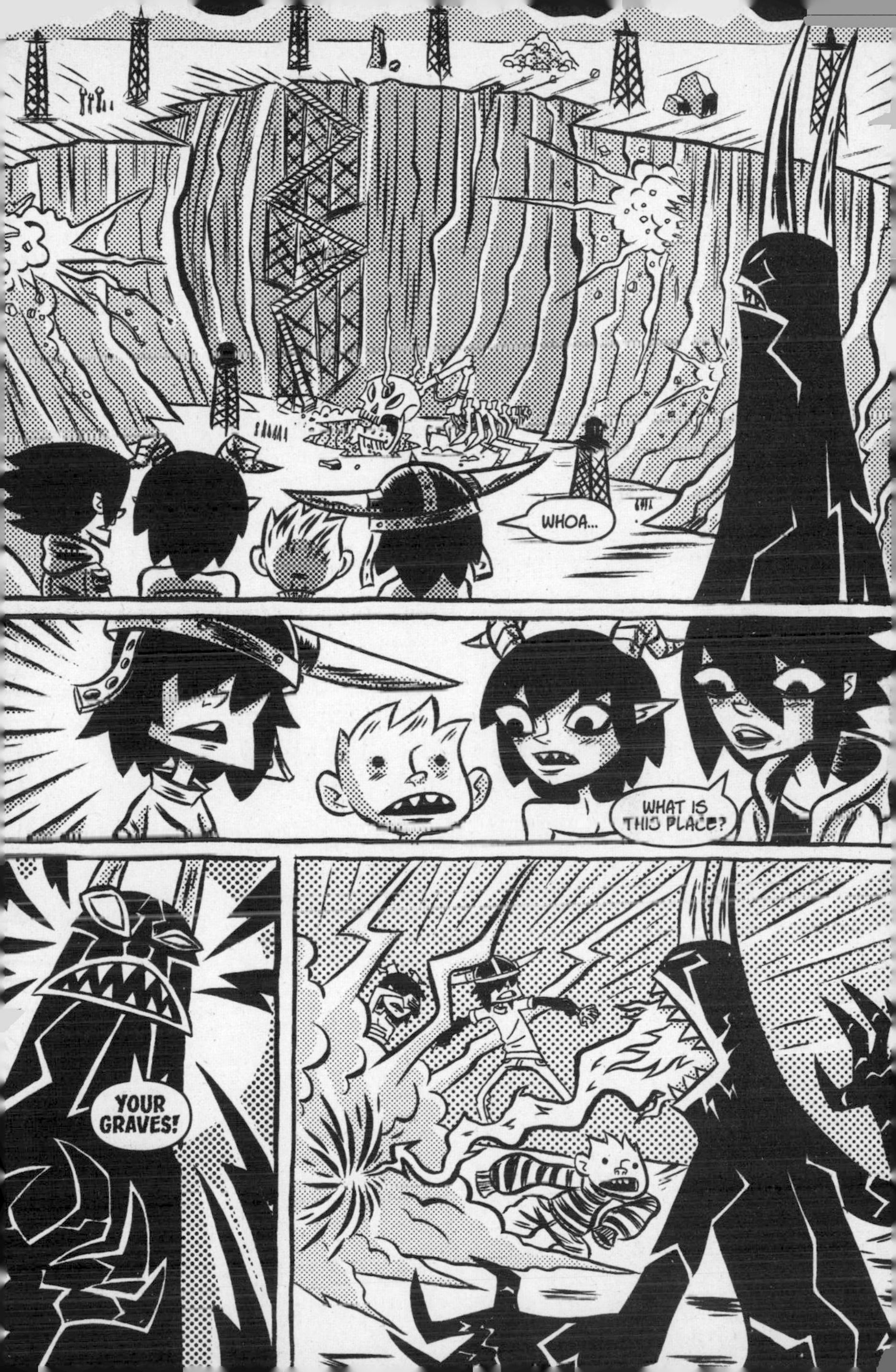
WHOA...
WHAT IS THIS PLACE?
YOUR GRAVES!

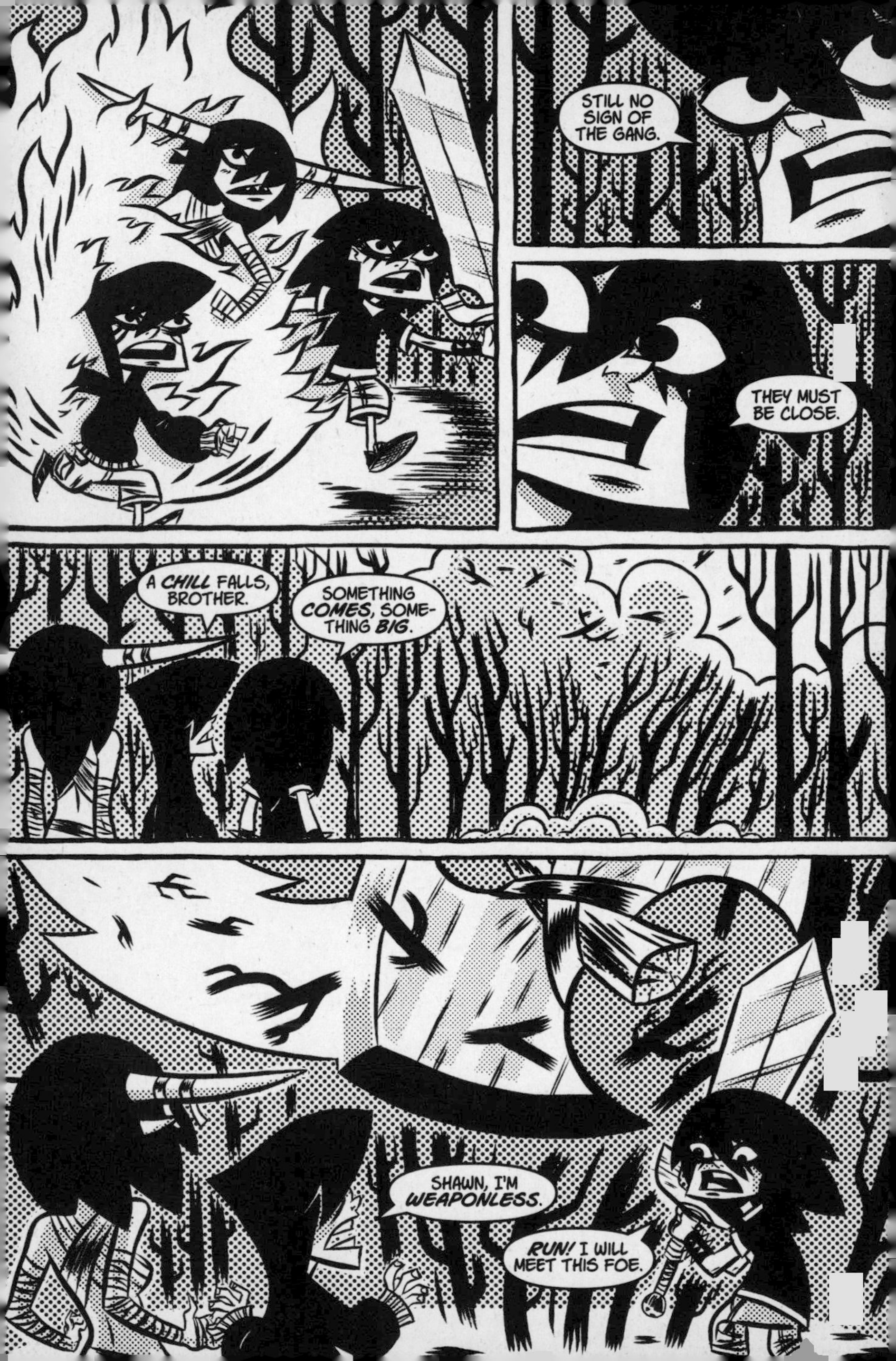
STILL NO SIGN OF THE GANG.
THEY MUST BE CLOSE.
A *CHILL* FALLS, BROTHER.
SOMETHING *COMES*, SOMETHING *BIG*.
SHAWN, I'M *WEAPONLESS*.
RUN! I WILL MEET THIS FOE.

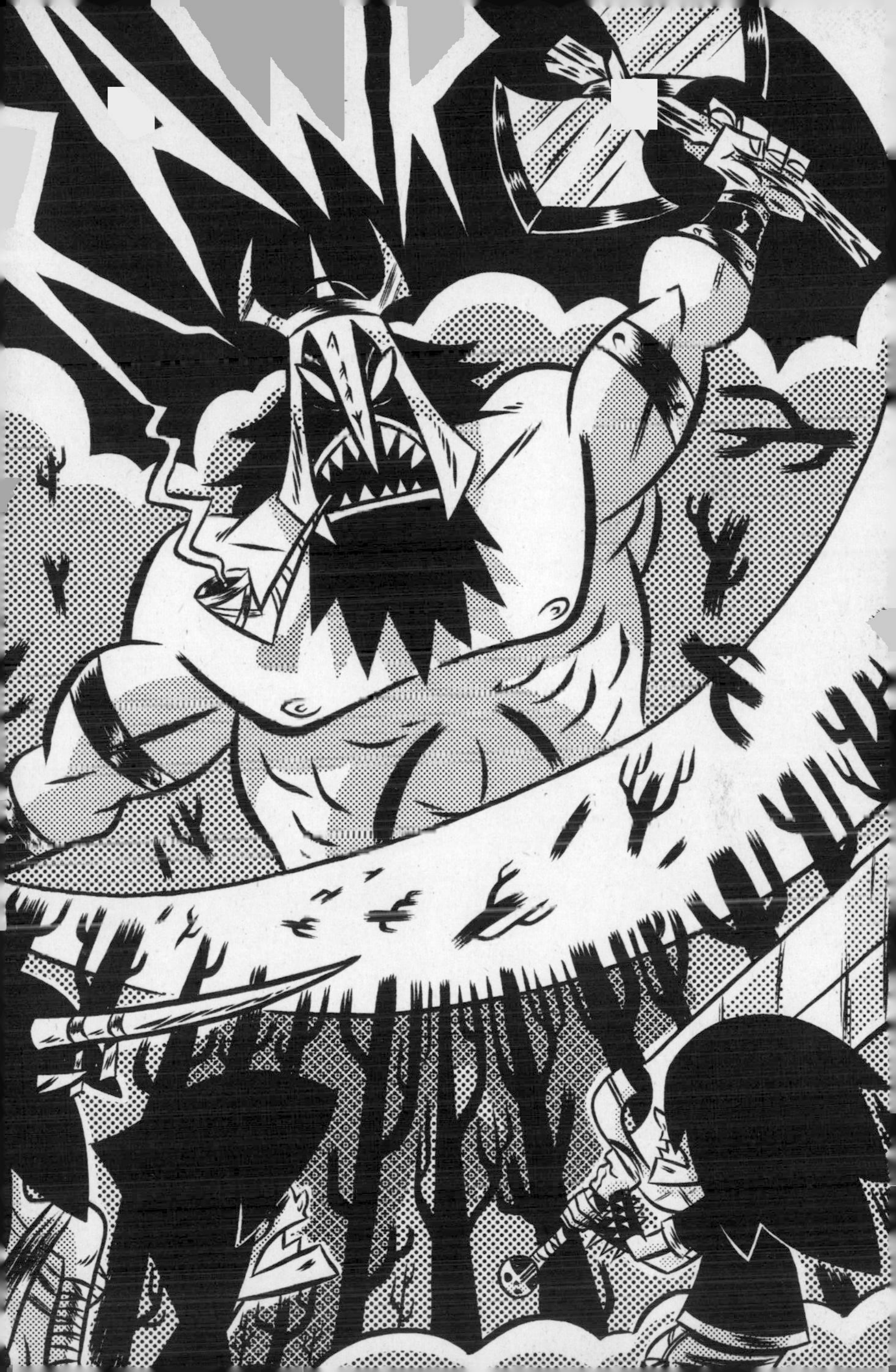

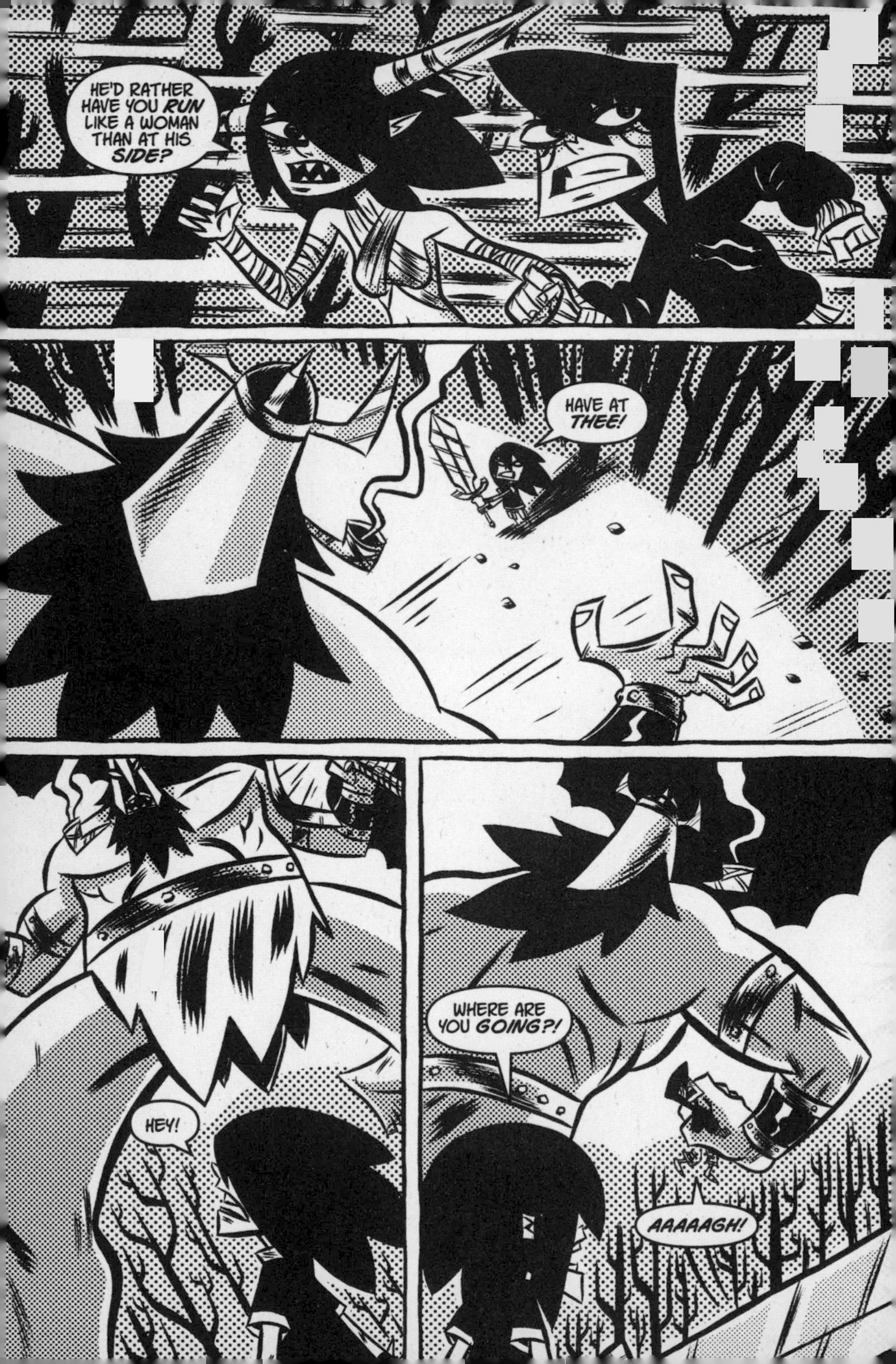
HE'D RATHER HAVE YOU RUN LIKE A WOMAN THAN AT HIS SIDE?
HAVE AT THEE!
HEY!
WHERE ARE YOU GOING?!
AAAAAGH!

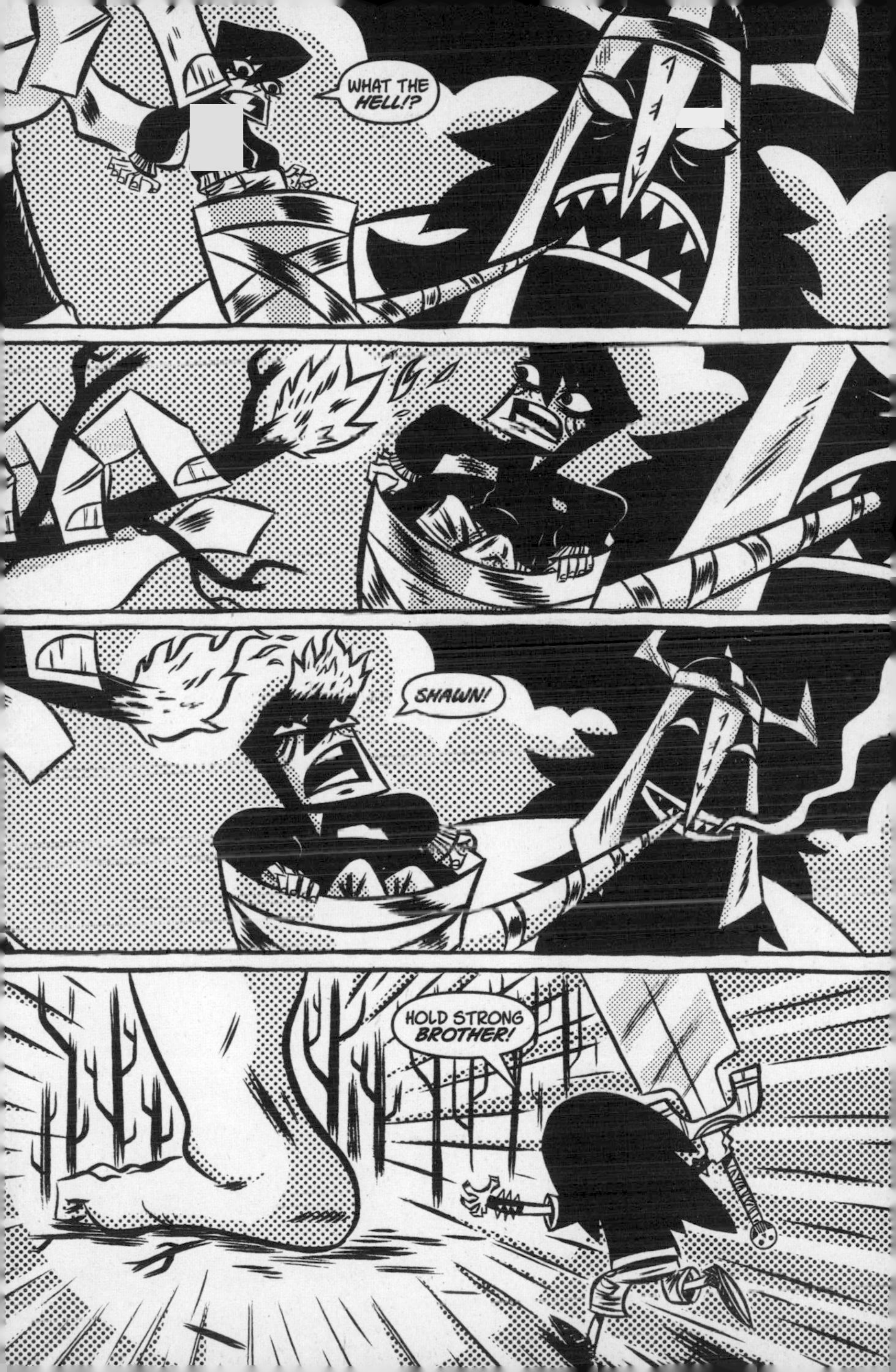
WHAT THE HELL!?
SHAWN!
HOLD STRONG BROTHER!

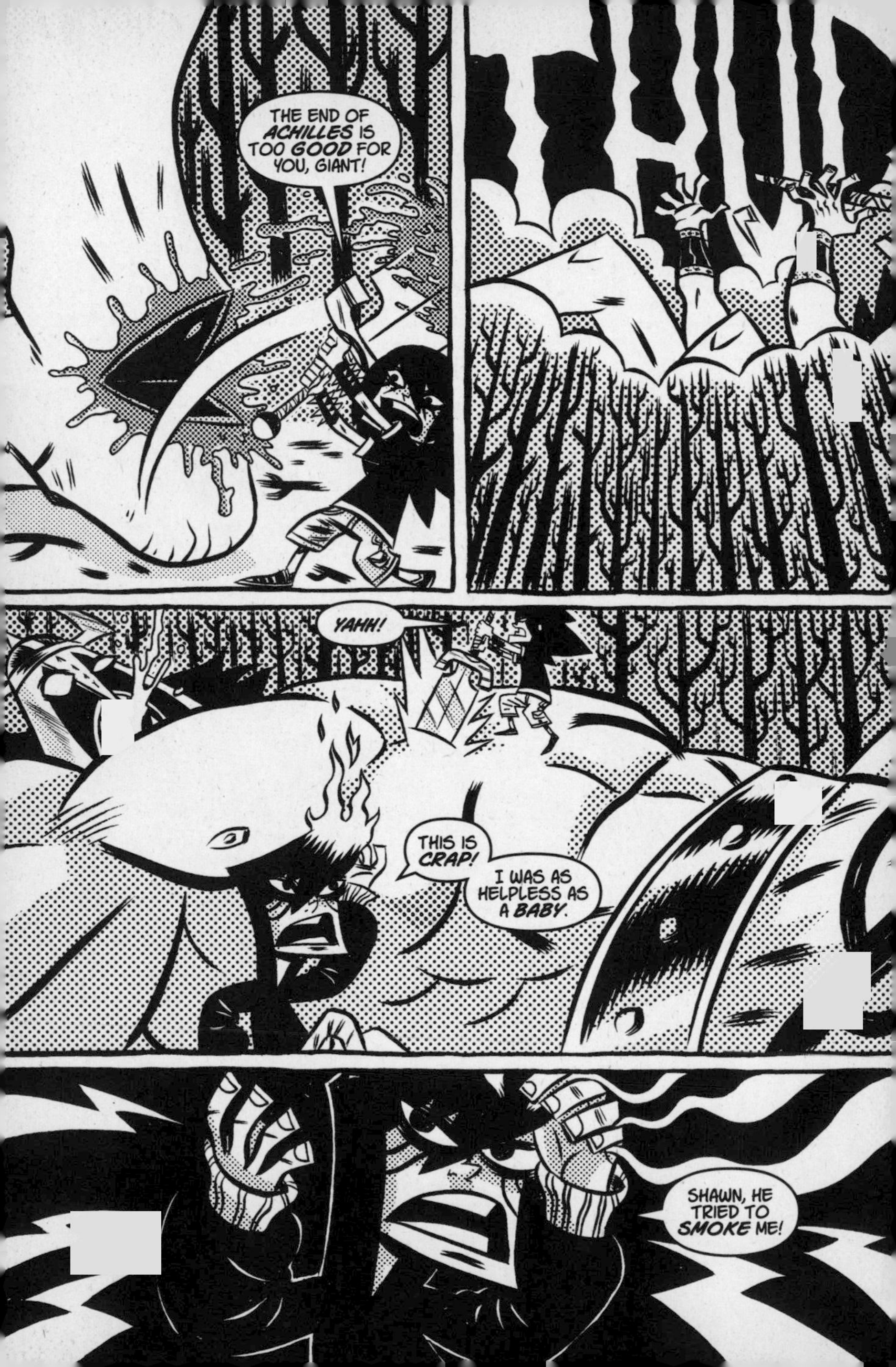
THE END OF ACHILLES IS TOO GOOD FOR YOU, GIANT!
YAHH!
THIS IS CRAP!
I WAS AS HELPLESS AS A BABY.
SHAWN, HE TRIED TO SMOKE ME!

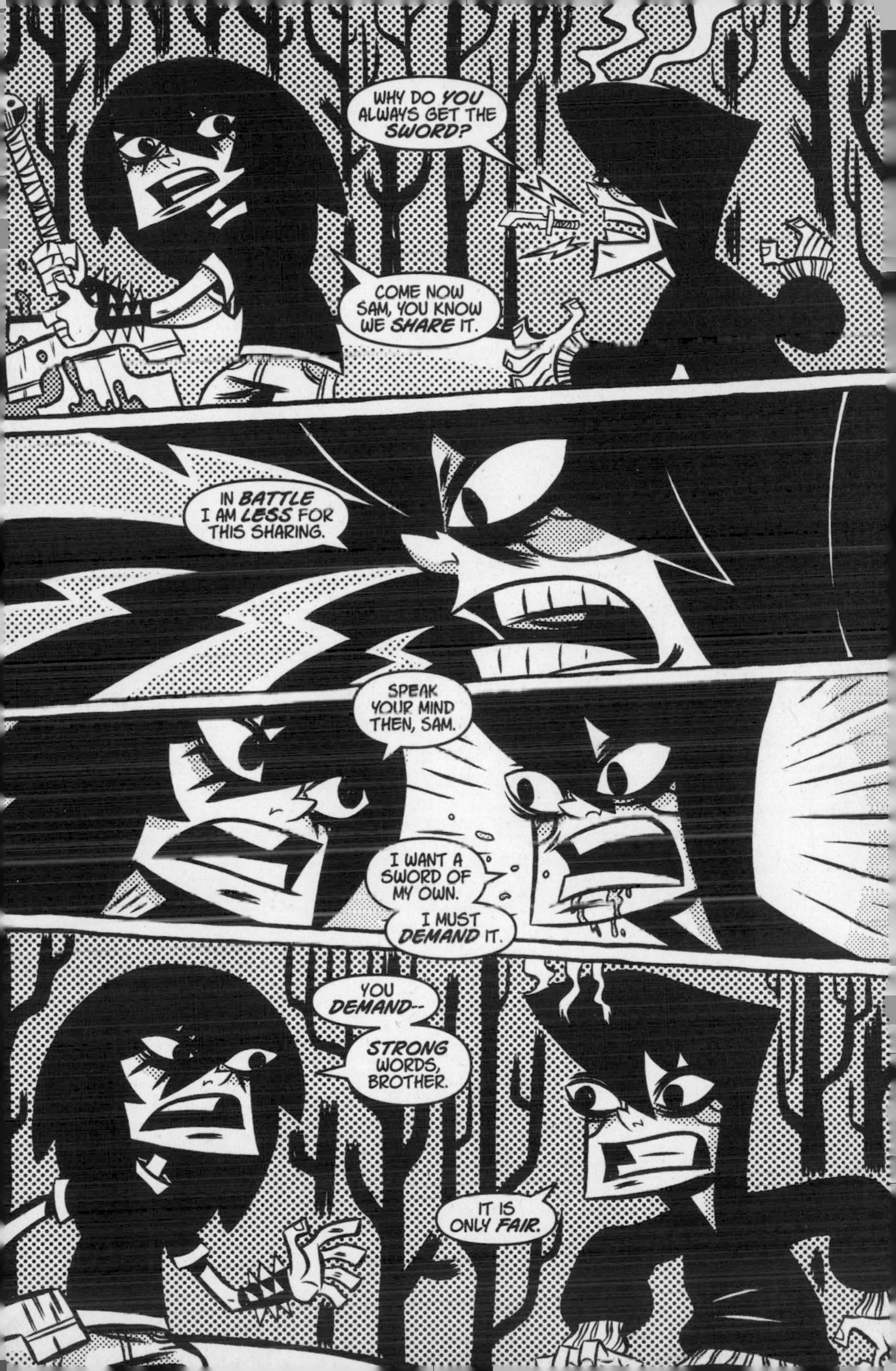
WHY DO YOU ALWAYS GET THE SWORD?
COME NOW SAM, YOU KNOW WE SHARE IT.
IN BATTLE I AM LESS FOR THIS SHARING.
SPEAK YOUR MIND THEN, SAM.
I WANT A SWORD OF MY OWN.
I MUST DEMAND IT.
YOU DEMAND--
STRONG WORDS, BROTHER.
IT IS ONLY FAIR.

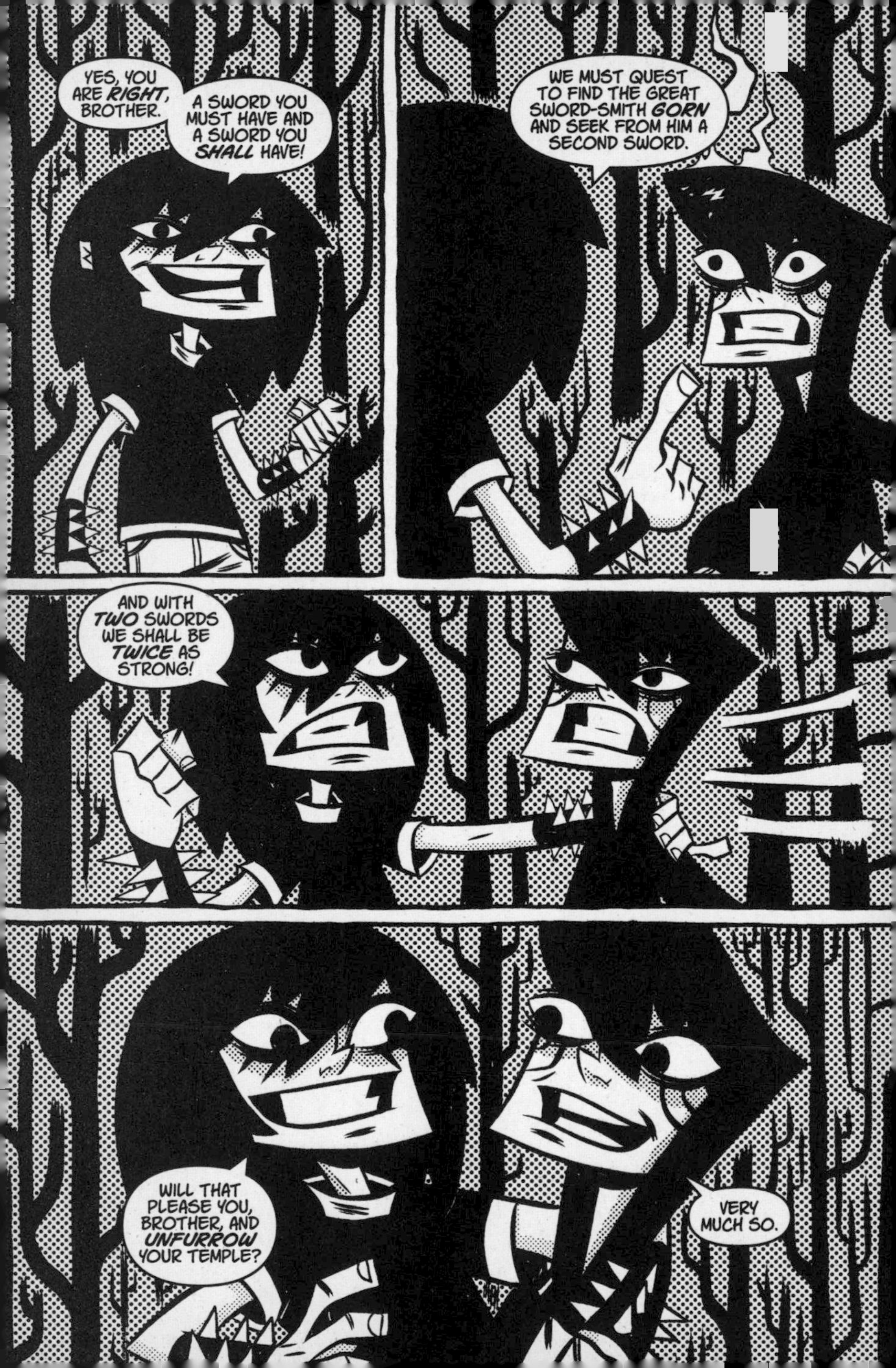
YES, YOU ARE RIGHT, BROTHER.
A SWORD YOU MUST HAVE AND A SWORD YOU SHALL HAVE!
WE MUST QUEST TO FIND THE GREAT SWORD-SMITH GORN AND SEEK FROM HIM A SECOND SWORD.
AND WITH TWO SWORDS WE SHALL BE TWICE AS STRONG!
WILL THAT PLEASE YOU, BROTHER, AND UNFURROW YOUR TEMPLE?
VERY MUCH SO.

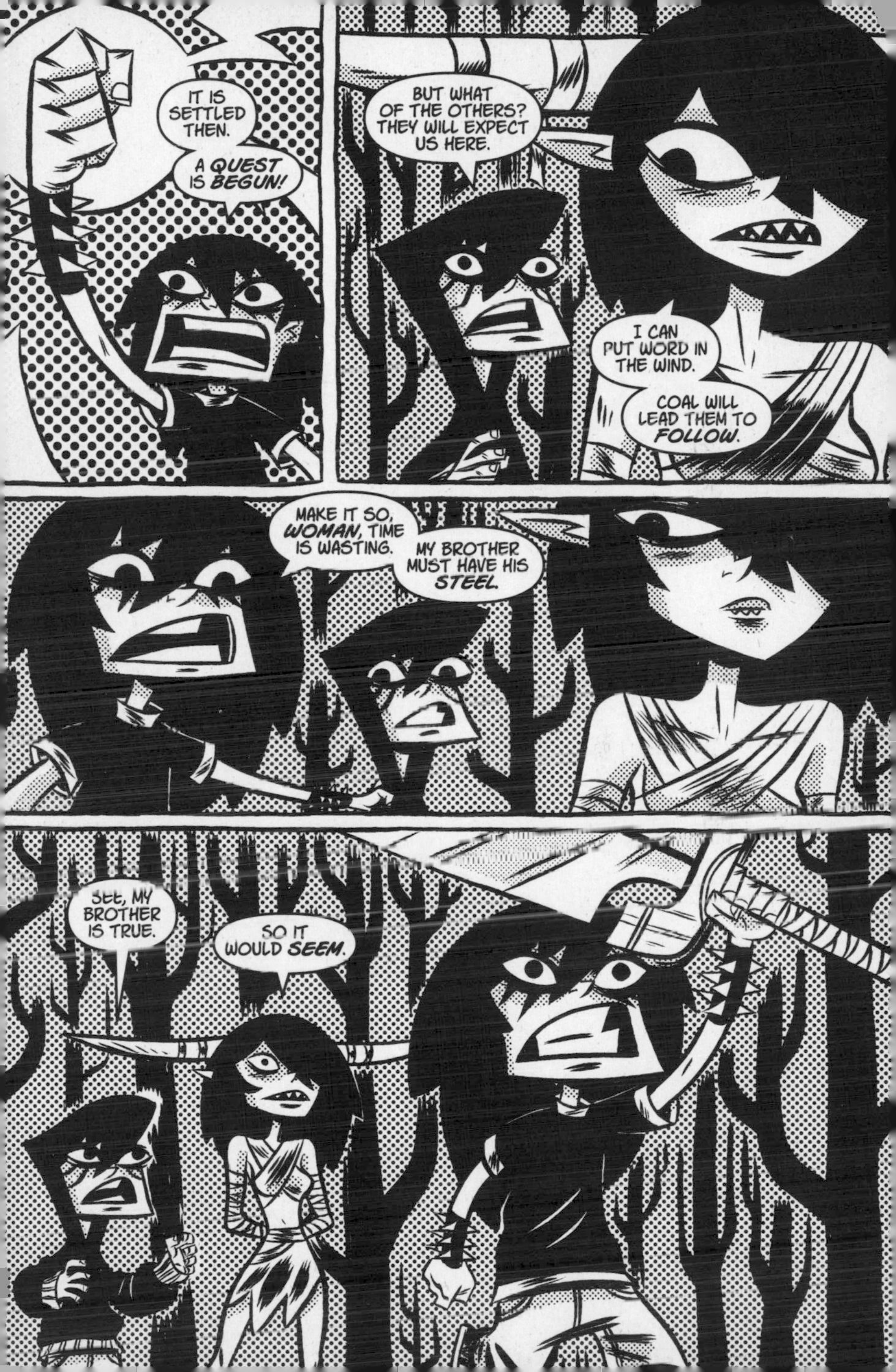
IT IS SETTLED THEN.
A QUEST IS BEGUN!
BUT WHAT OF THE OTHERS? THEY WILL EXPECT US HERE.
I CAN PUT WORD IN THE WIND.
COAL WILL LEAD THEM TO FOLLOW.
MAKE IT SO, WOMAN, TIME IS WASTING.
MY BROTHER MUST HAVE HIS STEEL.
SEE, MY BROTHER IS TRUE.
SO IT WOULD SEEM.

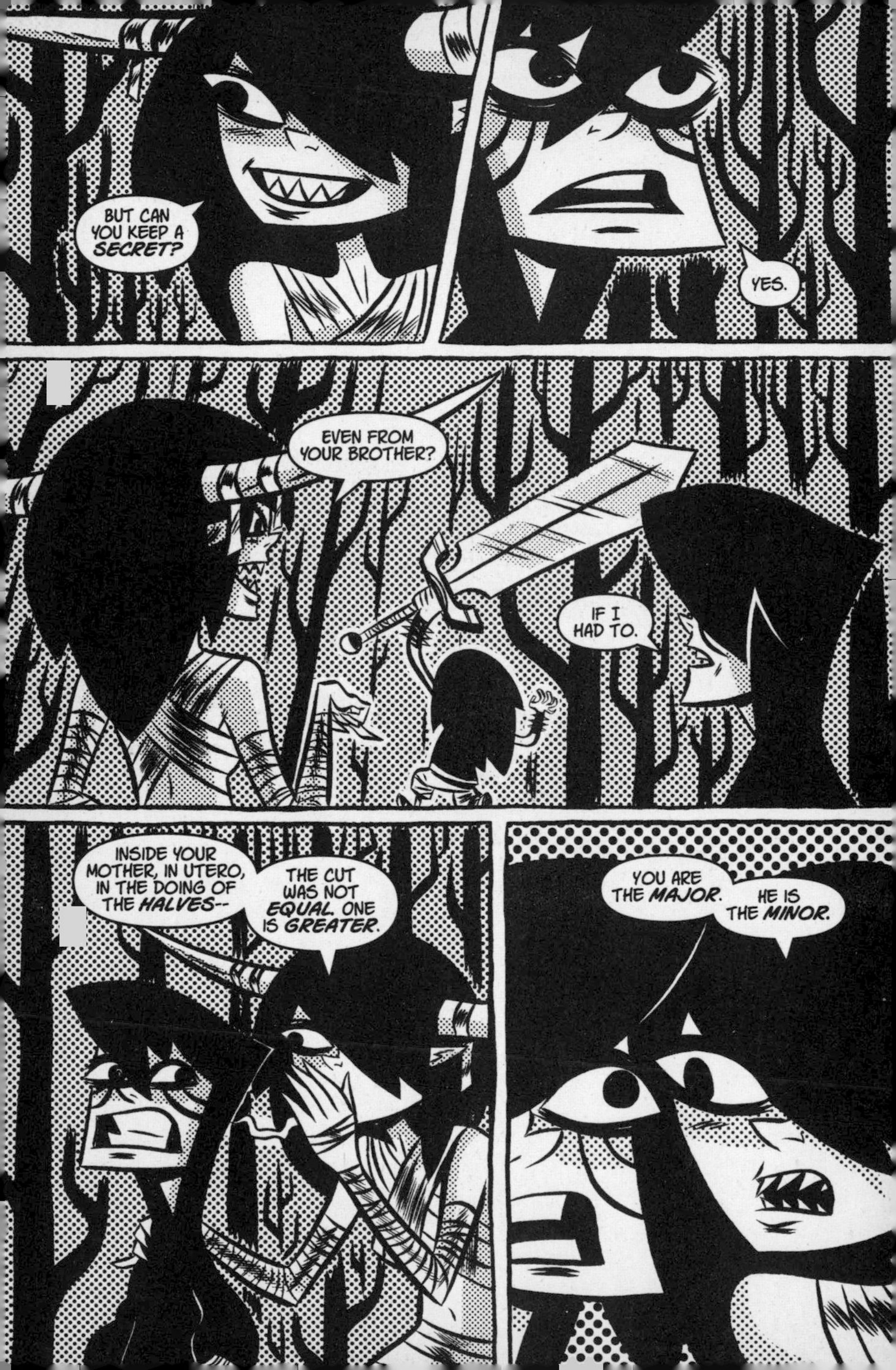
BUT CAN YOU KEEP A SECRET?
YES.
EVEN FROM YOUR BROTHER?
IF I HAD TO.
INSIDE YOUR MOTHER, IN UTERO, IN THE DOING OF THE HALVES--
THE CUT WAS NOT EQUAL. ONE IS GREATER.
YOU ARE THE MAJOR.
HE IS THE MINOR.

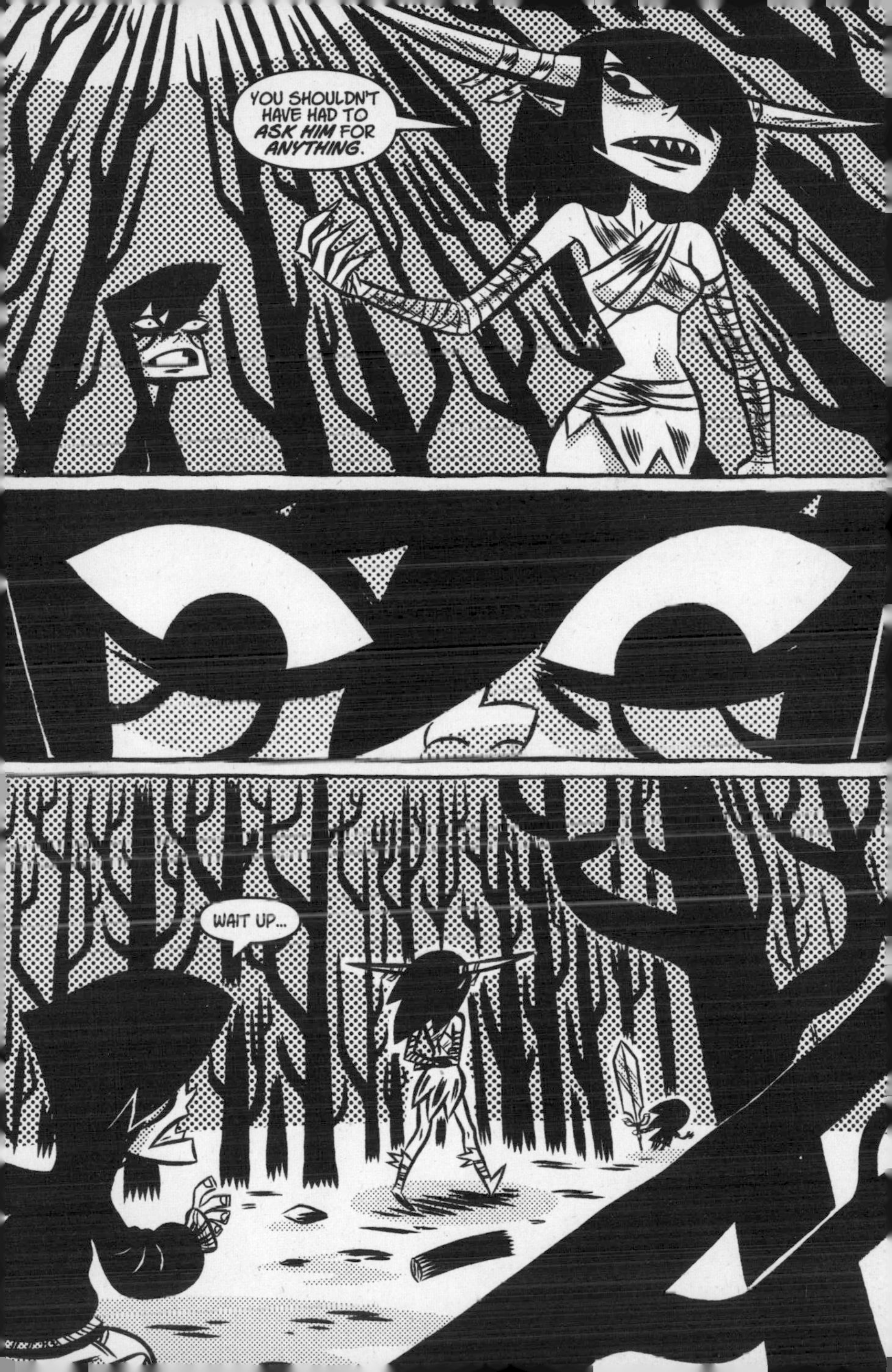
YOU SHOULDN'T HAVE HAD TO ASK HIM FOR ANYTHING.
WAIT UP...

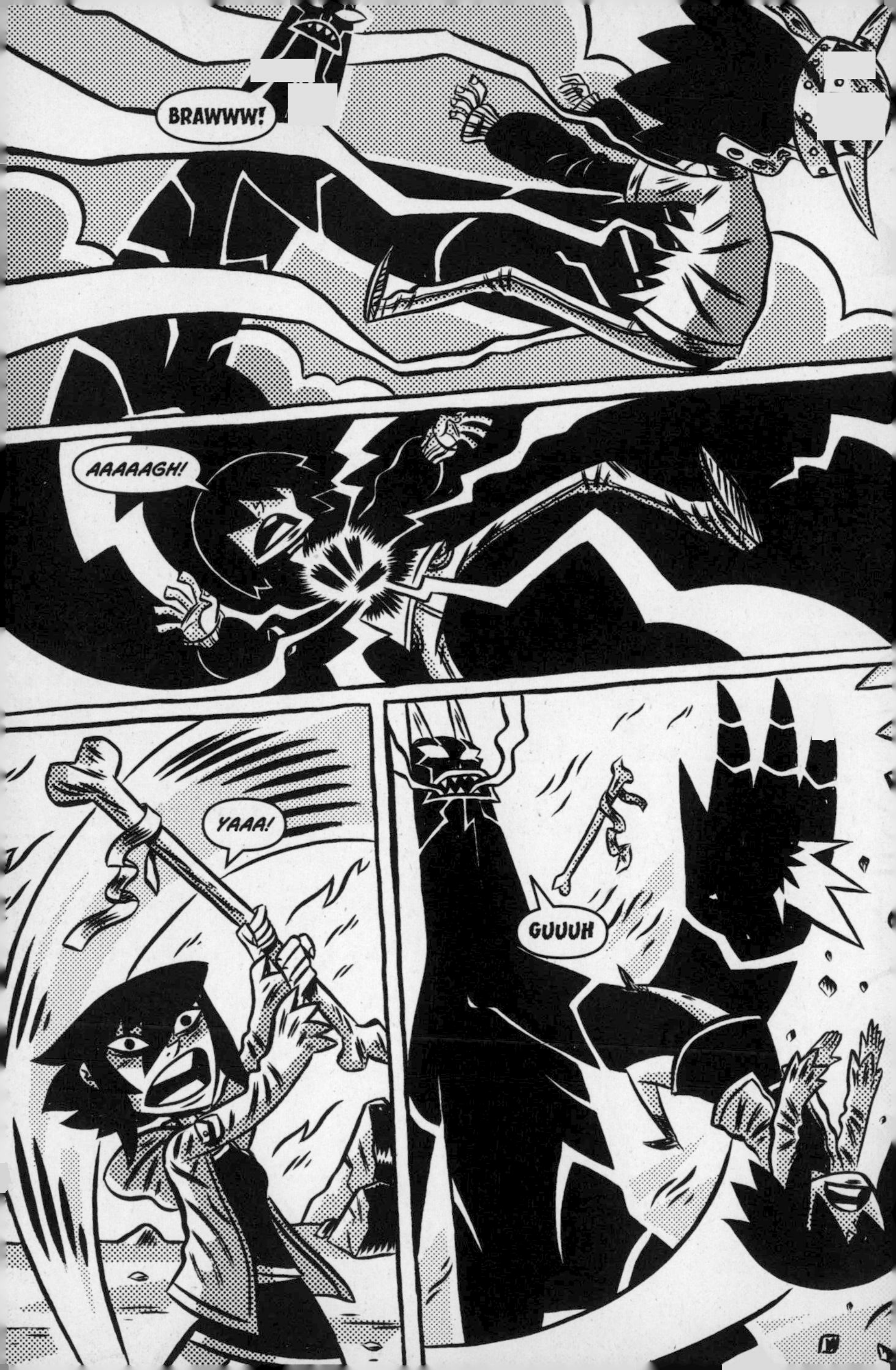
BRAWWW!
AAAAAGH!
YAAA!
GUUUH

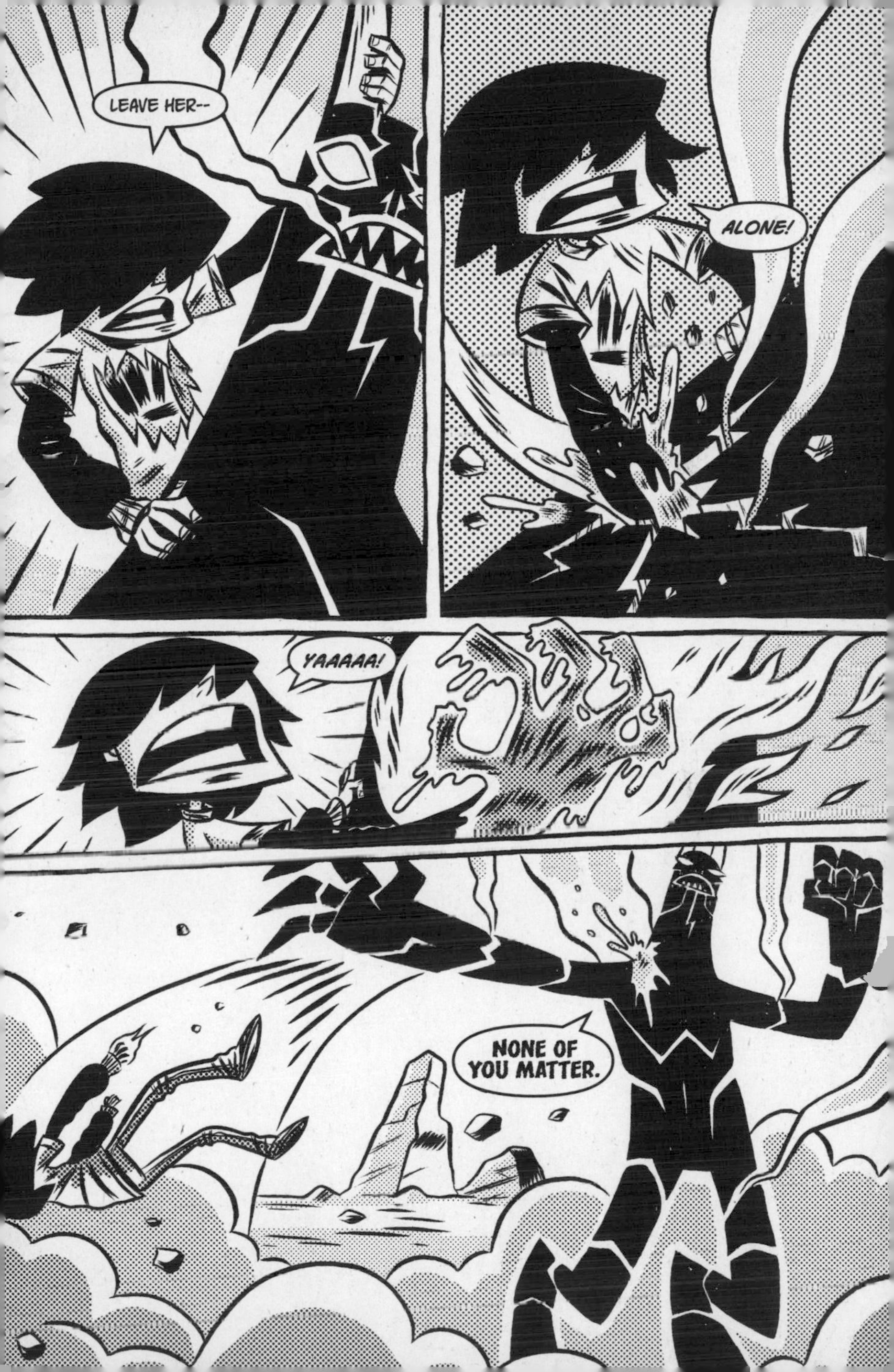
LEAVE HER--
ALONE!
YAAAAA!
NONE OF YOU MATTER.

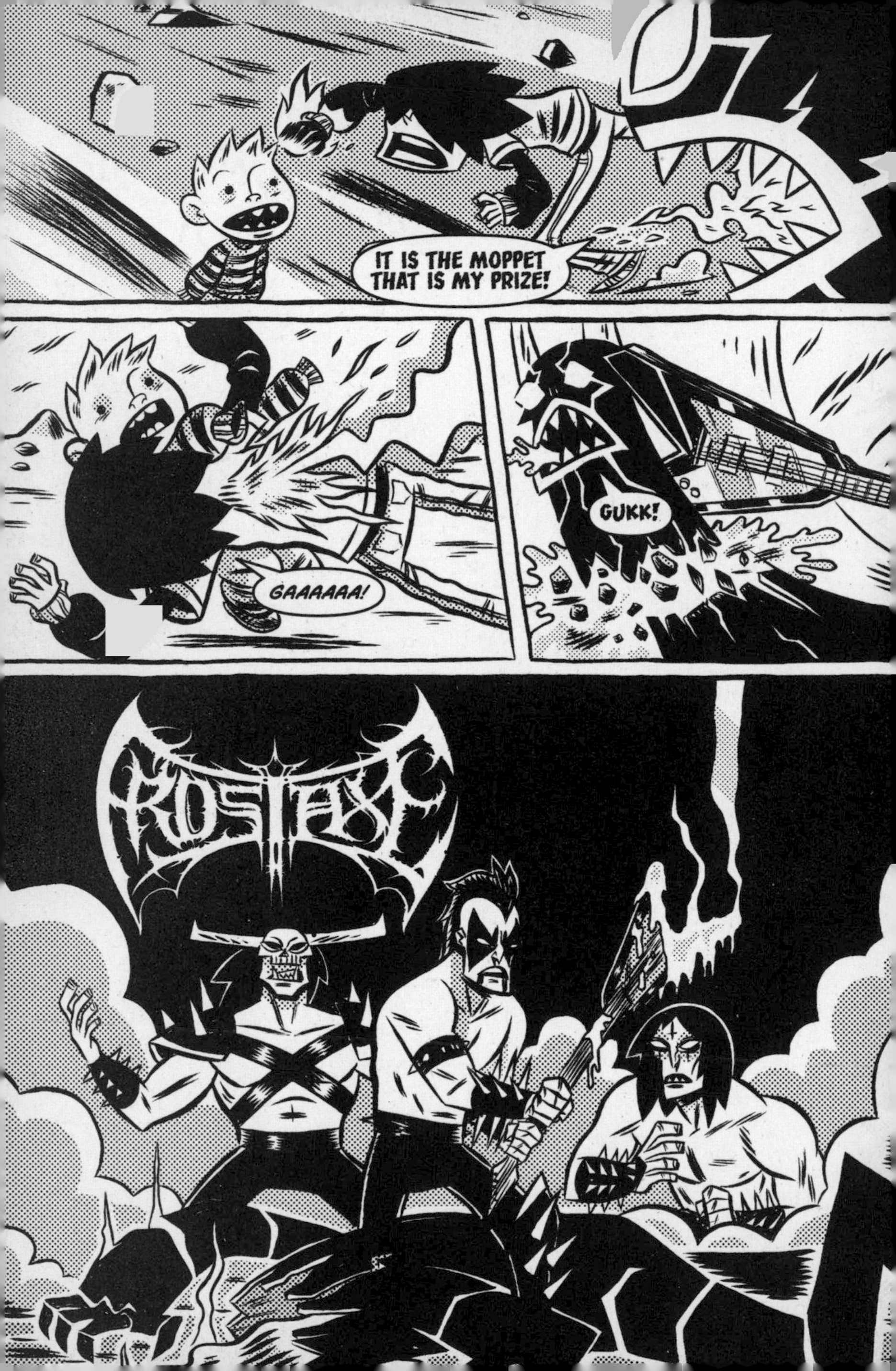
IT IS THE MOPPET THAT IS MY PRIZE!
GAAAAAA!
GUKK!

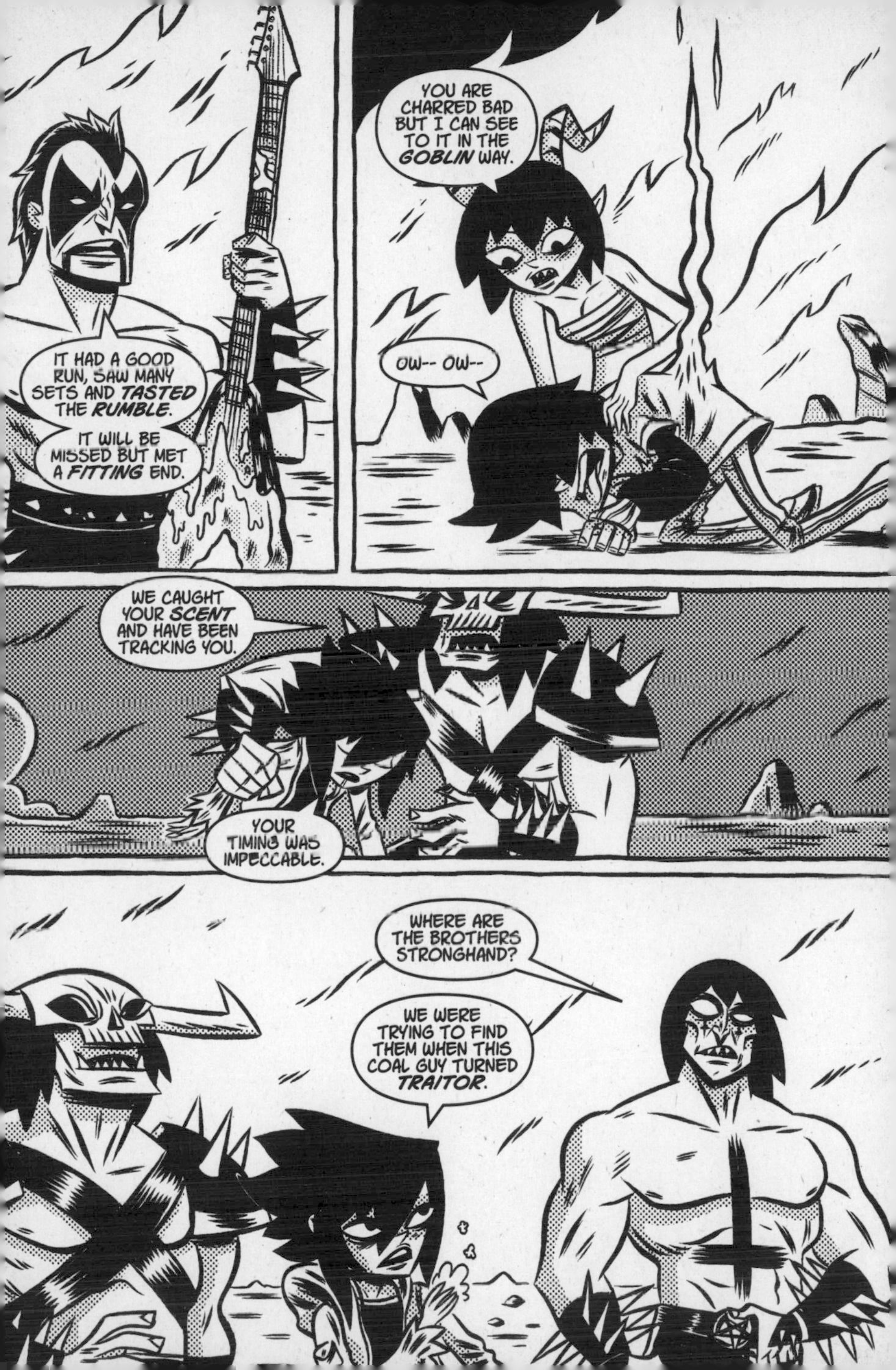
IT HAD A GOOD RUN, SAW MANY SETS AND TASTED THE RUMBLE.
IT WILL BE MISSED BUT MET A FITTING END.
YOU ARE CHARRED BAD BUT I CAN SEE TO IT IN THE GOBLIN WAY.
OW-- OW--
WE CAUGHT YOUR SCENT AND HAVE BEEN TRACKING YOU.
YOUR TIMING WAS IMPECCABLE.
WHERE ARE THE BROTHERS STRONGHAND?
WE WERE TRYING TO FIND THEM WHEN THIS COAL GUY TURNED TRAITOR.

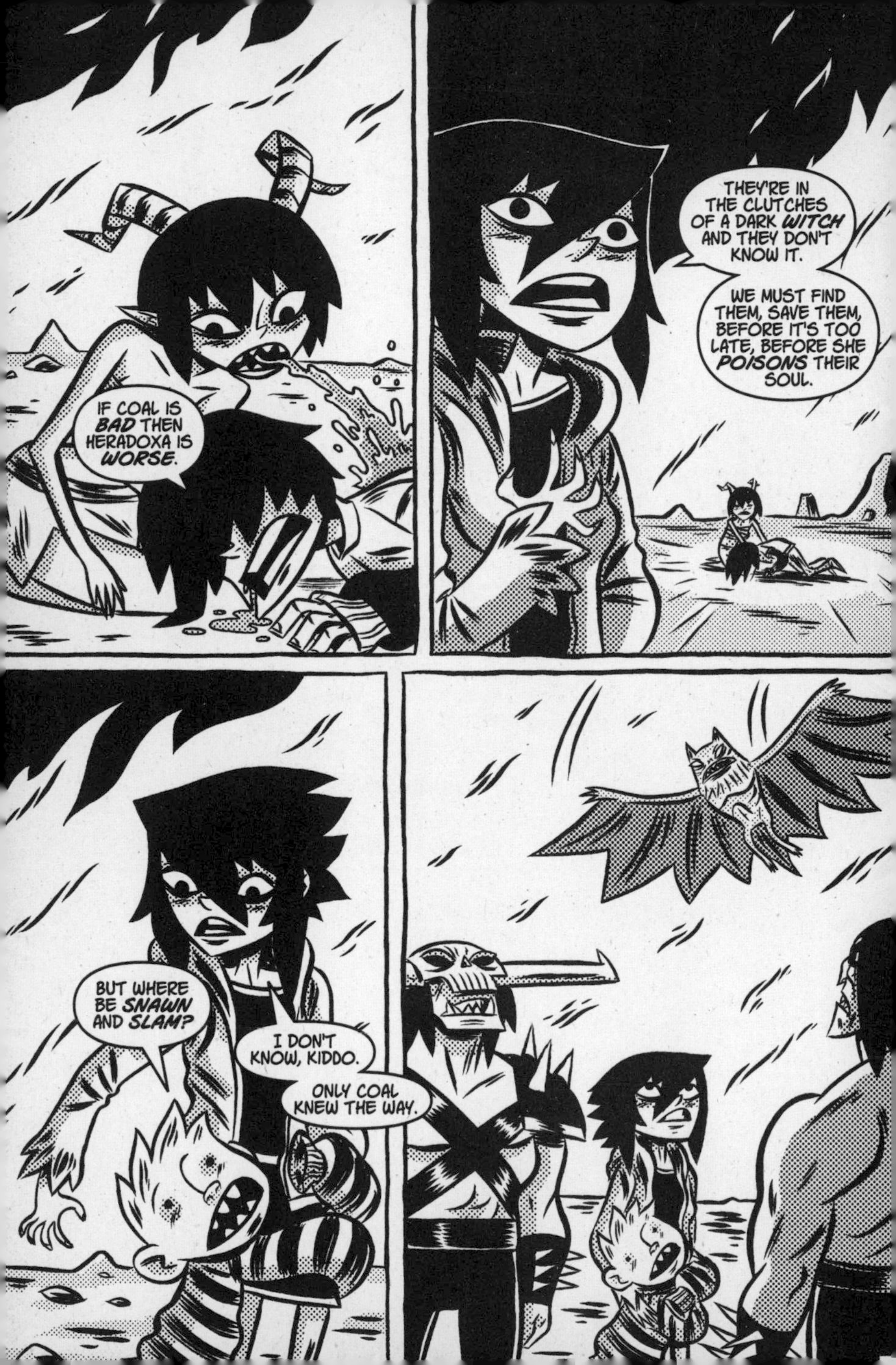
IF COAL IS BAD THEN HERADOXA IS WORSE.
THEY'RE IN THE CLUTCHES OF A DARK WITCH AND THEY DON'T KNOW IT.
WE MUST FIND THEM, SAVE THEM, BEFORE IT'S TOO LATE, BEFORE SHE POISONS THEIR SOUL.
BUT WHERE BE SNAWN AND SLAM?
I DON'T KNOW, KIDDO.
ONLY COAL KNEW THE WAY.

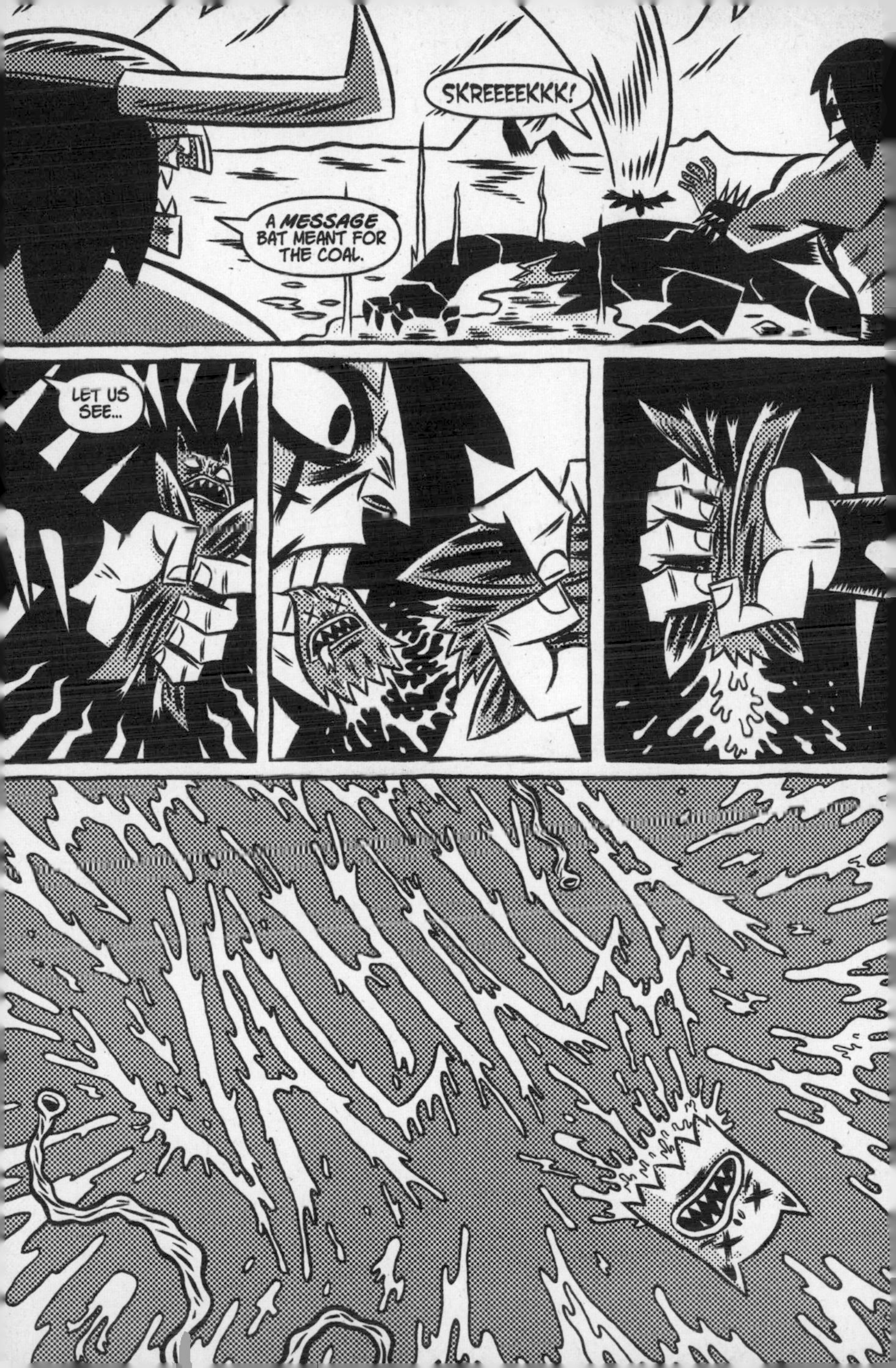

SKREEEEKKK!
A MESSAGE BAT MEANT FOR THE COAL.
LET US SEE...

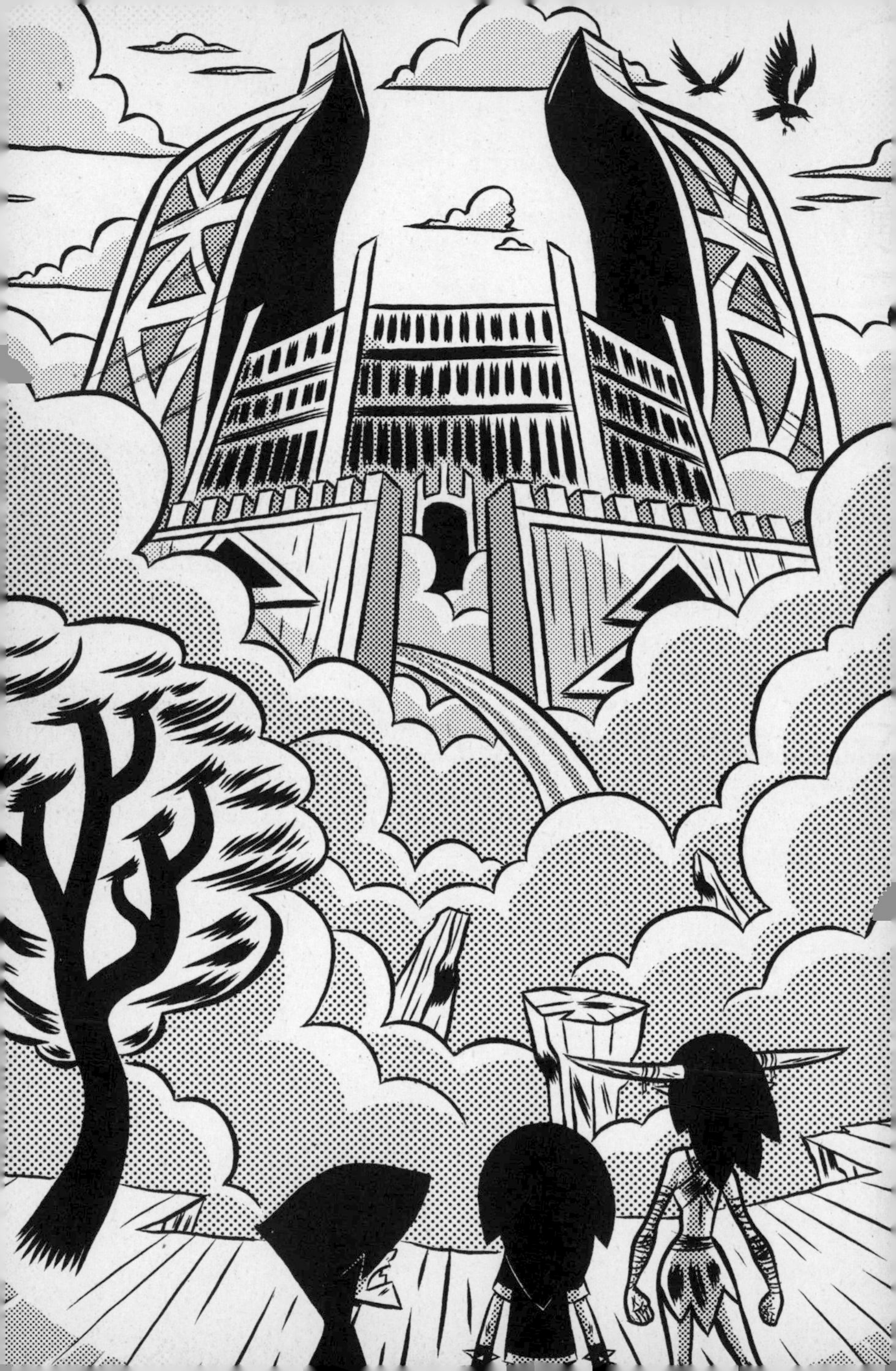

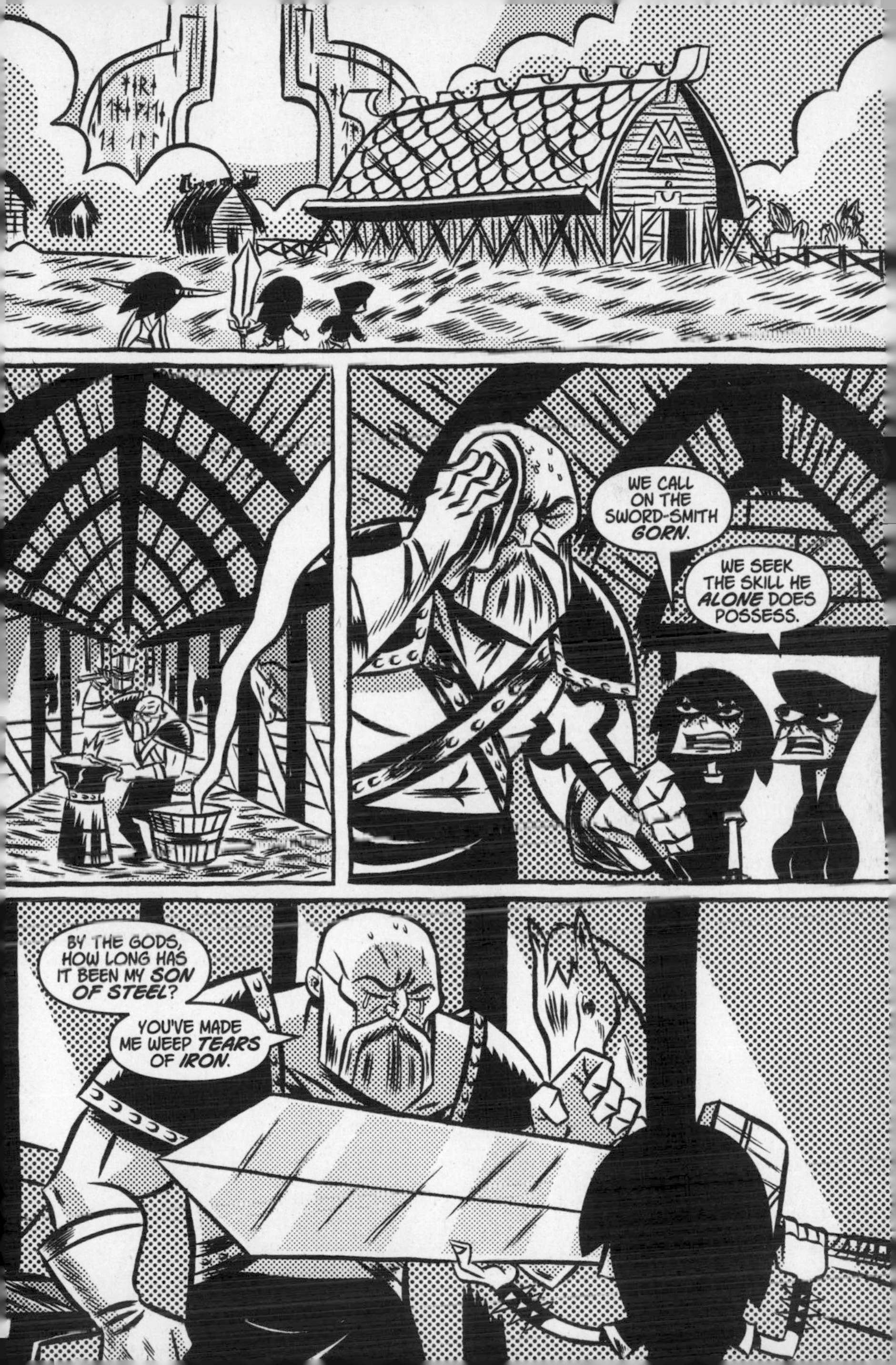
WE CALL ON THE SWORD-SMITH *GORN*.
WE SEEK THE SKILL HE *ALONE* DOES POSSESS.
BY THE GODS, HOW LONG HAS IT BEEN MY *SON OF STEEL*?
YOU'VE MADE ME WEEP *TEARS OF IRON*.

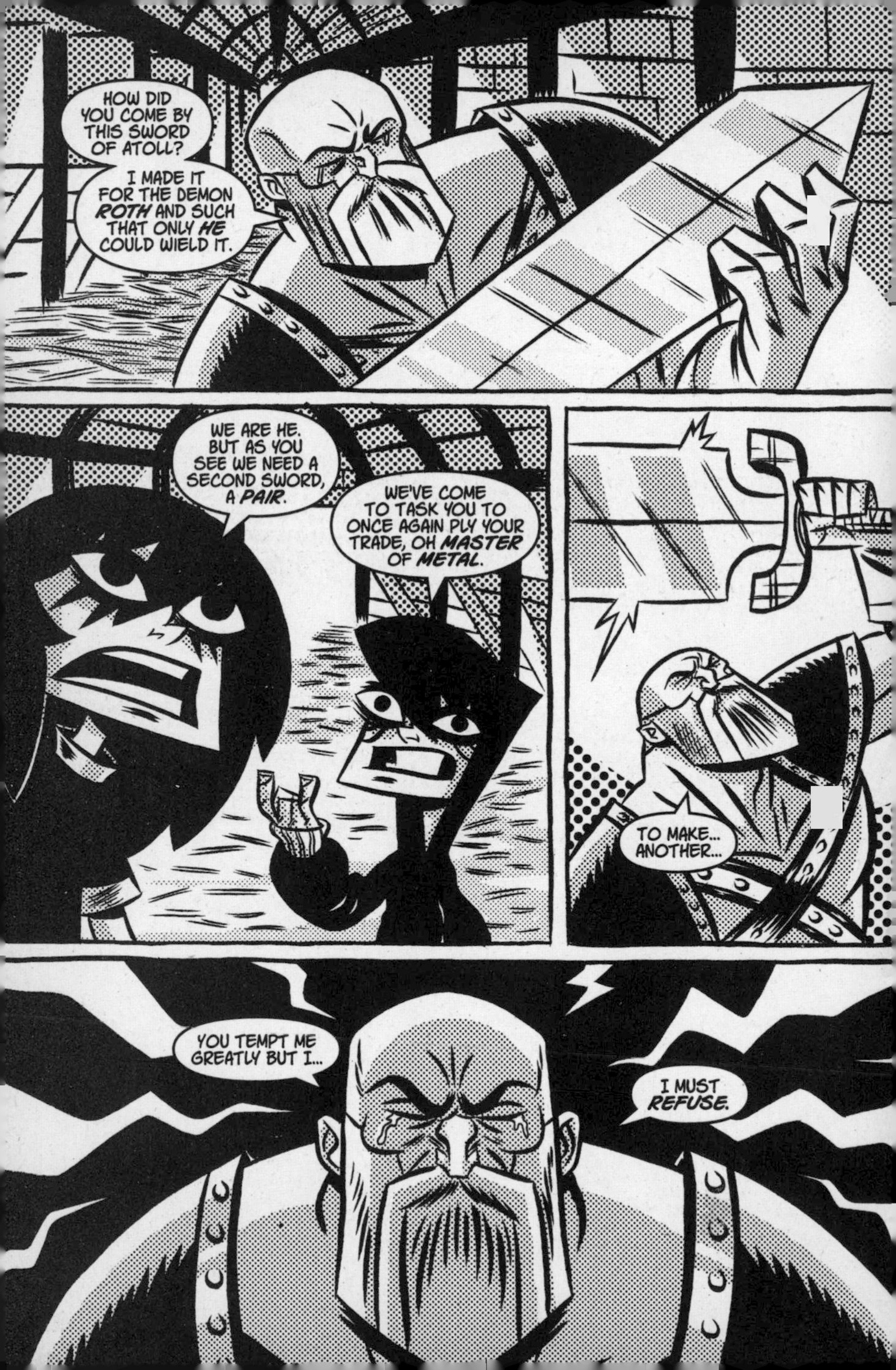
HOW DID YOU COME BY THIS SWORD OF ATOLL?
I MADE IT FOR THE DEMON ROTH AND SUCH THAT ONLY HE COULD WIELD IT.
WE ARE HE. BUT AS YOU SEE WE NEED A SECOND SWORD, A PAIR.
WE'VE COME TO TASK YOU TO ONCE AGAIN PLY YOUR TRADE, OH MASTER OF METAL.
TO MAKE... ANOTHER...
YOU TEMPT ME GREATLY BUT I...
I MUST REFUSE.

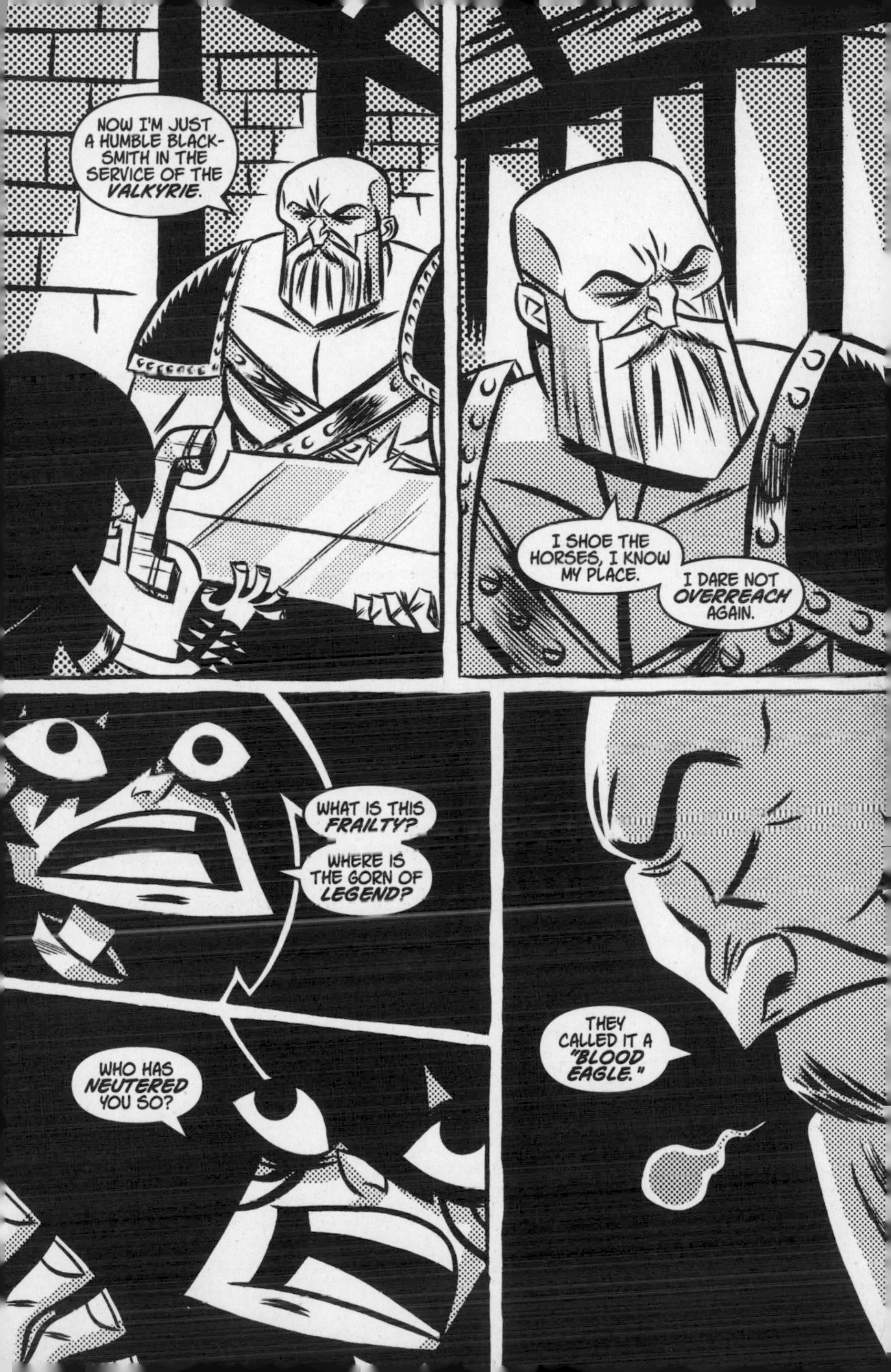
NOW I'M JUST A HUMBLE BLACK-SMITH IN THE SERVICE OF THE VALKYRIE.
I SHOE THE HORSES, I KNOW MY PLACE.
I DARE NOT OVERREACH AGAIN.
WHAT IS THIS FRAILTY?
WHERE IS THE GORN OF LEGEND?
WHO HAS NEUTERED YOU SO?
THEY CALLED IT A "BLOOD EAGLE."

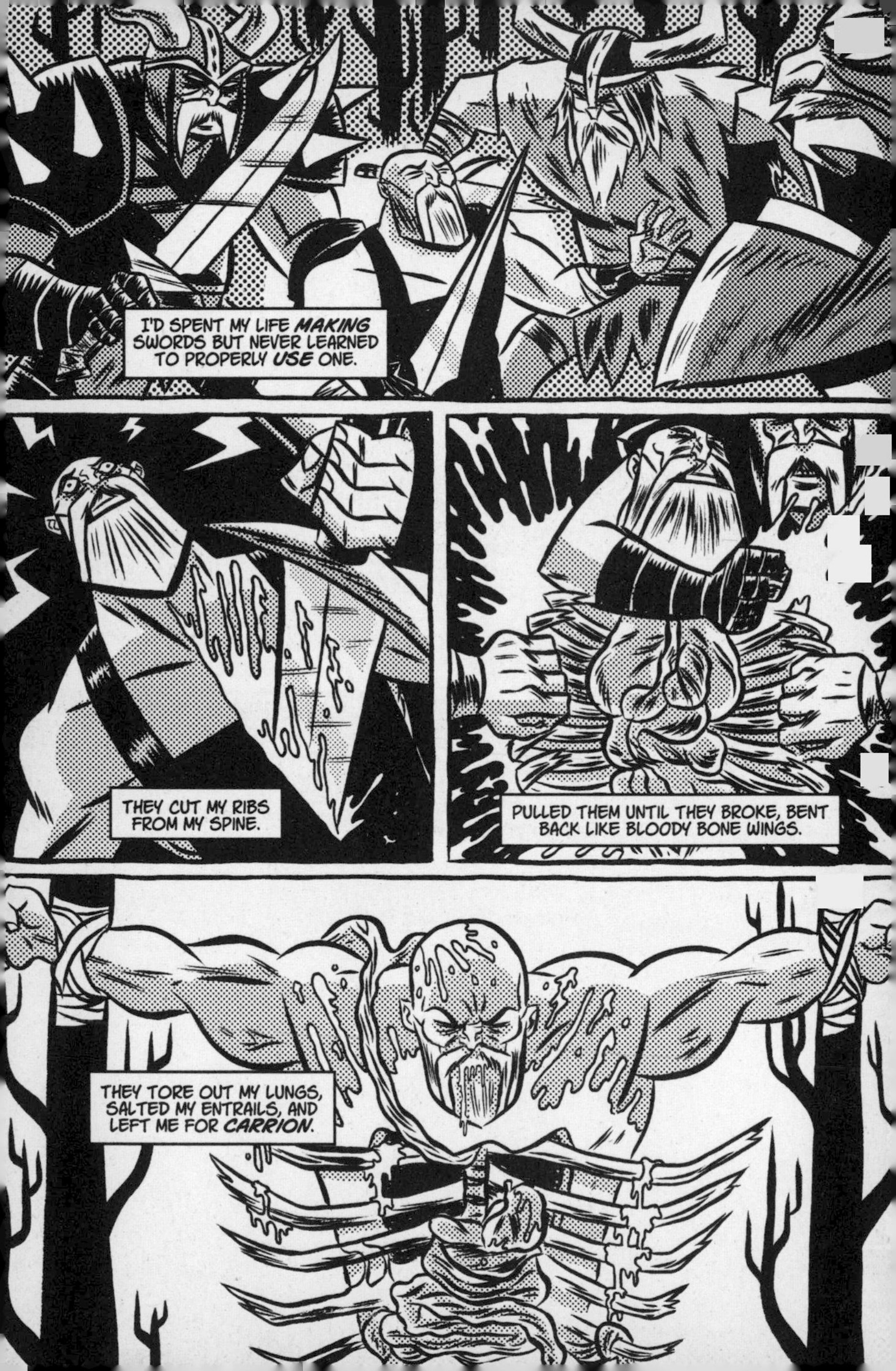
I'D SPENT MY LIFE MAKING SWORDS BUT NEVER LEARNED TO PROPERLY USE ONE.
THEY CUT MY RIBS FROM MY SPINE.
PULLED THEM UNTIL THEY BROKE, BENT BACK LIKE BLOODY BONE WINGS.
THEY TORE OUT MY LUNGS, SALTED MY ENTRAILS, AND LEFT ME FOR CARRION.

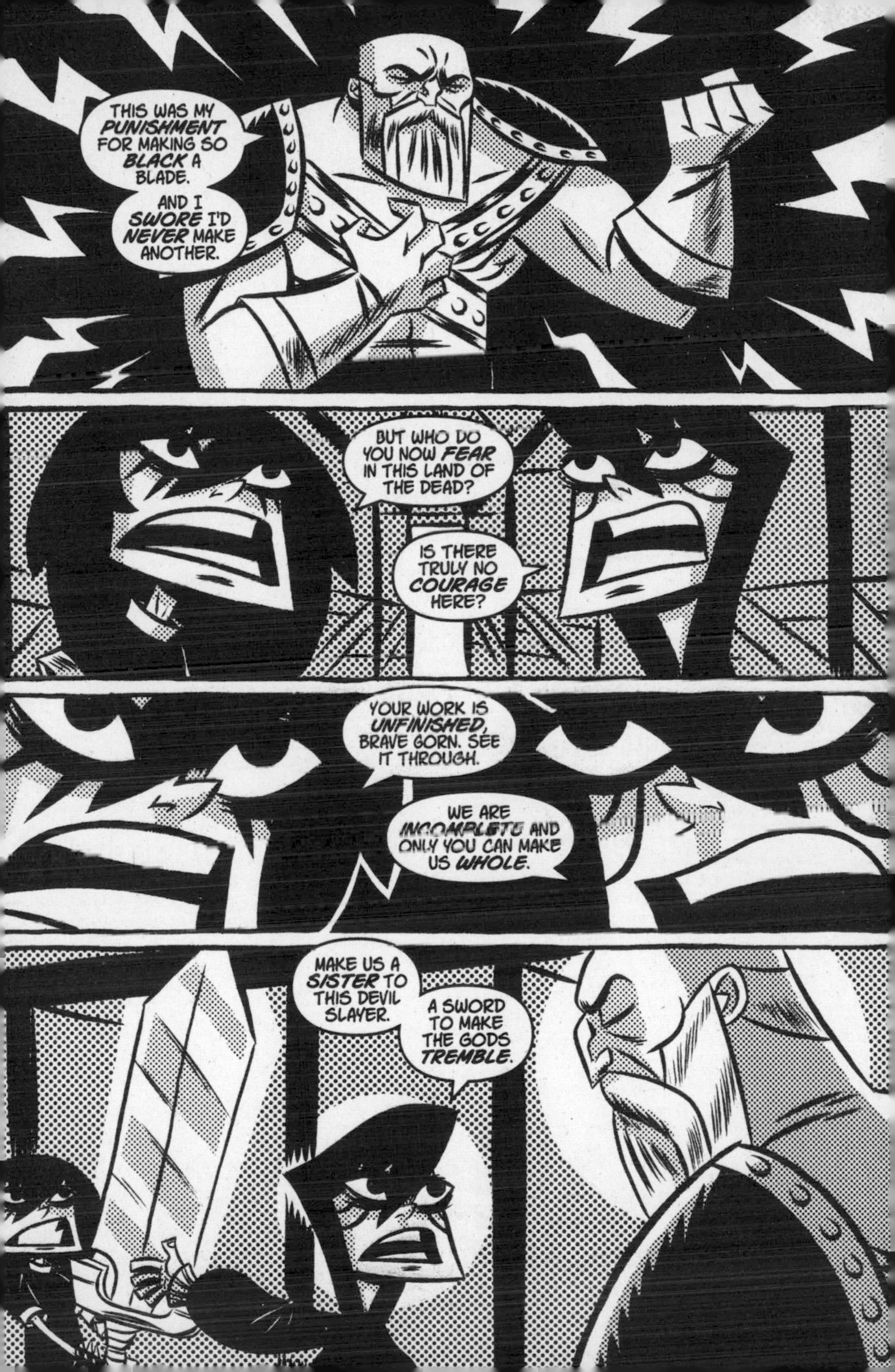
THIS WAS MY PUNISHMENT FOR MAKING SO BLACK A BLADE.
AND I SWORE I'D NEVER MAKE ANOTHER.
BUT WHO DO YOU NOW FEAR IN THIS LAND OF THE DEAD?
IS THERE TRULY NO COURAGE HERE?
YOUR WORK IS UNFINISHED, BRAVE GORN. SEE IT THROUGH.
WE ARE INCOMPLETE AND ONLY YOU CAN MAKE US WHOLE.
MAKE US A SISTER TO THIS DEVIL SLAYER.
A SWORD TO MAKE THE GODS TREMBLE.

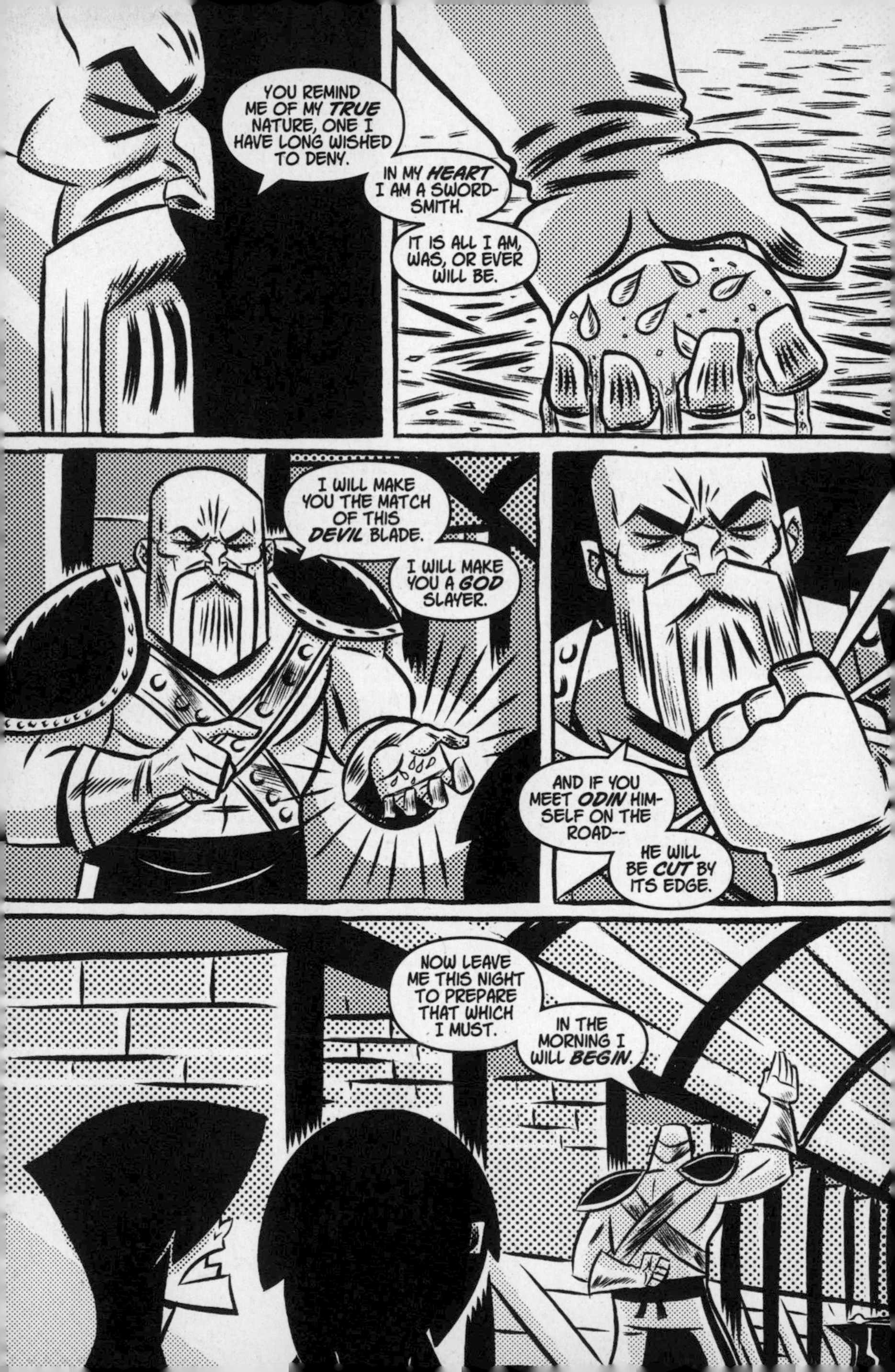
YOU REMIND ME OF MY TRUE NATURE, ONE I HAVE LONG WISHED TO DENY.
IN MY HEART I AM A SWORD-SMITH.
IT IS ALL I AM, WAS, OR EVER WILL BE.
I WILL MAKE YOU THE MATCH OF THIS DEVIL BLADE.
I WILL MAKE YOU A GOD SLAYER.
AND IF YOU MEET ODIN HIM-SELF ON THE ROAD--
HE WILL BE CUT BY ITS EDGE.
NOW LEAVE ME THIS NIGHT TO PREPARE THAT WHICH I MUST.
IN THE MORNING I WILL BEGIN.

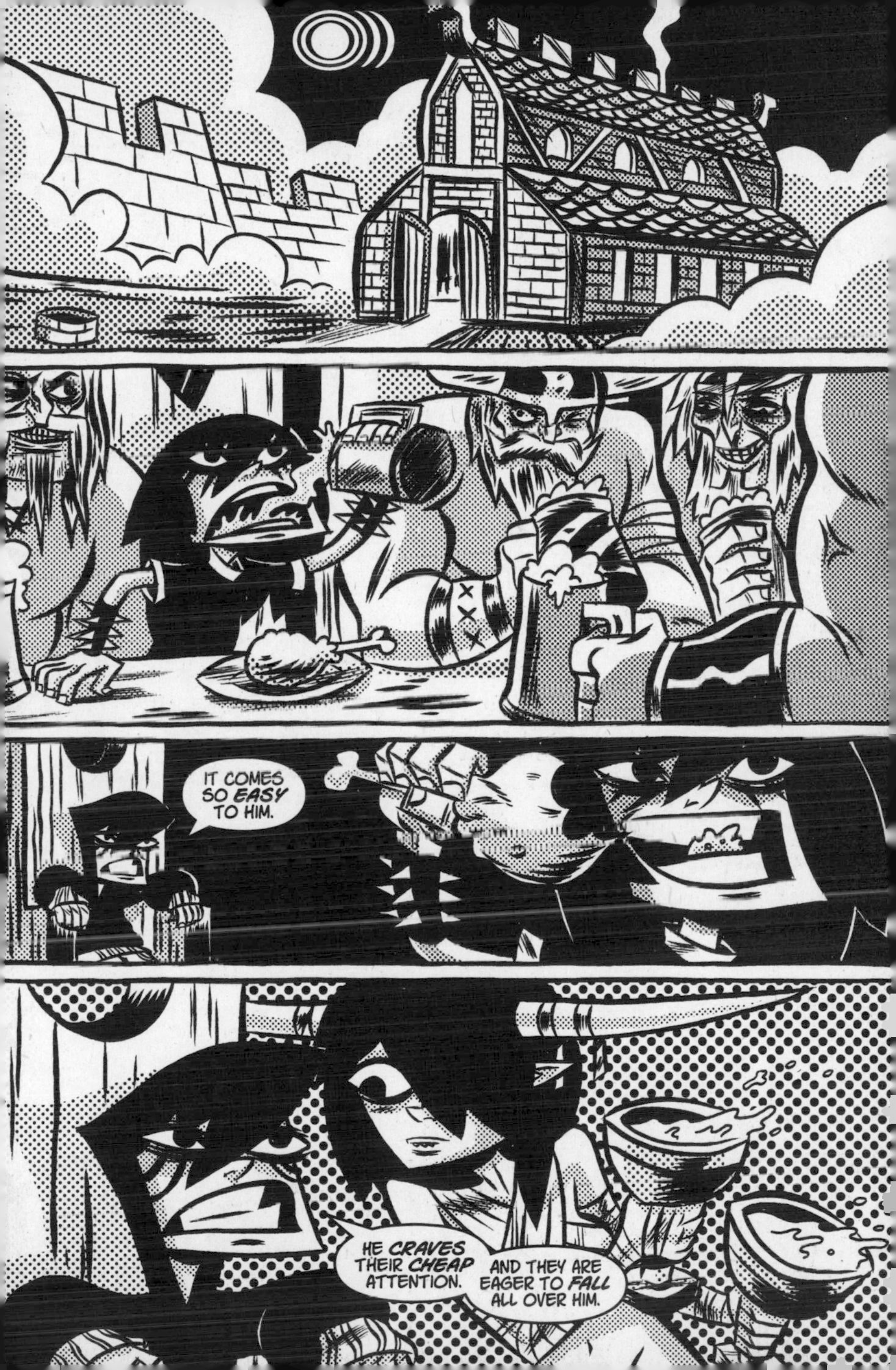
IT COMES SO EASY TO HIM.
HE CRAVES THEIR CHEAP ATTENTION.
AND THEY ARE EAGER TO FALL ALL OVER HIM.

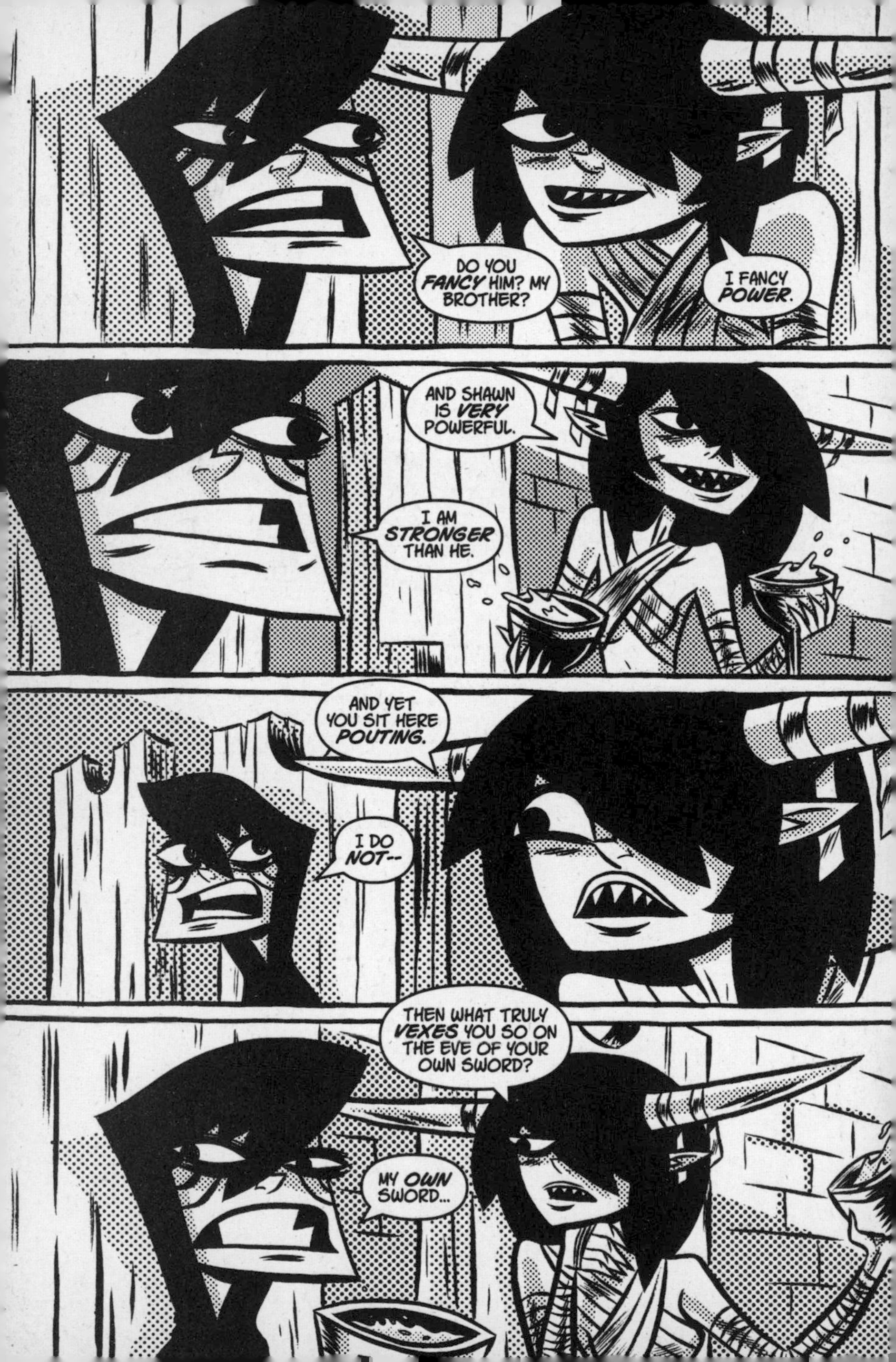
DO YOU FANCY HIM? MY BROTHER?
I FANCY POWER.
AND SHAWN IS VERY POWERFUL.
I AM STRONGER THAN HE.
AND YET YOU SIT HERE POUTING.
I DO NOT--
THEN WHAT TRULY VEXES YOU SO ON THE EVE OF YOUR OWN SWORD?
MY OWN SWORD...

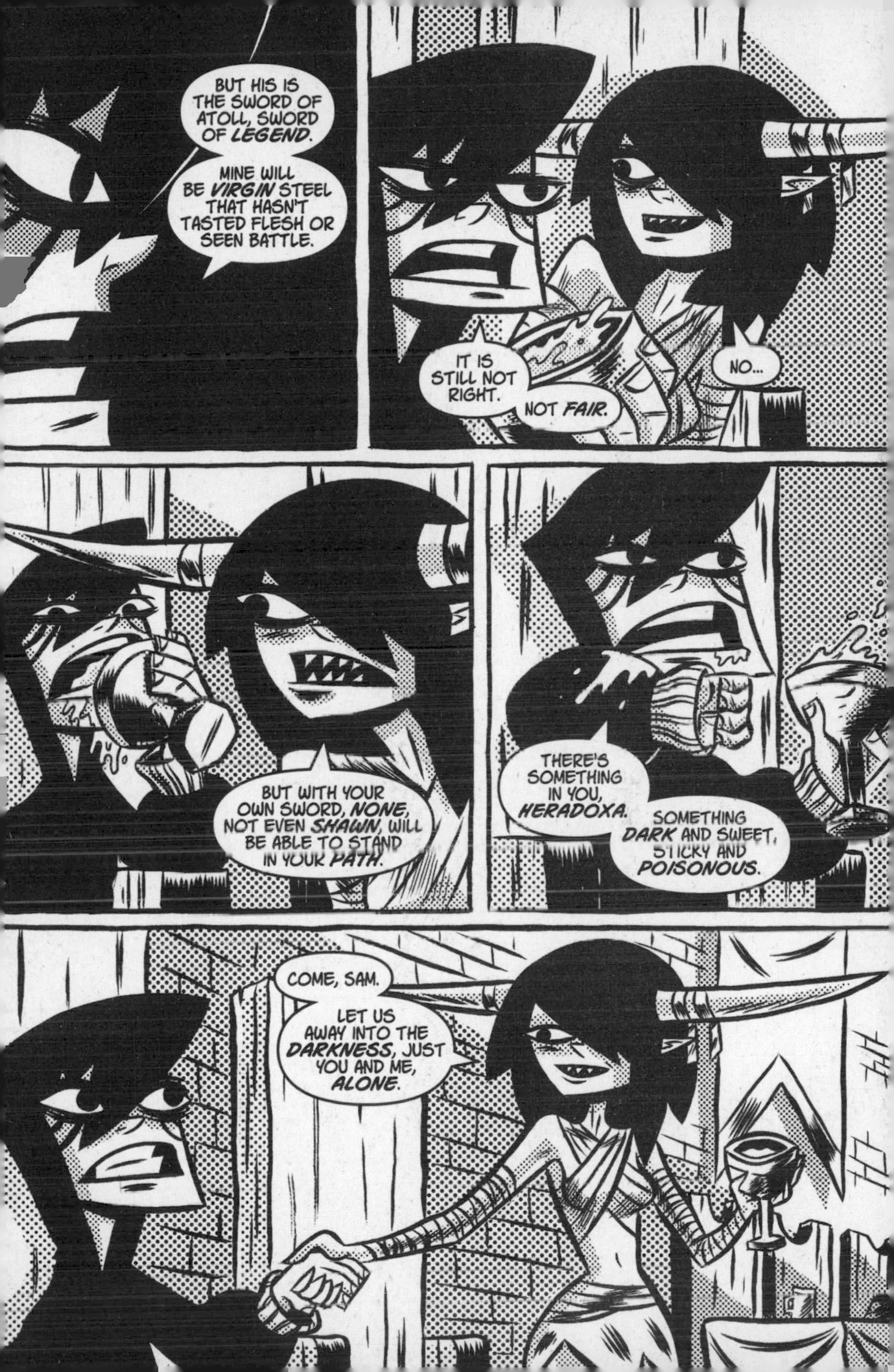

BUT HIS IS THE SWORD OF ATOLL, SWORD OF LEGEND.
MINE WILL BE VIRGIN STEEL THAT HASN'T TASTED FLESH OR SEEN BATTLE.
IT IS STILL NOT RIGHT.
NOT FAIR.
NO...
BUT WITH YOUR OWN SWORD, NONE, NOT EVEN SHAWN, WILL BE ABLE TO STAND IN YOUR PATH.
THERE'S SOMETHING IN YOU, HERADOXA.
SOMETHING DARK AND SWEET, STICKY AND POISONOUS.
COME, SAM.
LET US AWAY INTO THE DARKNESS, JUST YOU AND ME, ALONE.

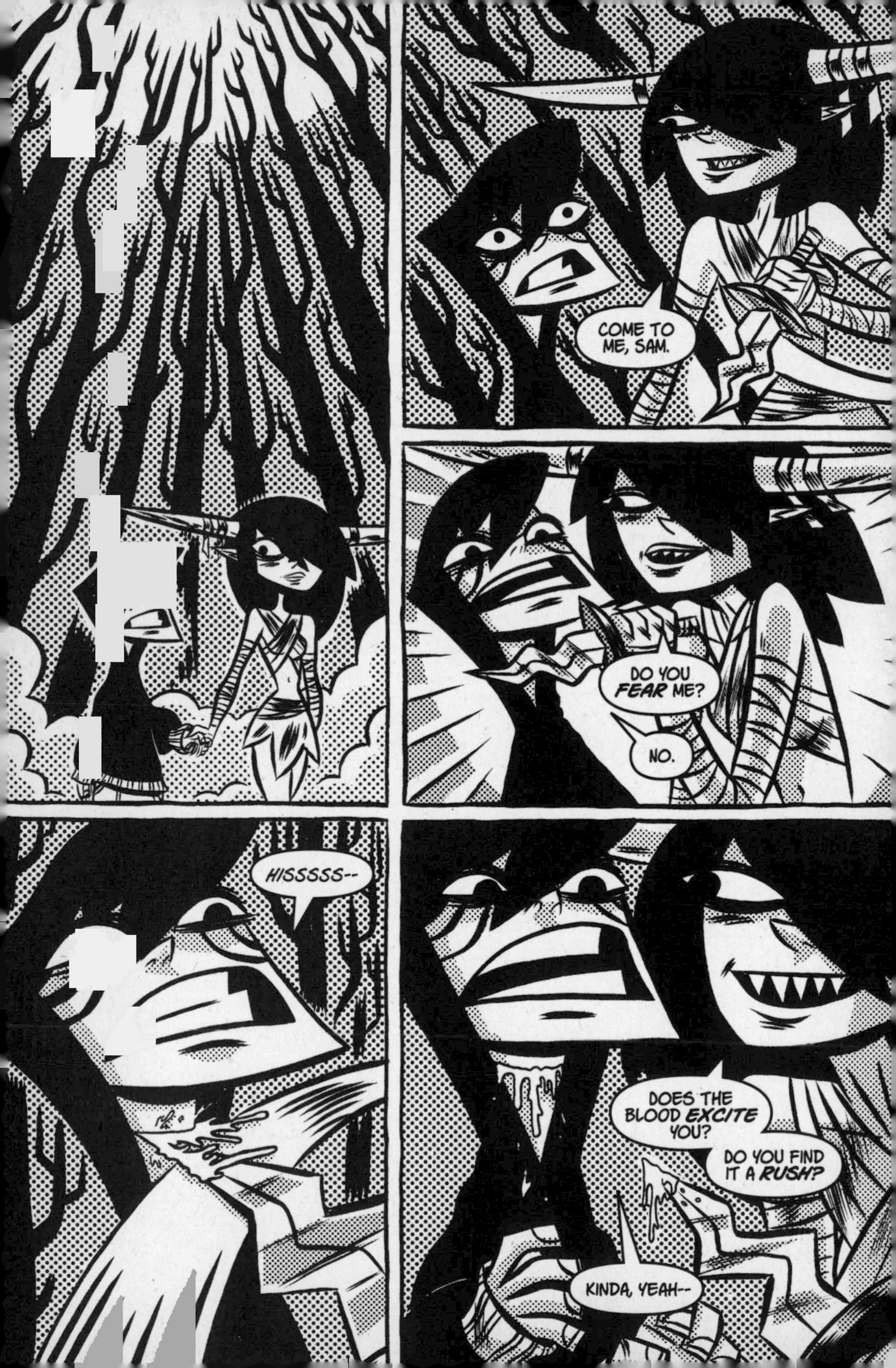
COME TO ME, SAM.
DO YOU FEAR ME?
NO.
HISSSSS--
DOES THE BLOOD EXCITE YOU?
DO YOU FIND IT A RUSH?
KINDA, YEAH--

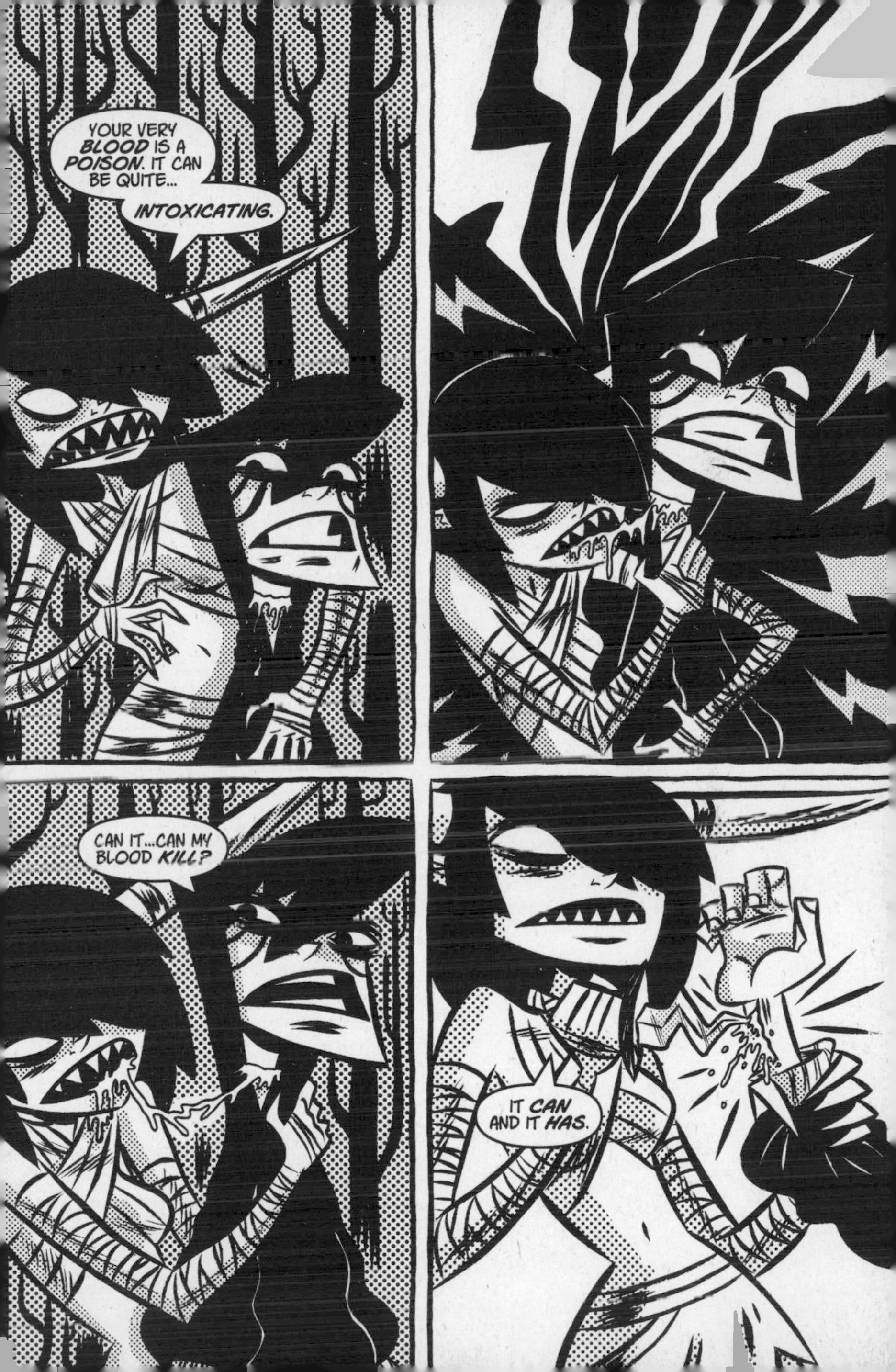
YOUR VERY BLOOD IS A POISON. IT CAN BE QUITE...
INTOXICATING.
CAN IT...CAN MY BLOOD KILL?
IT CAN AND IT HAS.

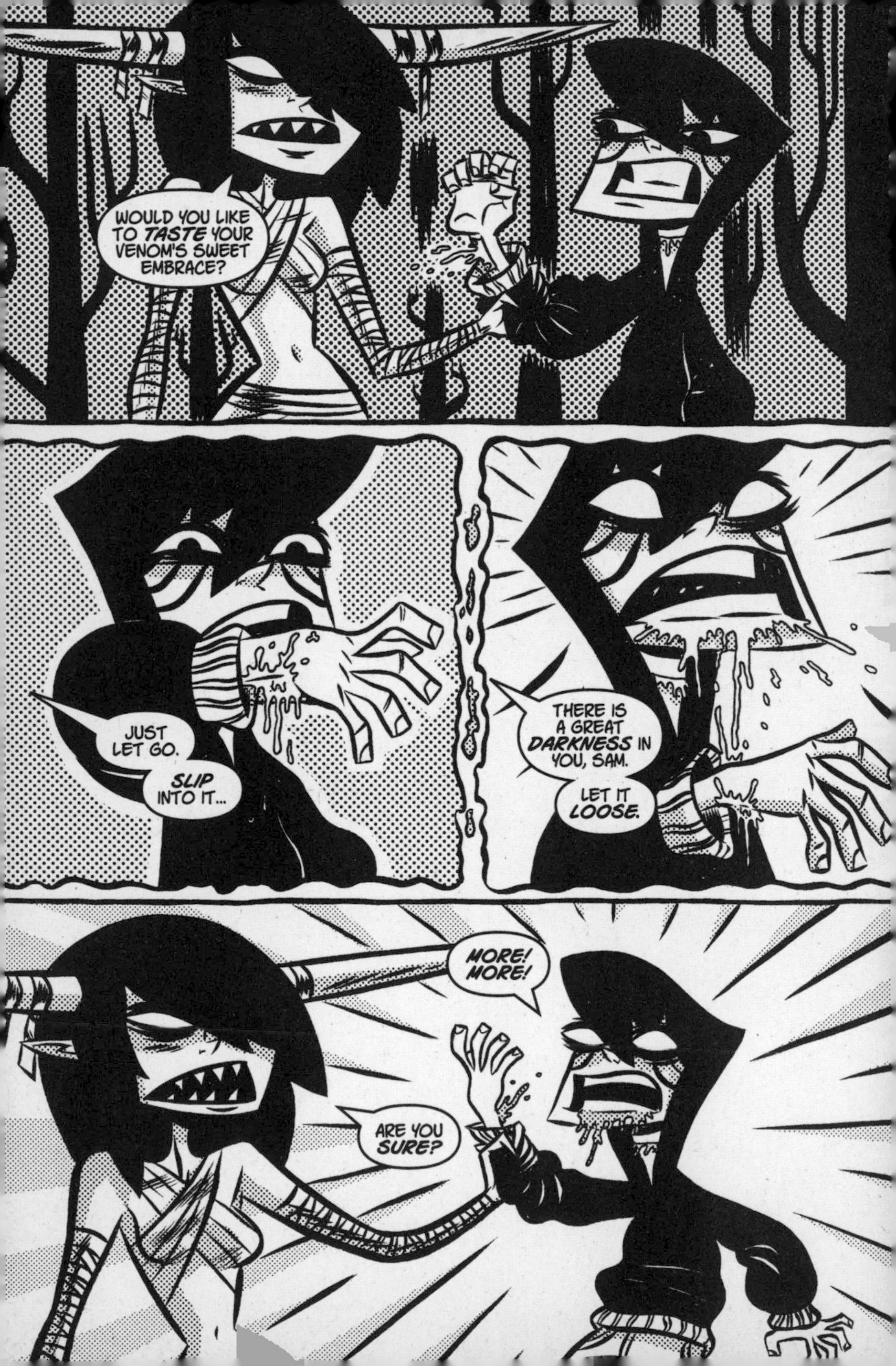
WOULD YOU LIKE TO TASTE YOUR VENOM'S SWEET EMBRACE?
JUST LET GO.
SLIP INTO IT...
THERE IS A GREAT DARKNESS IN YOU, SAM.
LET IT LOOSE.
MORE! MORE!
ARE YOU SURE?

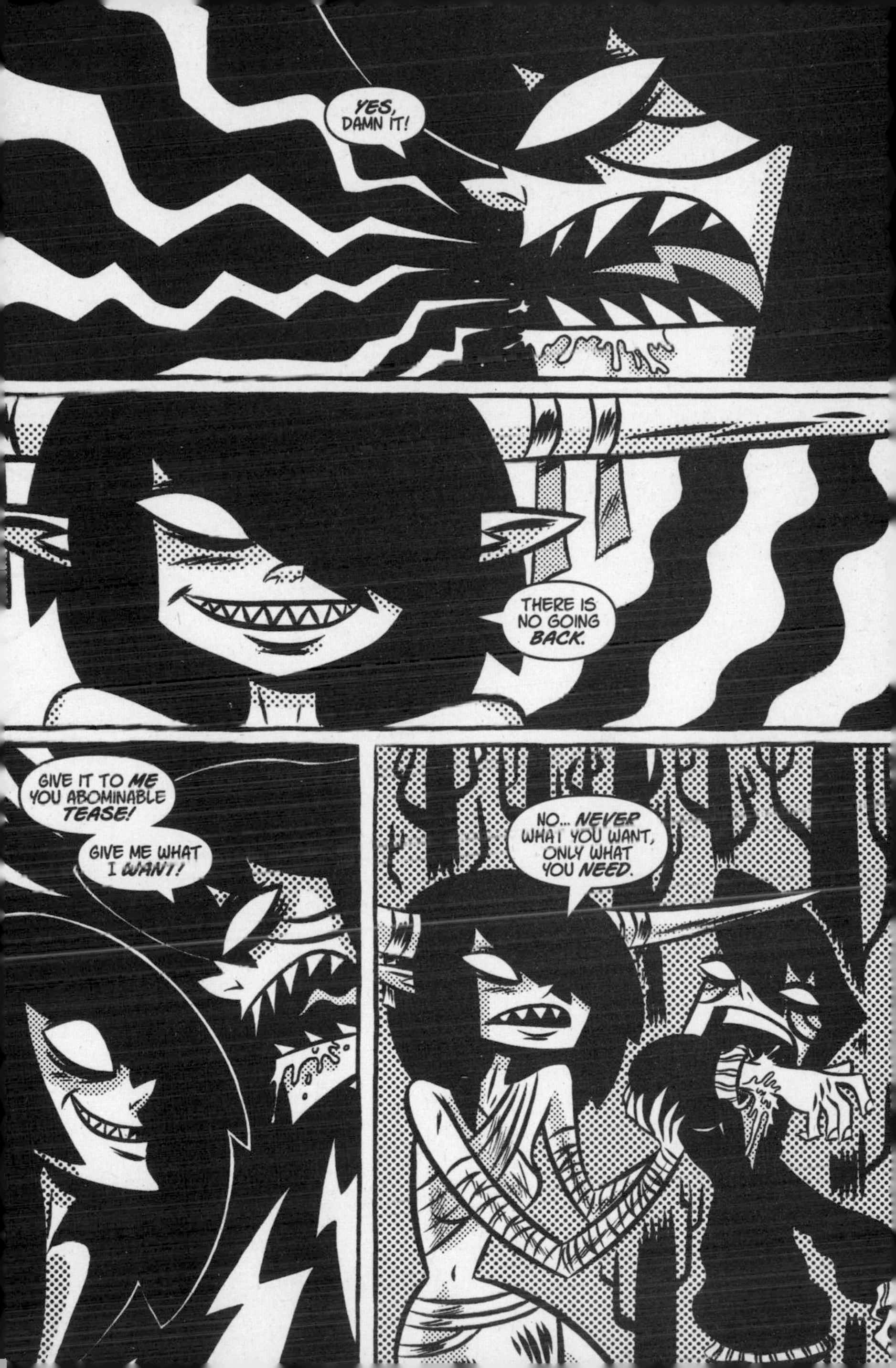
YES, DAMN IT!
THERE IS NO GOING BACK.
GIVE IT TO ME YOU ABOMINABLE TEASE!
GIVE ME WHAT I WANT!
NO... NEVER WHAT YOU WANT, ONLY WHAT YOU NEED.

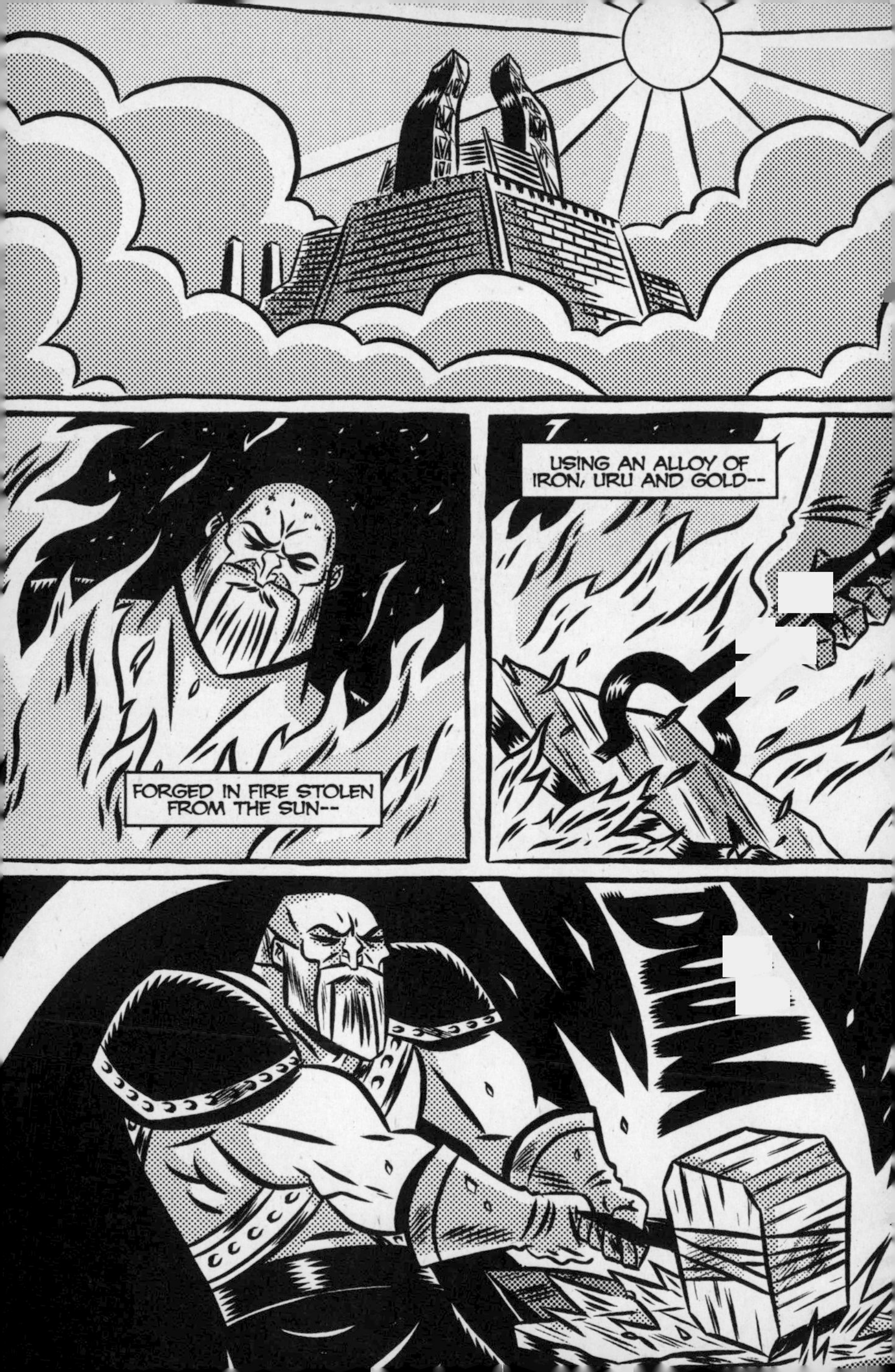
FORGED IN FIRE STOLEN FROM THE SUN--
USING AN ALLOY OF IRON, URU AND GOLD--

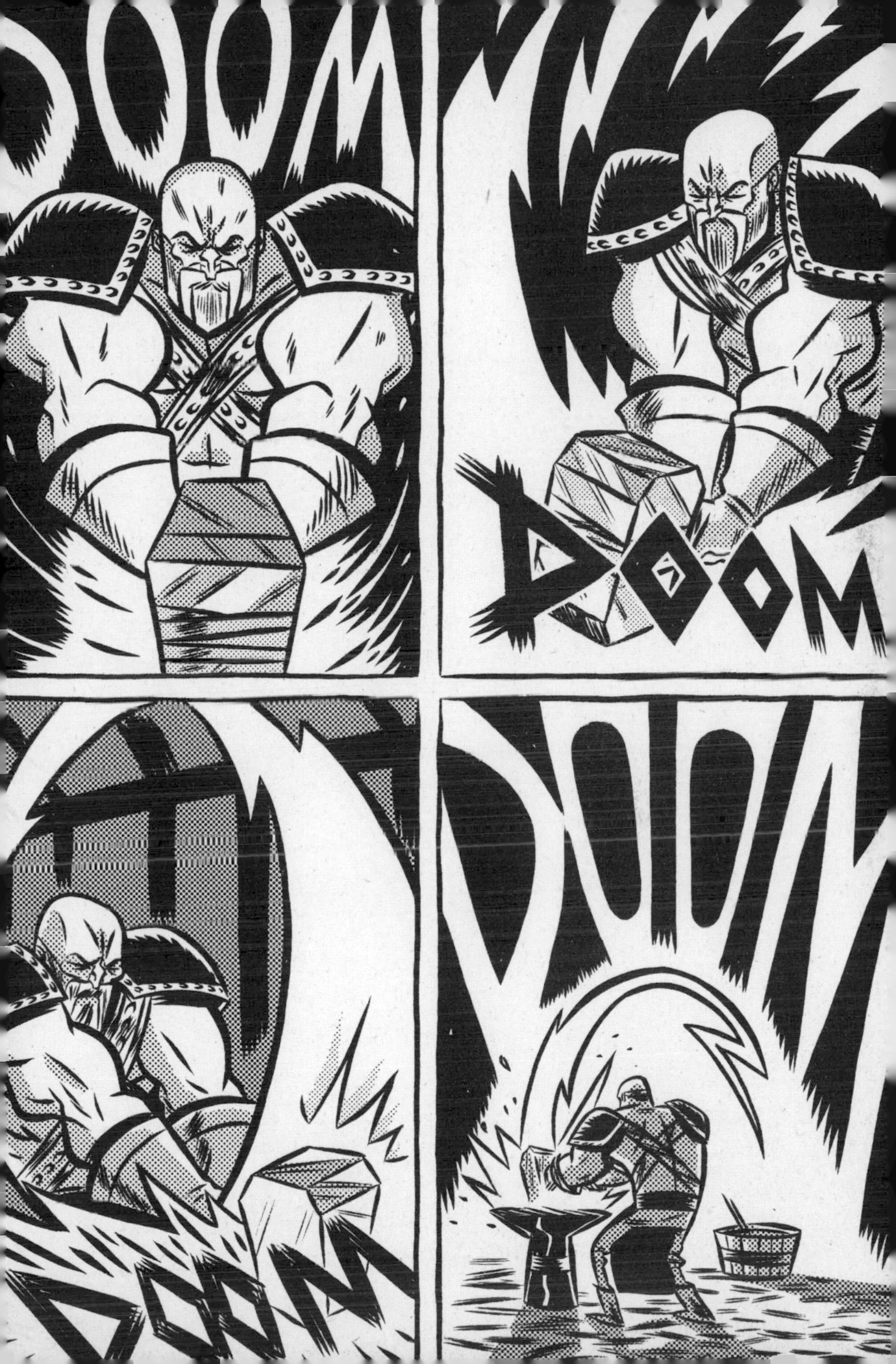
DOOM
DOOM

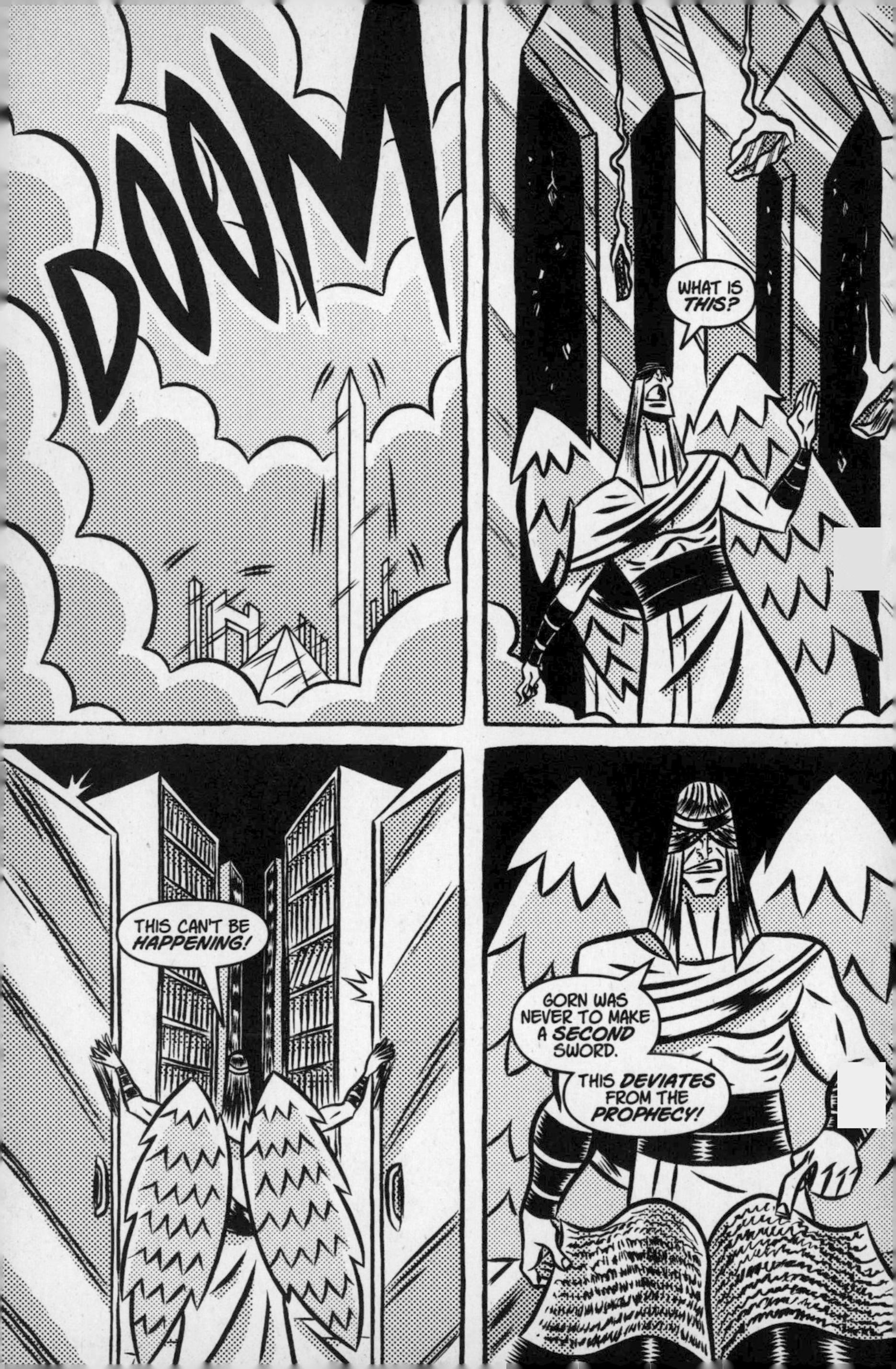
DOOM
WHAT IS THIS?
THIS CAN'T BE HAPPENING!
GORN WAS NEVER TO MAKE A SECOND SWORD.
THIS DEVIATES FROM THE PROPHECY!

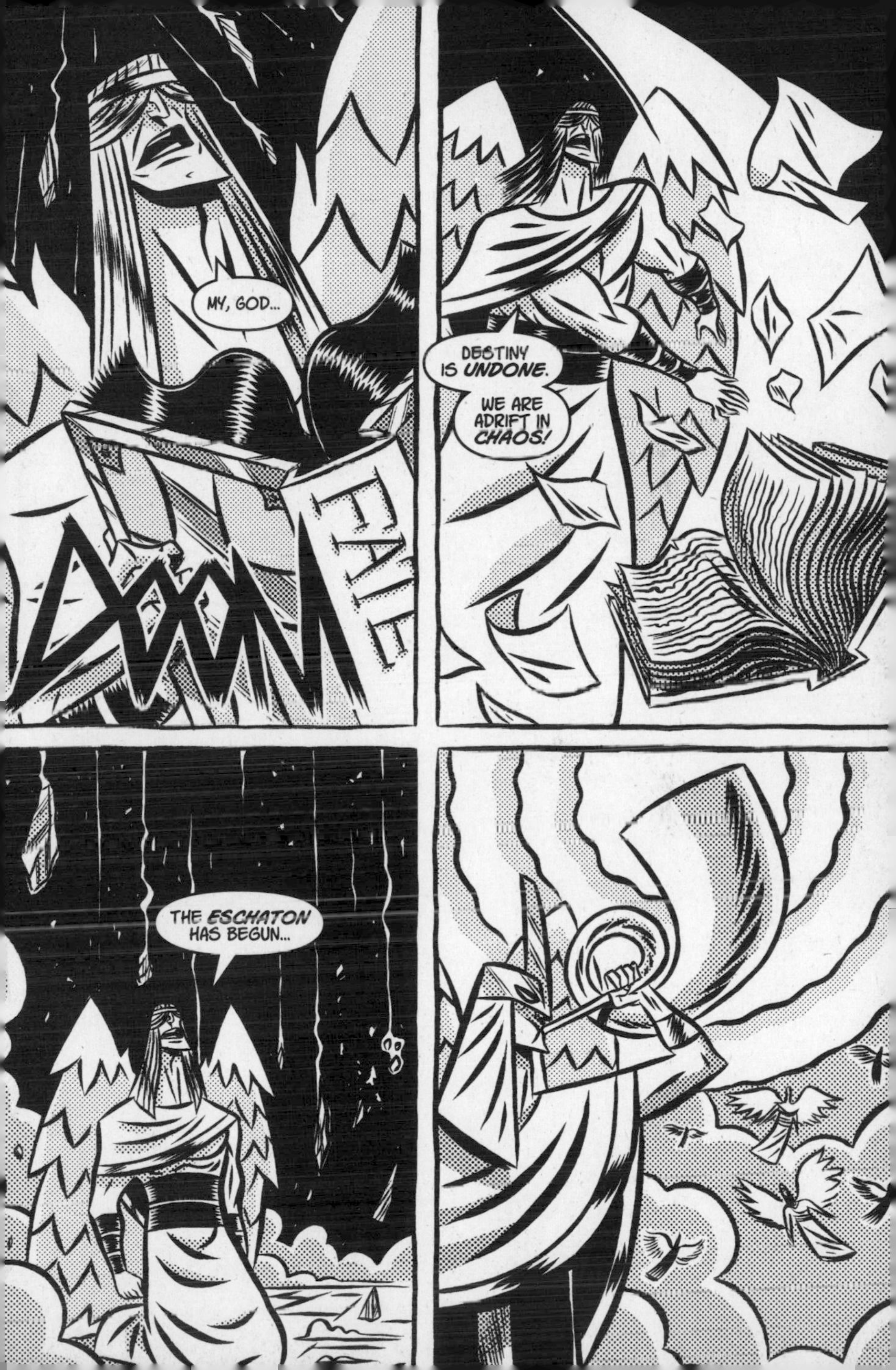
MY, GOD...
FATE
DESTINY IS *UNDONE*.
WE ARE ADRIFT IN *CHAOS!*
THE *ESCHATON* HAS BEGUN...

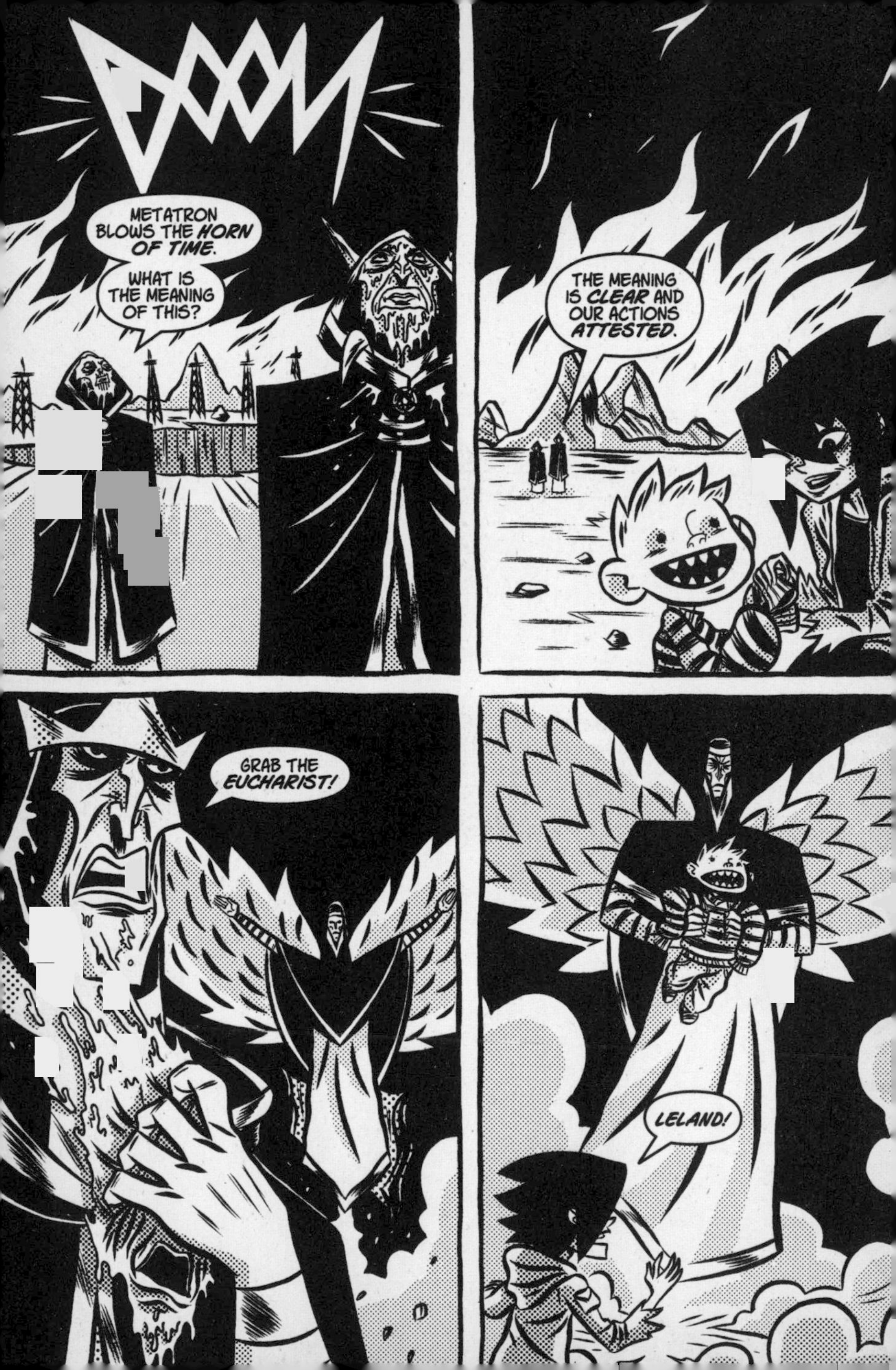

DOOM
METATRON BLOWS THE *HORN OF TIME*.
WHAT IS THE MEANING OF THIS?
THE MEANING IS *CLEAR* AND OUR ACTIONS *ATTESTED*.
GRAB THE *EUCHARIST!*
LELAND!

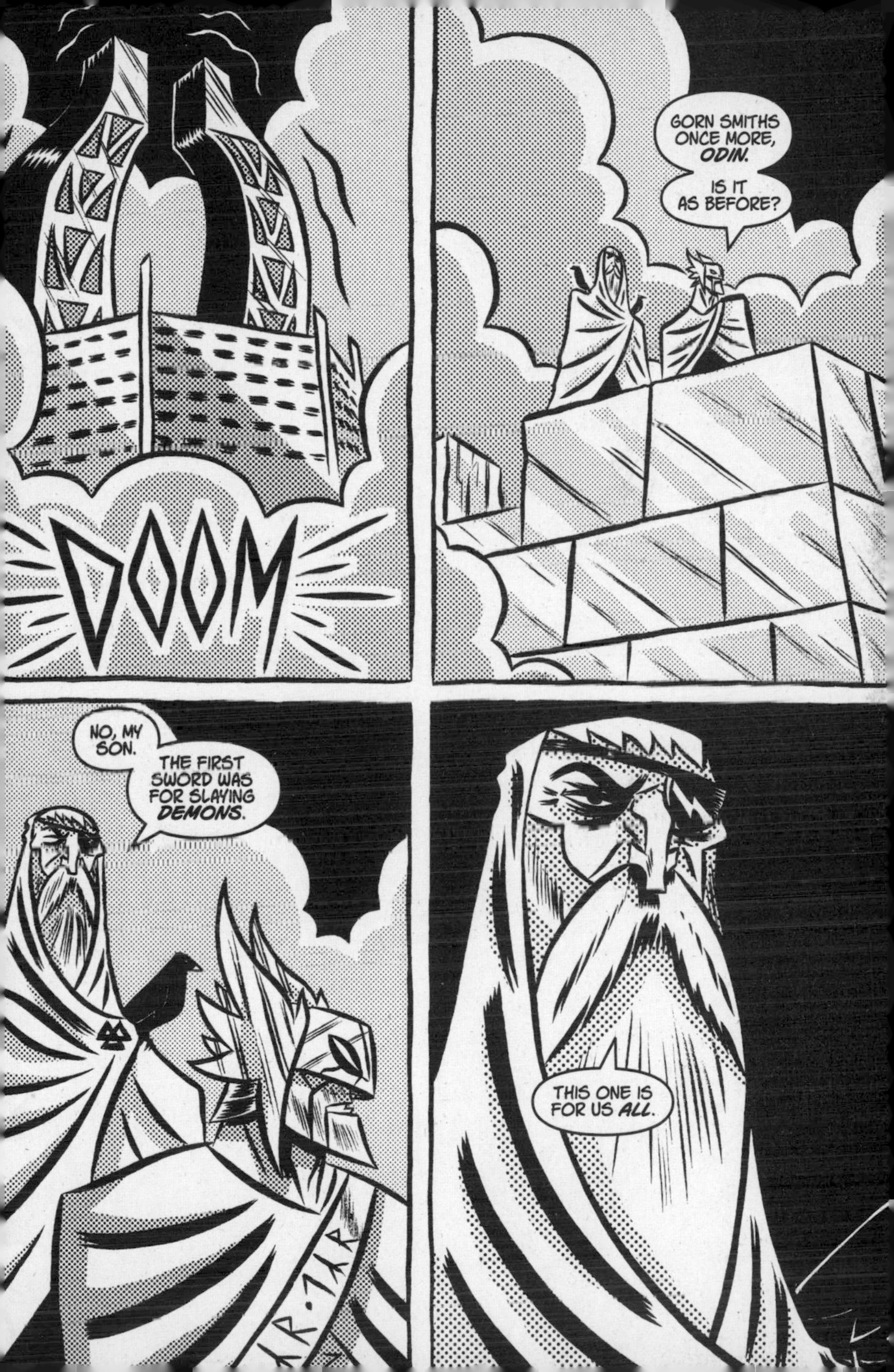
DOOM
GORN SMITHS ONCE MORE, *ODIN*.
IS IT AS BEFORE?
NO, MY SON.
THE FIRST SWORD WAS FOR SLAYING *DEMONS*.
THIS ONE IS FOR US *ALL*.

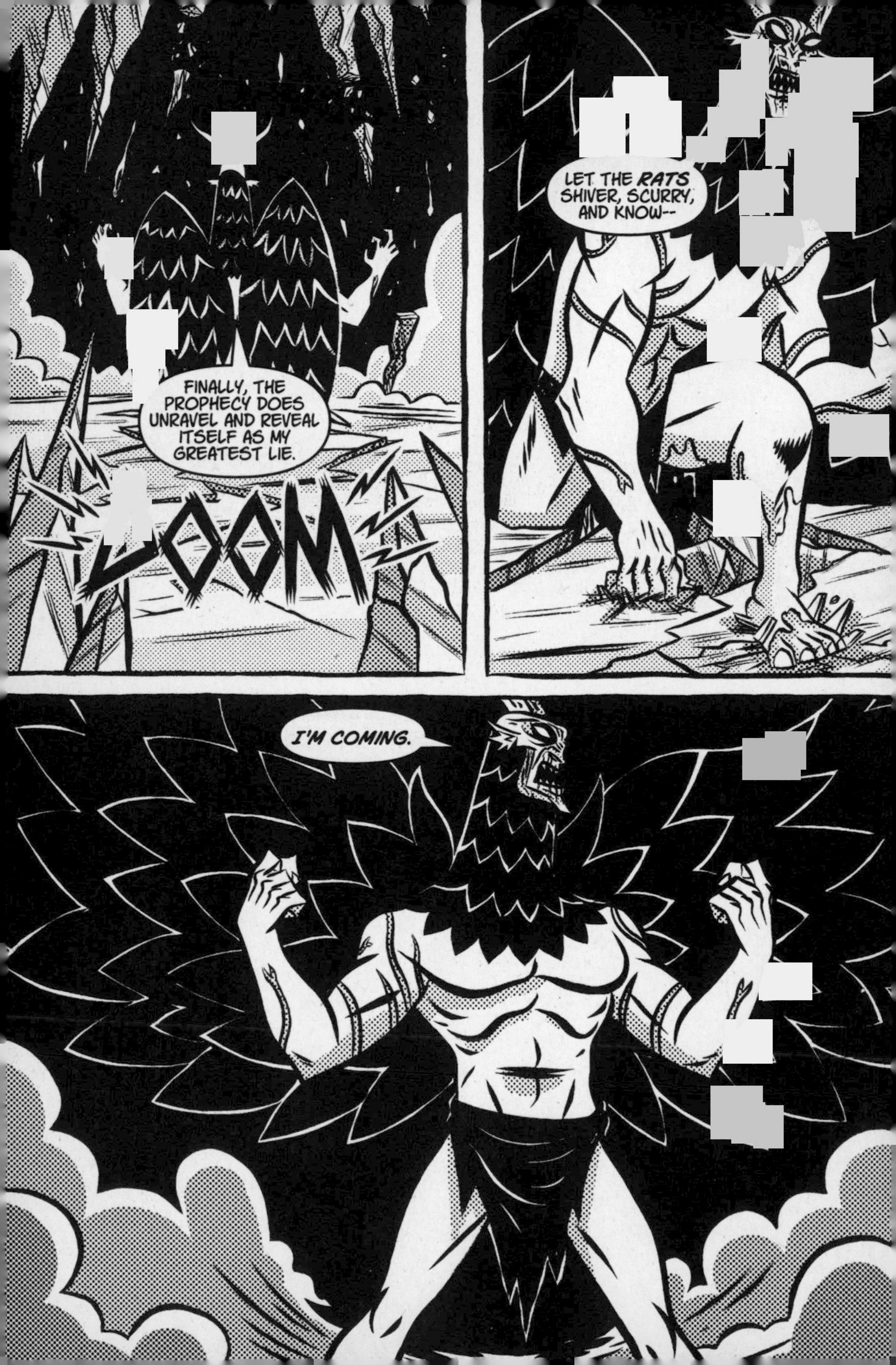
FINALLY, THE PROPHECY DOES UNRAVEL AND REVEAL ITSELF AS MY GREATEST LIE.
DOOM
LET THE *RATS* SHIVER, SCURRY, AND KNOW--
I'M COMING.

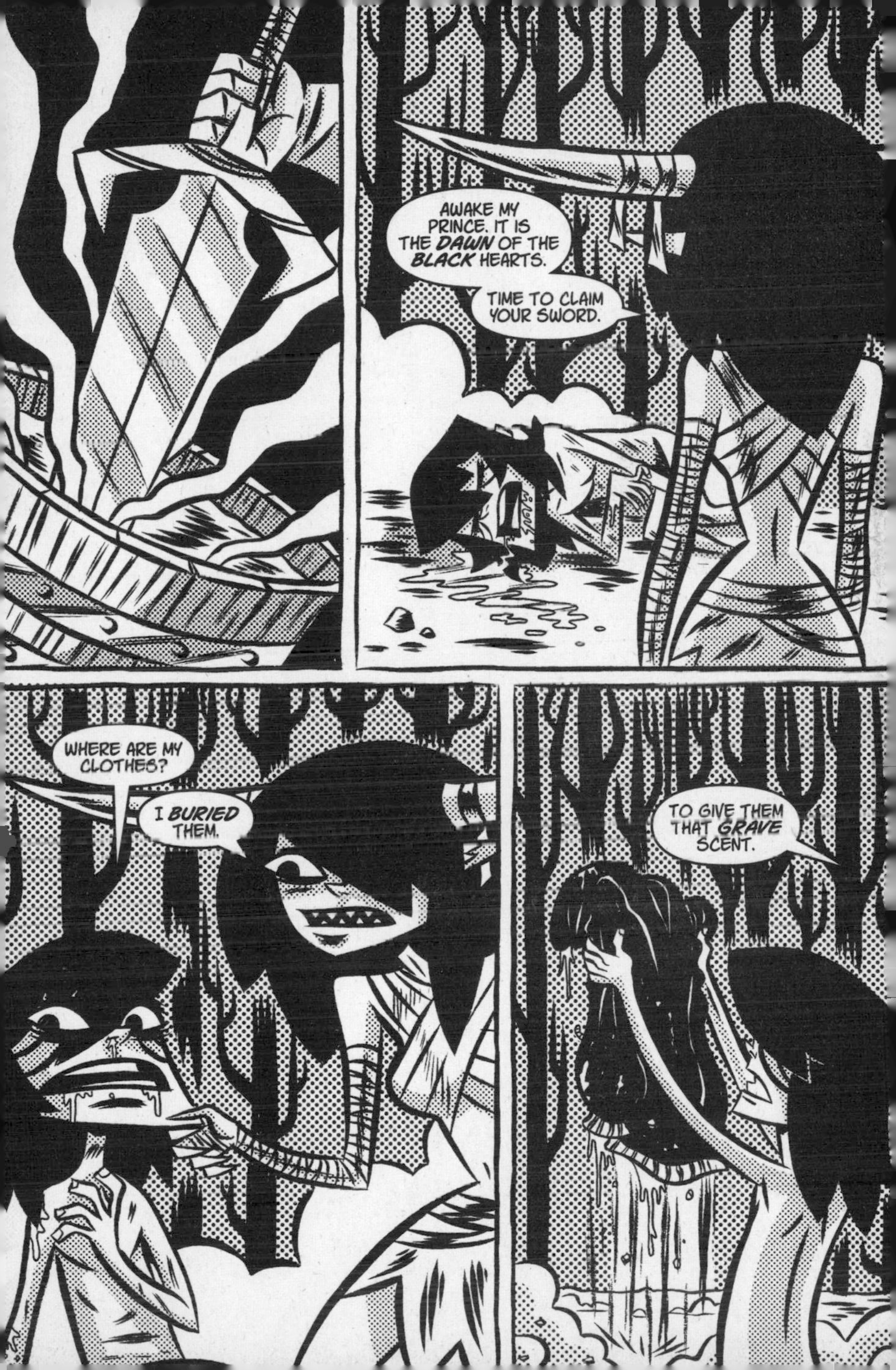
AWAKE MY PRINCE. IT IS THE DAWN OF THE BLACK HEARTS.
TIME TO CLAIM YOUR SWORD.
WHERE ARE MY CLOTHES?
I BURIED THEM.
TO GIVE THEM THAT GRAVE SCENT.

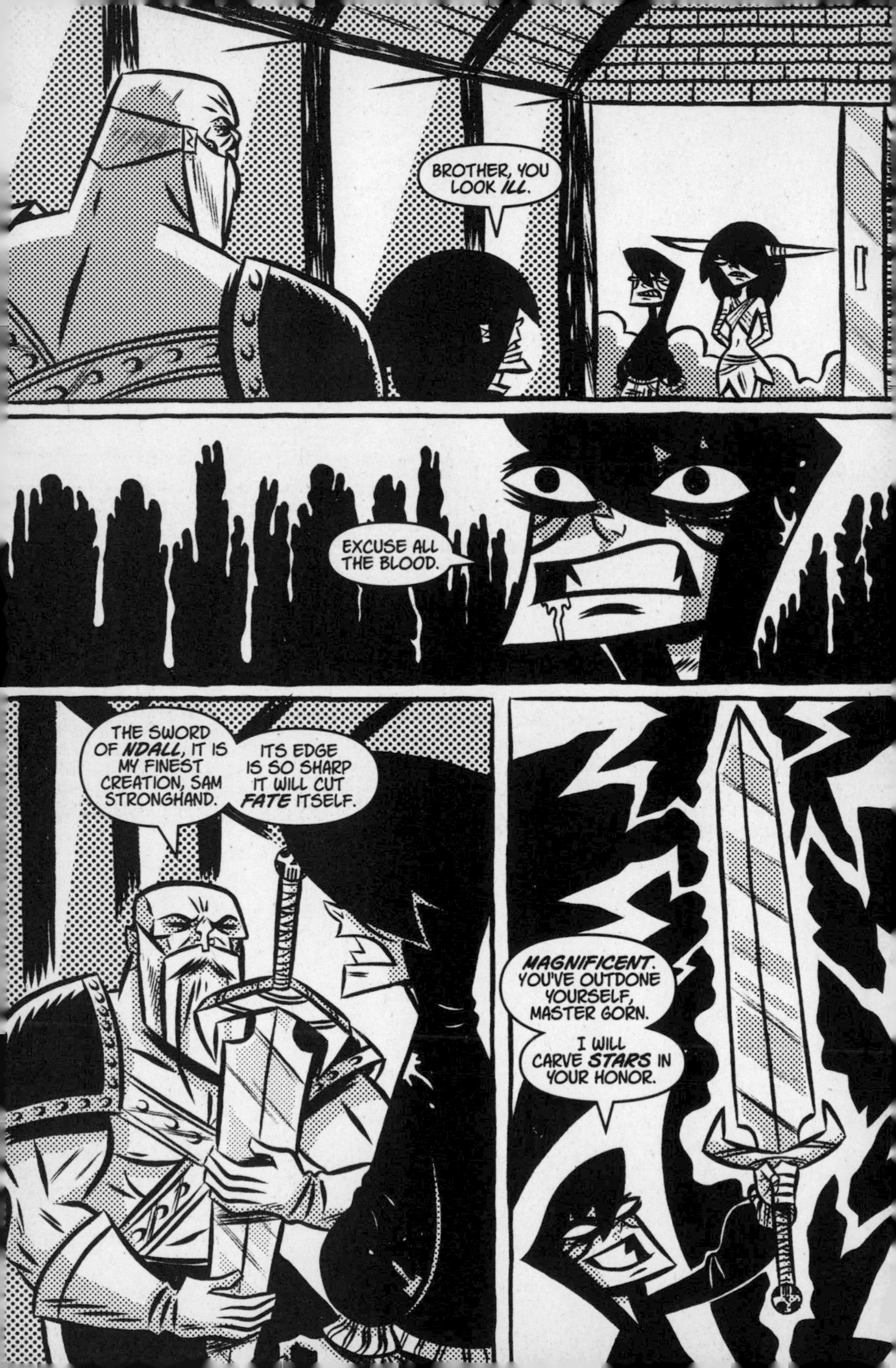
BROTHER, YOU LOOK ILL.
EXCUSE ALL THE BLOOD.
THE SWORD OF NDALL, IT IS MY FINEST CREATION, SAM STRONGHAND.
ITS EDGE IS SO SHARP IT WILL CUT FATE ITSELF.
MAGNIFICENT. YOU'VE OUTDONE YOURSELF, MASTER GORN.
I WILL CARVE STARS IN YOUR HONOR.

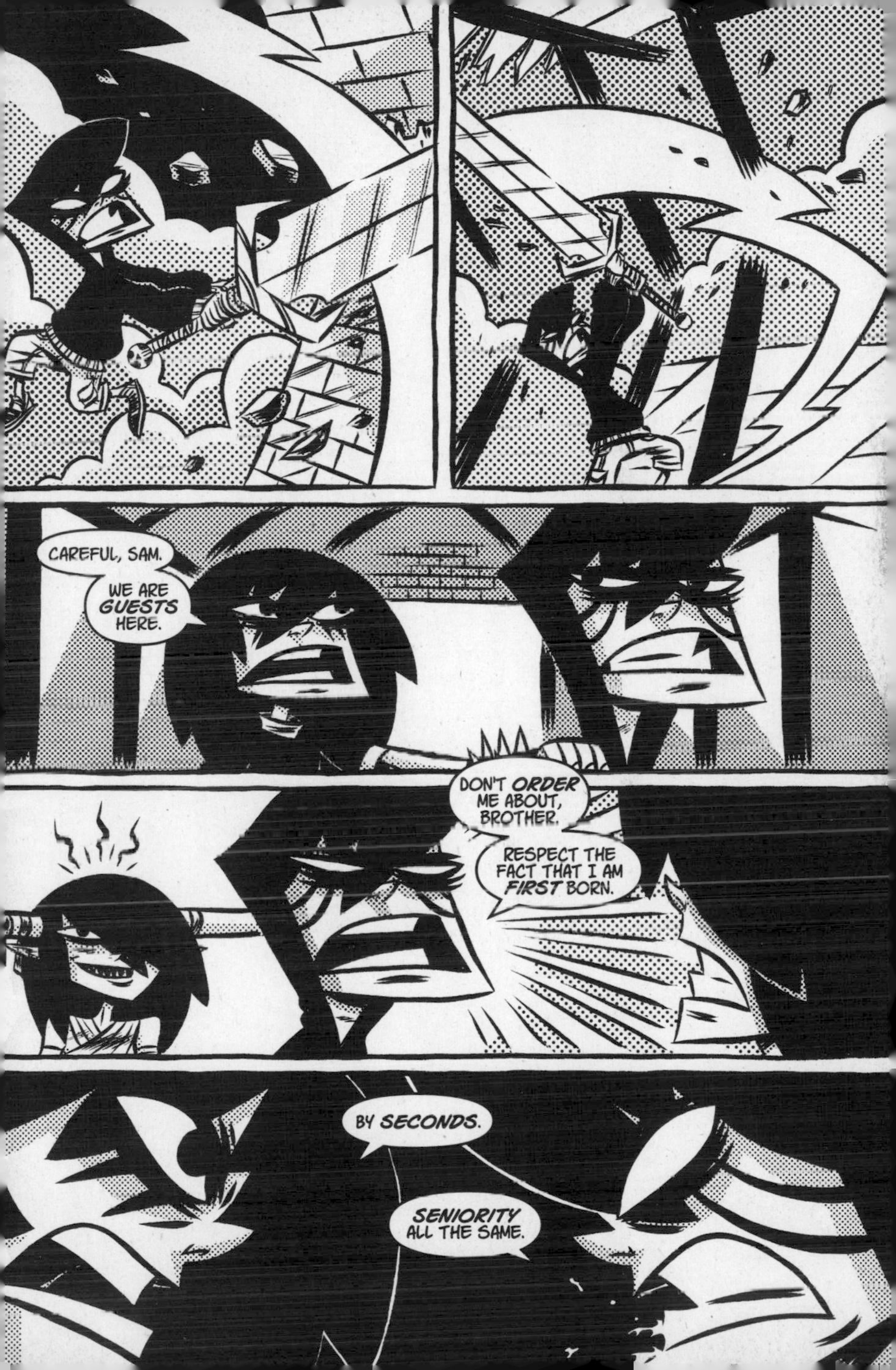

CAREFUL, SAM.
WE ARE GUESTS HERE.
DON'T ORDER ME ABOUT, BROTHER.
RESPECT THE FACT THAT I AM FIRST BORN.
BY SECONDS.
SENIORITY ALL THE SAME.

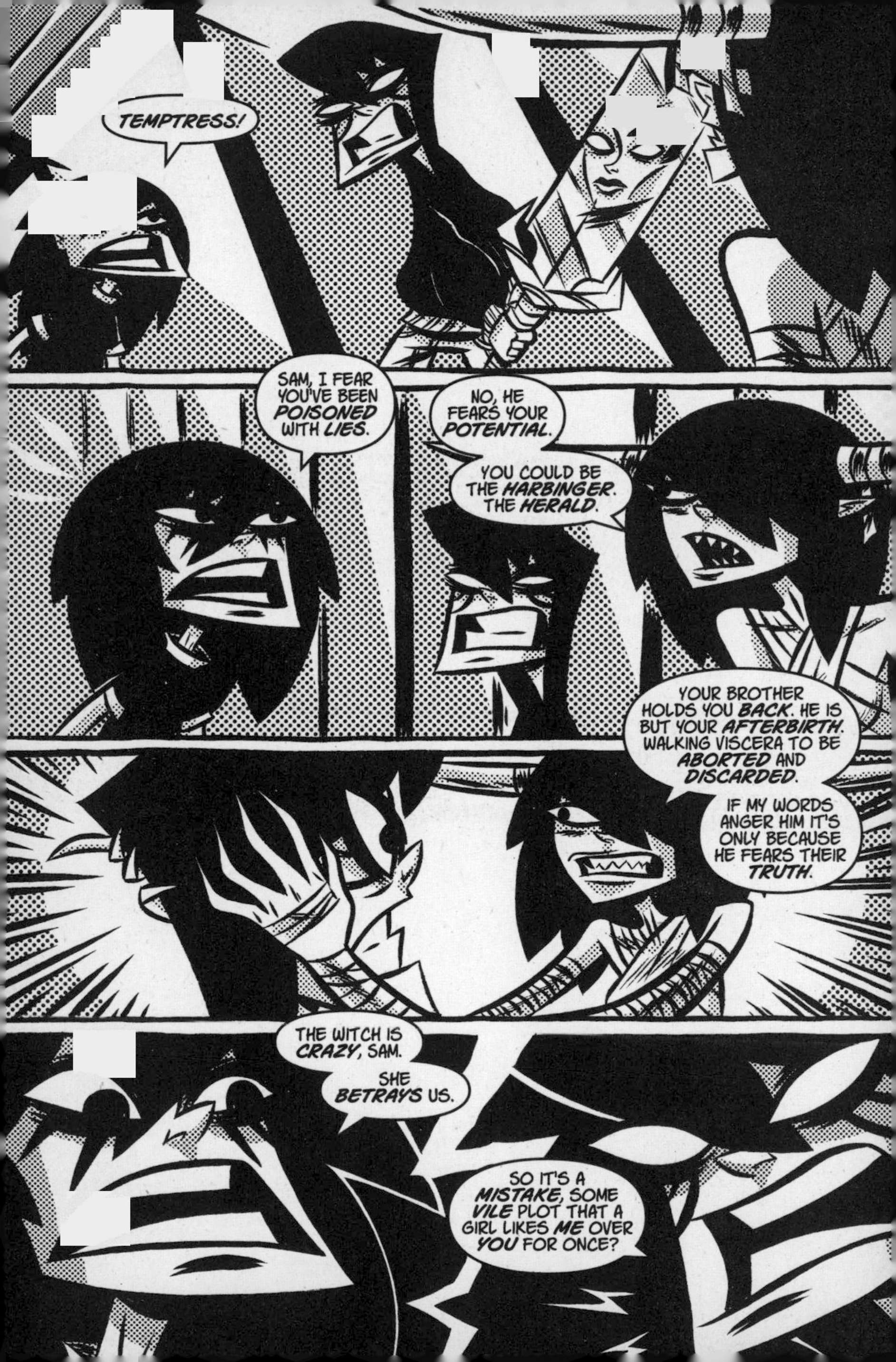
TEMPTRESS!
SAM, I FEAR YOU'VE BEEN POISONED WITH LIES.
NO, HE FEARS YOUR POTENTIAL.
YOU COULD BE THE HARBINGER. THE HERALD.
YOUR BROTHER HOLDS YOU BACK. HE IS BUT YOUR AFTERBIRTH. WALKING VISCERA TO BE ABORTED AND DISCARDED.
IF MY WORDS ANGER HIM IT'S ONLY BECAUSE HE FEARS THEIR TRUTH.
THE WITCH IS CRAZY, SAM.
SHE BETRAYS US.
SO IT'S A MISTAKE, SOME VILE PLOT THAT A GIRL LIKES ME OVER YOU FOR ONCE?

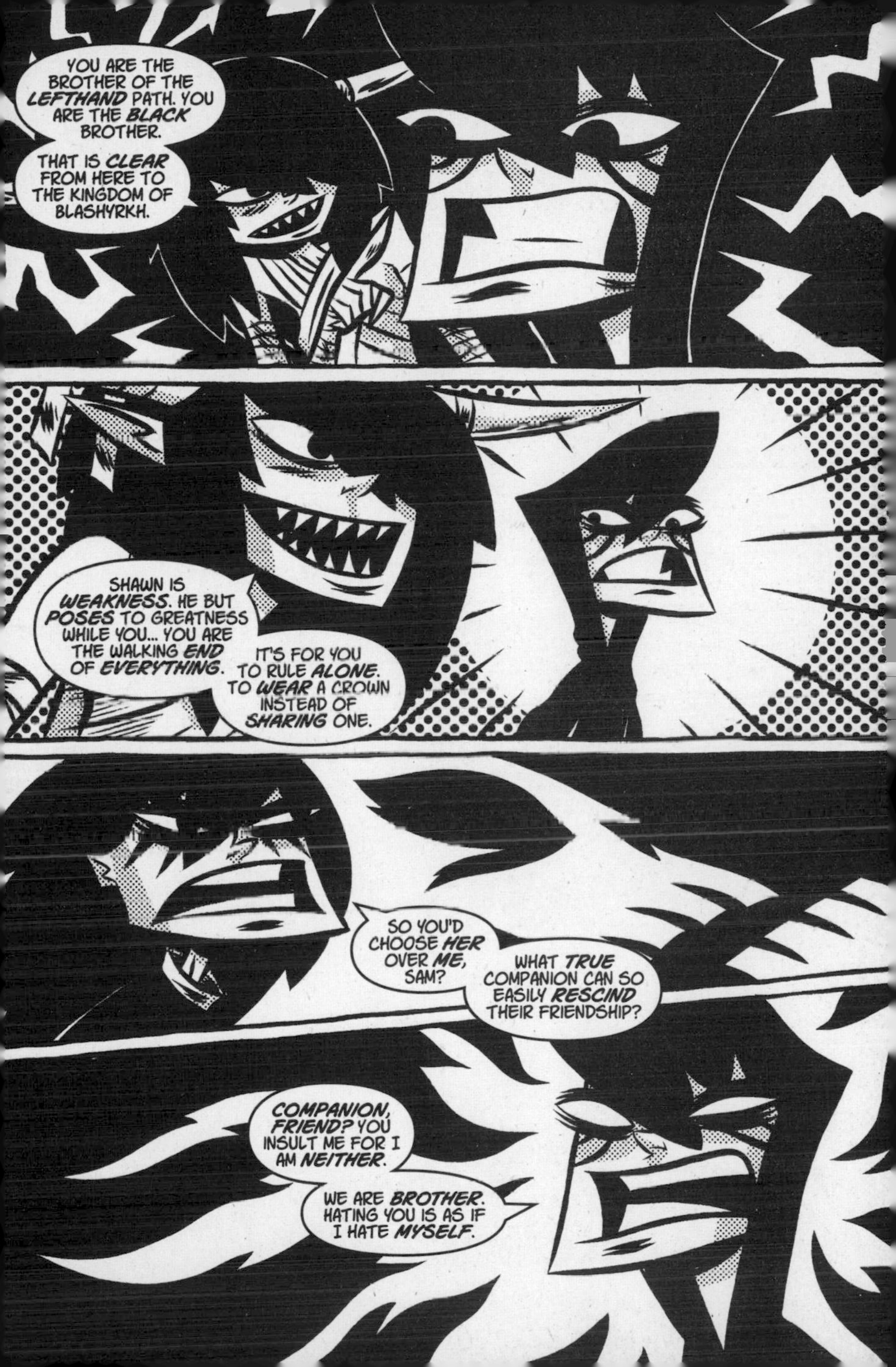
YOU ARE THE BROTHER OF THE LEFTHAND PATH. YOU ARE THE BLACK BROTHER.
THAT IS CLEAR FROM HERE TO THE KINGDOM OF BLASHYRKH.
SHAWN IS WEAKNESS. HE BUT POSES TO GREATNESS WHILE YOU... YOU ARE THE WALKING END OF EVERYTHING.
IT'S FOR YOU TO RULE ALONE. TO WEAR A CROWN INSTEAD OF SHARING ONE.
SO YOU'D CHOOSE HER OVER ME, SAM?
WHAT TRUE COMPANION CAN SO EASILY RESCIND THEIR FRIENDSHIP?
COMPANION, FRIEND? YOU INSULT ME FOR I AM NEITHER.
WE ARE BROTHER. HATING YOU IS AS IF I HATE MYSELF.

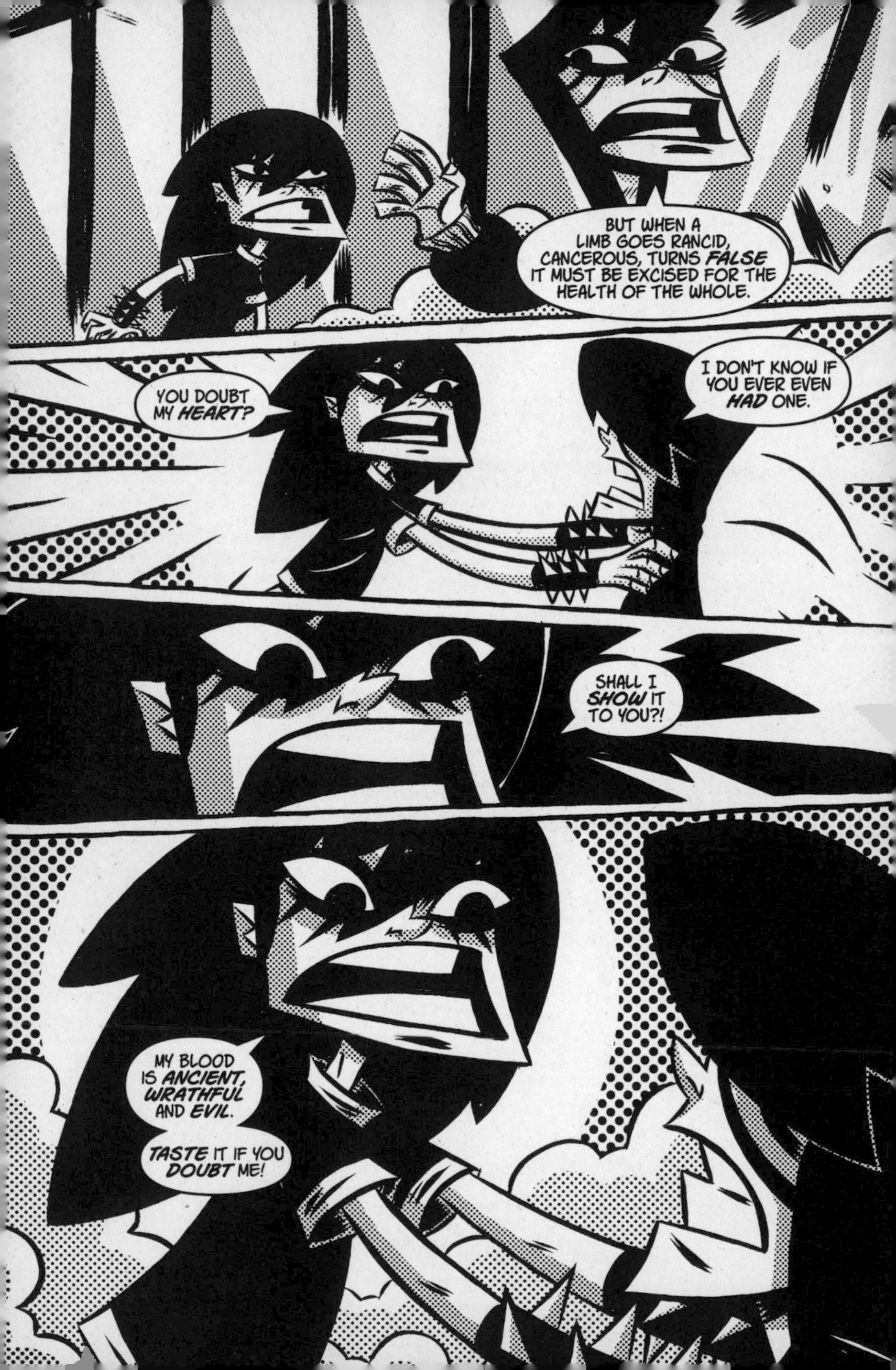
BUT WHEN A LIMB GOES RANCID, CANCEROUS, TURNS *FALSE* IT MUST BE EXCISED FOR THE HEALTH OF THE WHOLE.
YOU DOUBT MY *HEART?*
I DON'T KNOW IF YOU EVER EVEN *HAD* ONE.
SHALL I *SHOW* IT TO YOU?!
MY BLOOD IS *ANCIENT, WRATHFUL* AND *EVIL*.
TASTE IT IF YOU *DOUBT* ME!

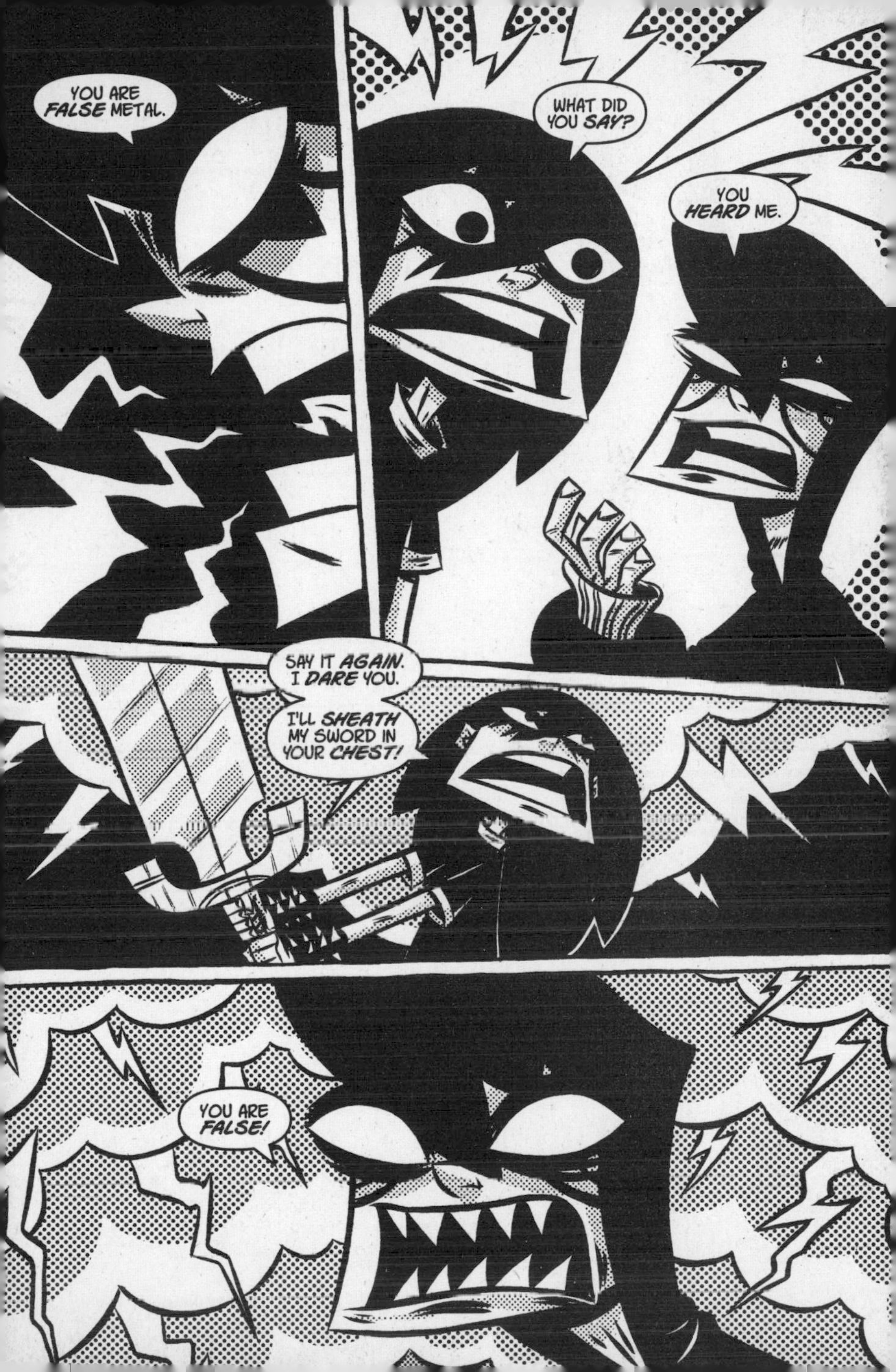
YOU ARE FALSE METAL.
WHAT DID YOU SAY?
YOU HEARD ME.
SAY IT AGAIN. I DARE YOU.
I'LL SHEATH MY SWORD IN YOUR CHEST!
YOU ARE FALSE!

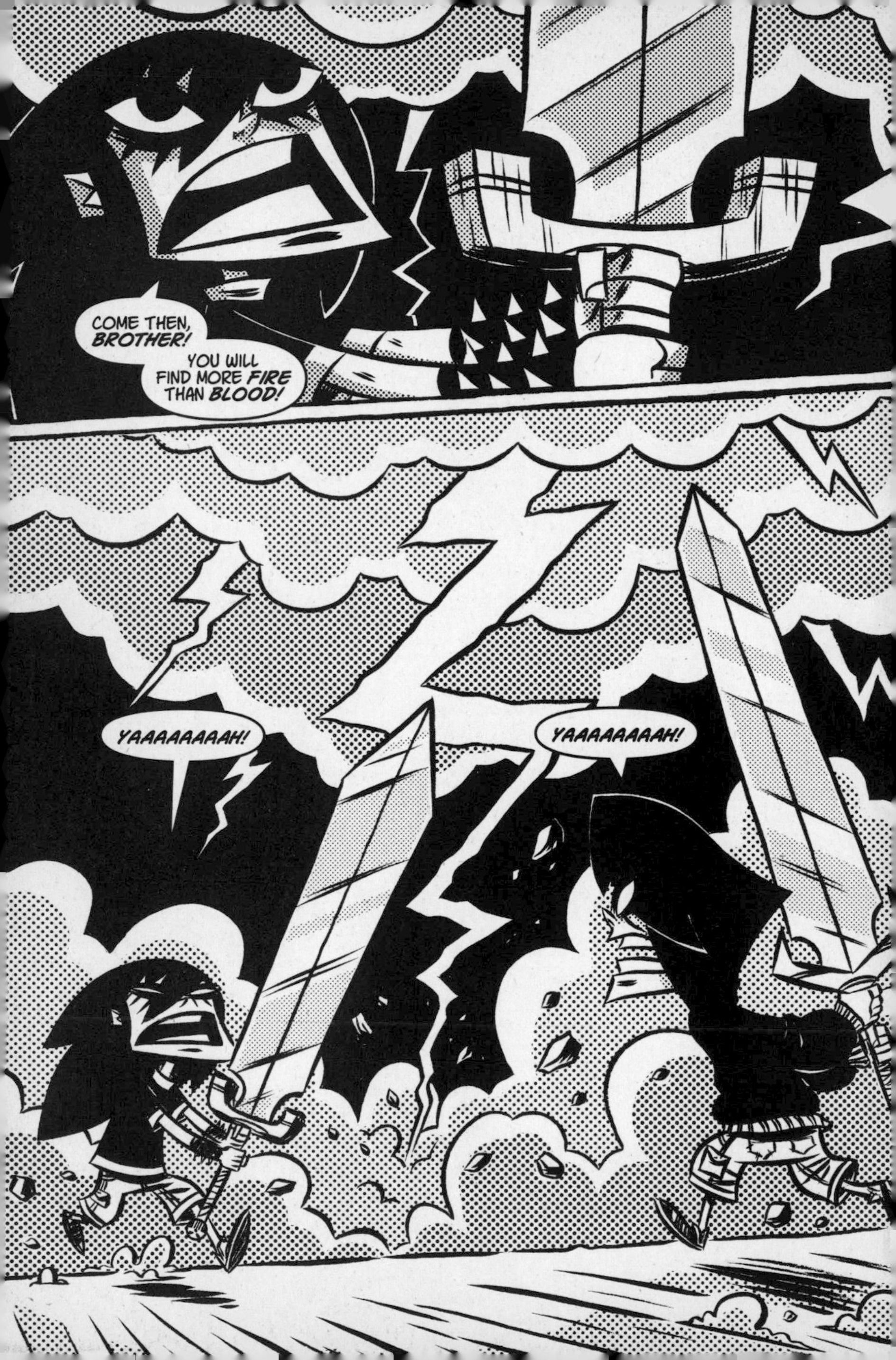
COME THEN, *BROTHER!*
YOU WILL FIND MORE *FIRE* THAN *BLOOD!*
YAAAAAAAAH!
YAAAAAAAAH!

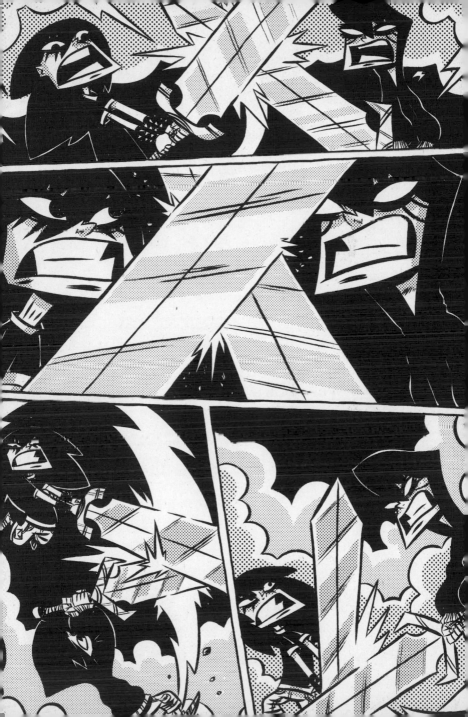

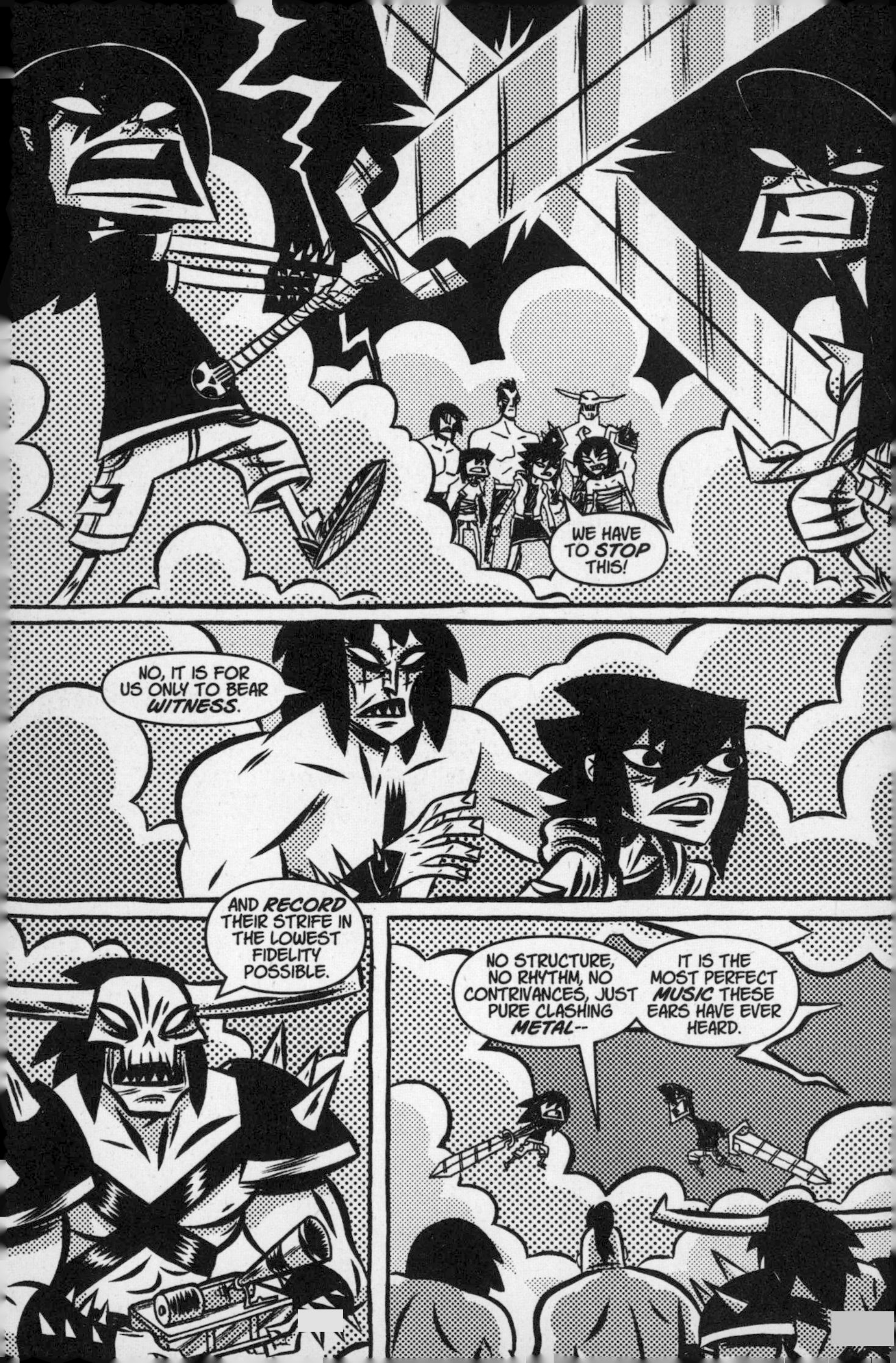
WE HAVE TO STOP THIS!
NO, IT IS FOR US ONLY TO BEAR WITNESS.
AND RECORD THEIR STRIFE IN THE LOWEST FIDELITY POSSIBLE.
NO STRUCTURE, NO RHYTHM, NO CONTRIVANCES, JUST PURE CLASHING METAL--
IT IS THE MOST PERFECT MUSIC THESE EARS HAVE EVER HEARD.

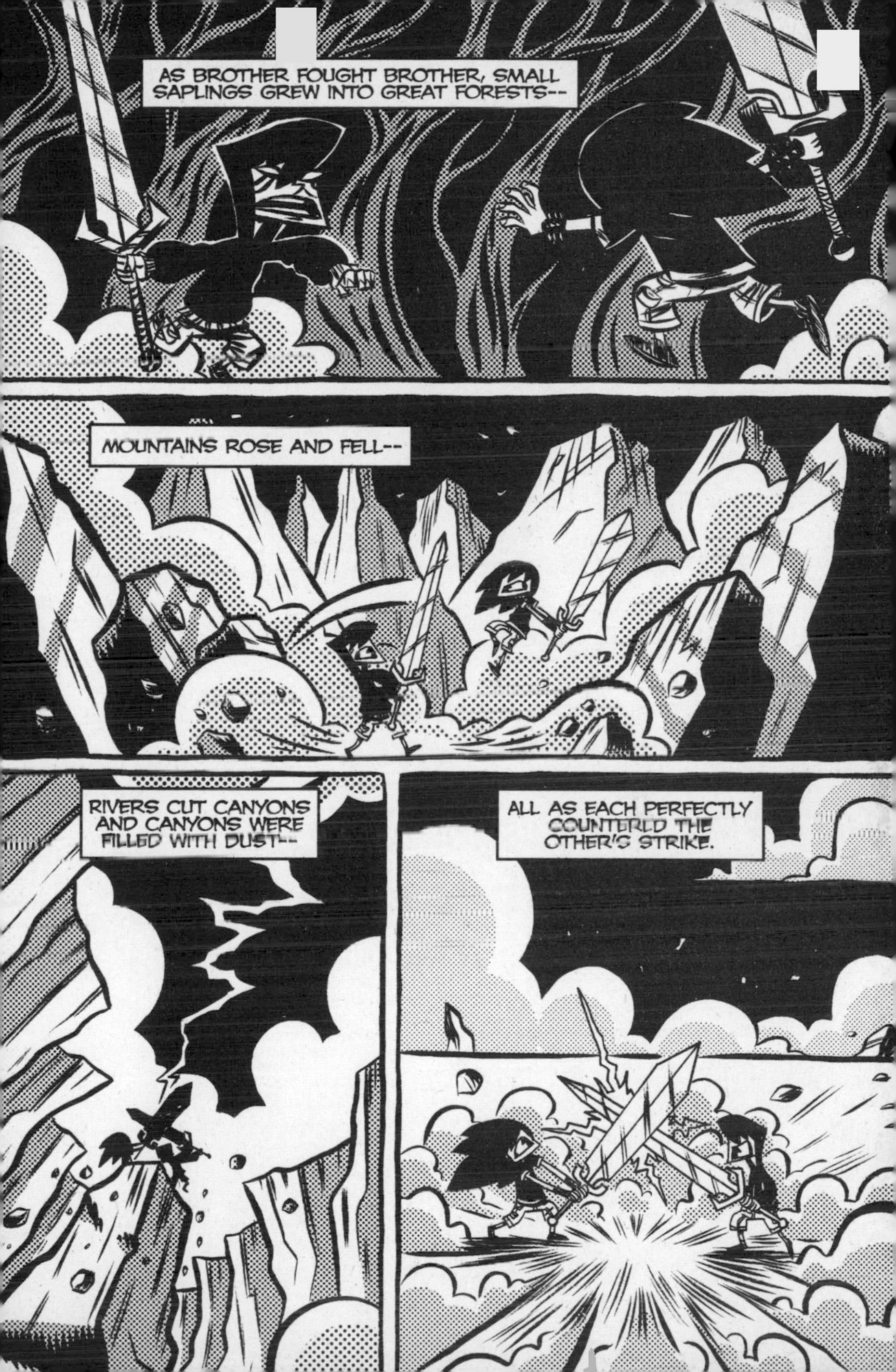
AS BROTHER FOUGHT BROTHER, SMALL SAPLINGS GREW INTO GREAT FORESTS--
MOUNTAINS ROSE AND FELL--
RIVERS CUT CANYONS AND CANYONS WERE FILLED WITH DUST--
ALL AS EACH PERFECTLY COUNTERED THE OTHER'S STRIKE.

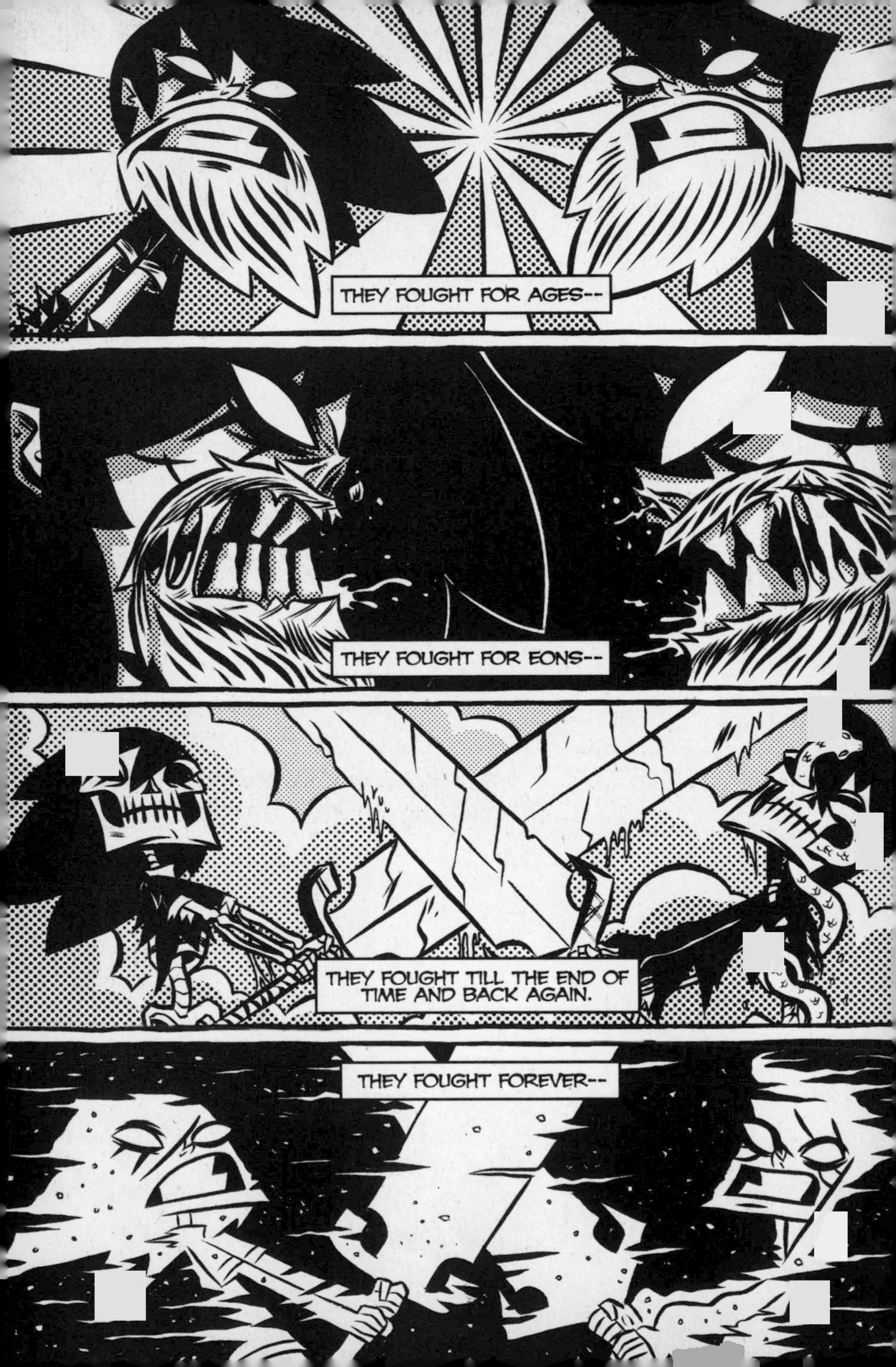
THEY FOUGHT FOR AGES--
THEY FOUGHT FOR EONS--
THEY FOUGHT TILL THE END OF TIME AND BACK AGAIN.
THEY FOUGHT FOREVER--

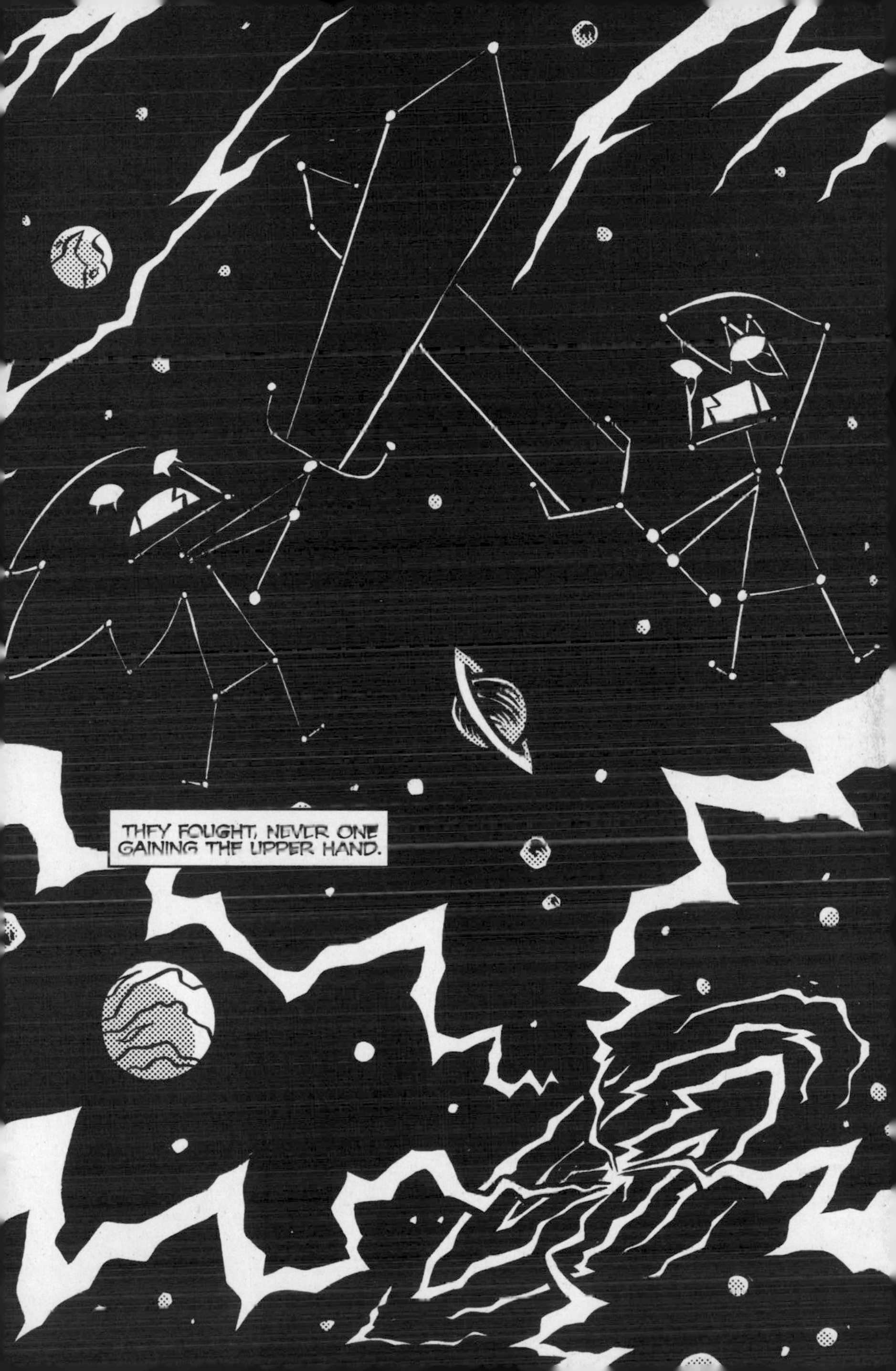
THEY FOUGHT, NEVER ONE GAINING THE UPPER HAND.

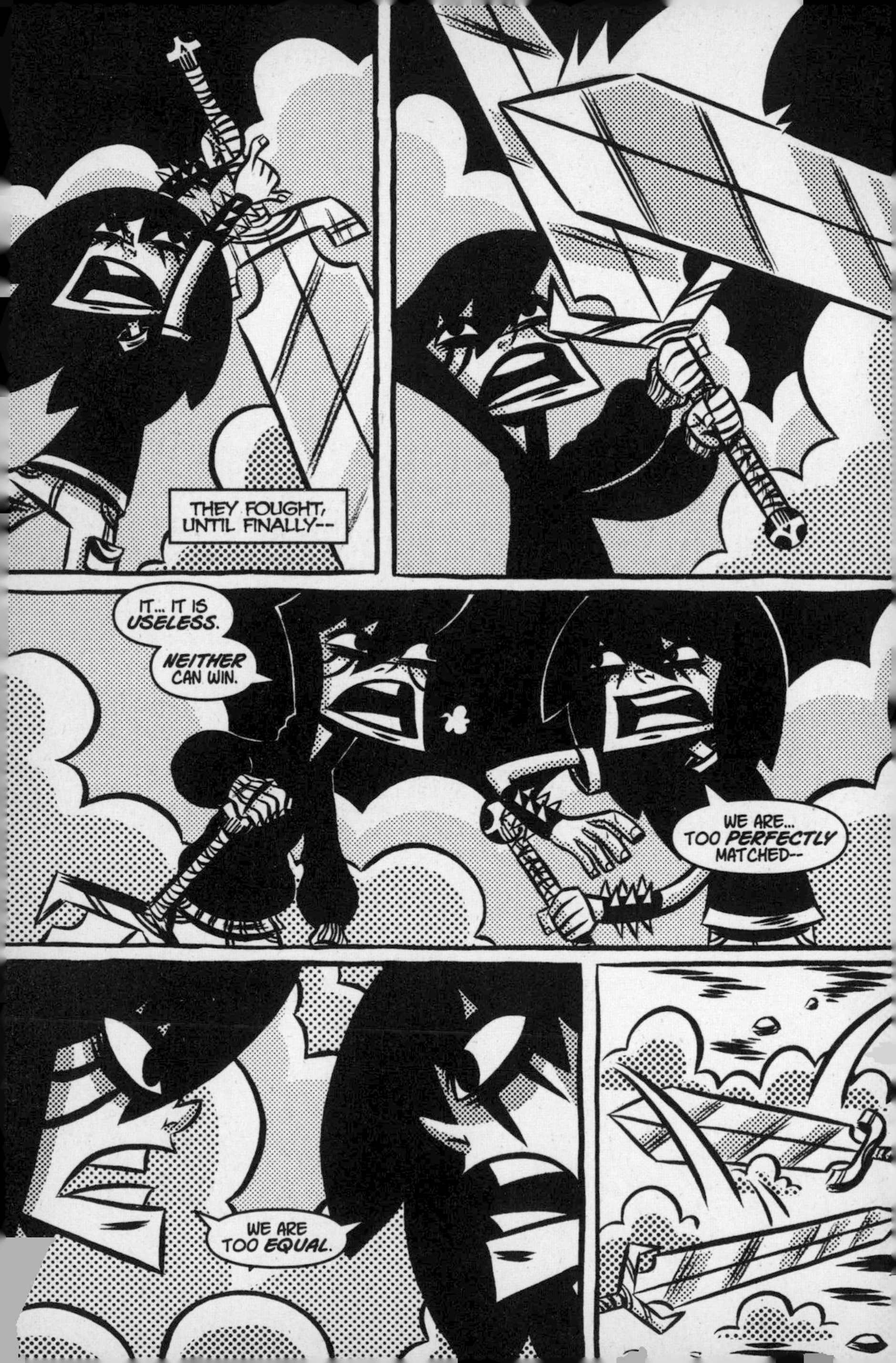
THEY FOUGHT, UNTIL FINALLY--
IT... IT IS USELESS.
NEITHER CAN WIN.
WE ARE... TOO PERFECTLY MATCHED--
WE ARE TOO EQUAL.

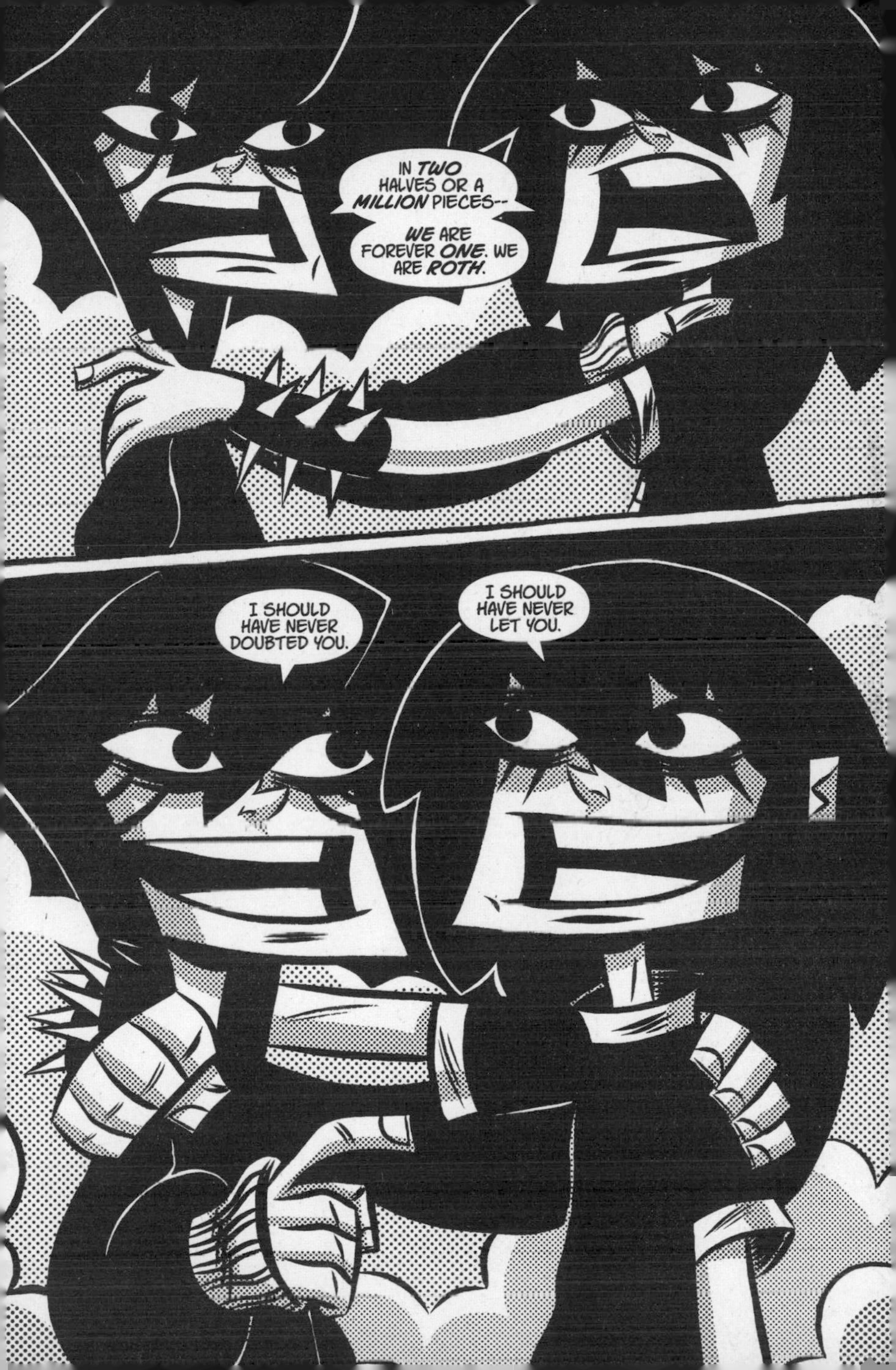
IN TWO HALVES OR A MILLION PIECES--
WE ARE FOREVER ONE. WE ARE ROTH.
I SHOULD HAVE NEVER DOUBTED YOU.
I SHOULD HAVE NEVER LET YOU.

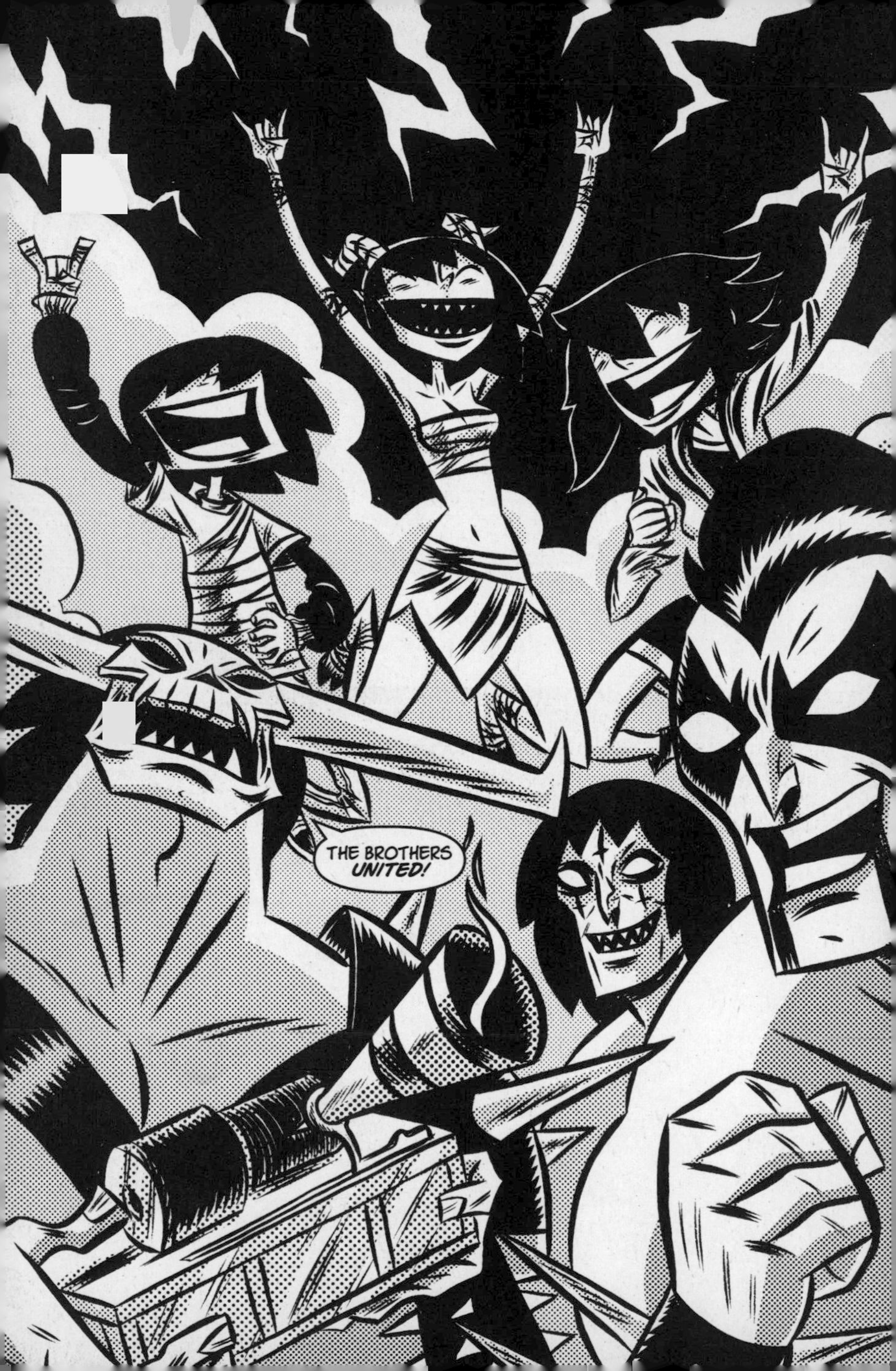
THE BROTHERS *UNITED!*

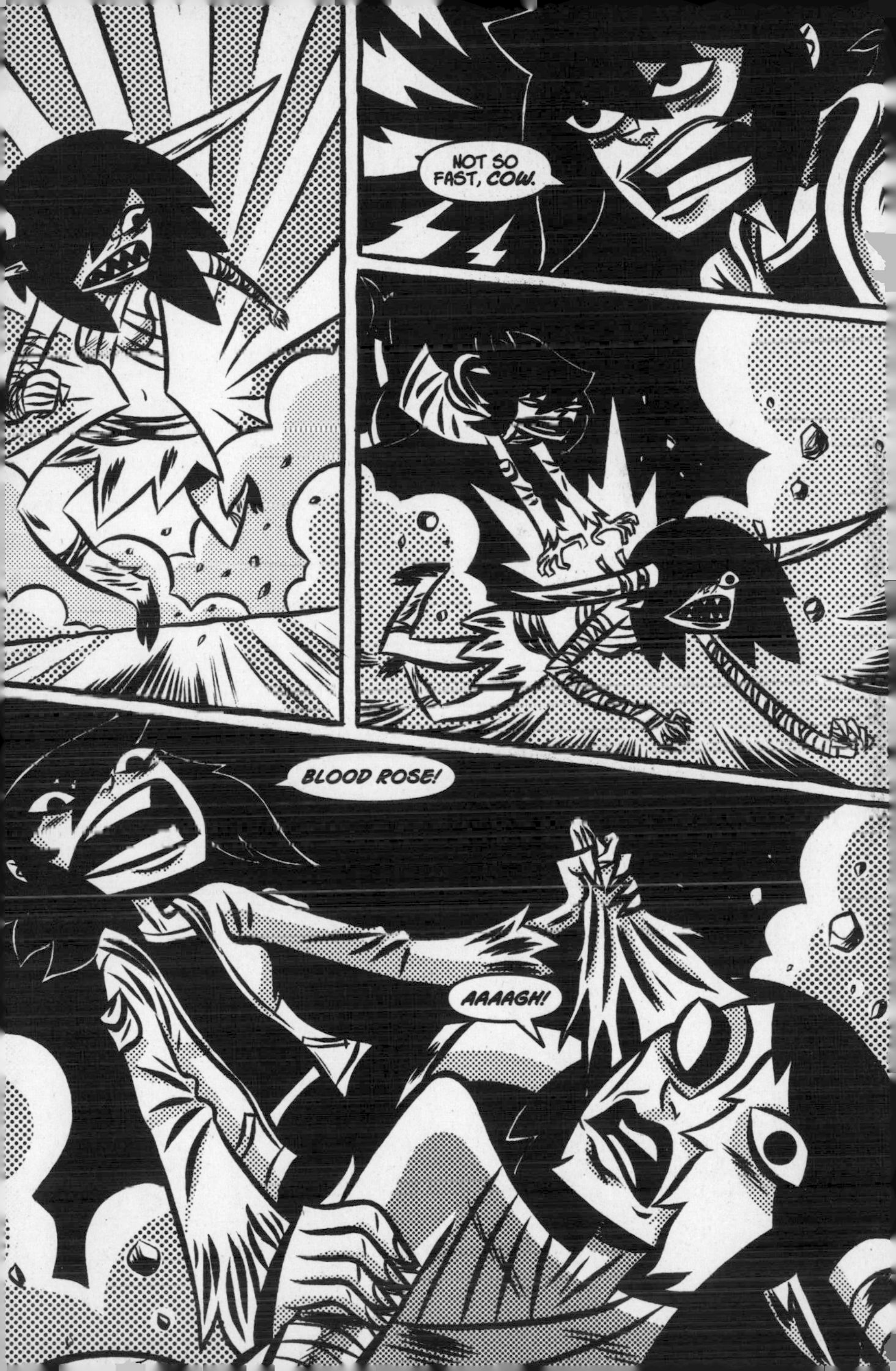
NOT SO FAST, COW.
BLOOD ROSE!
AAAAGH!

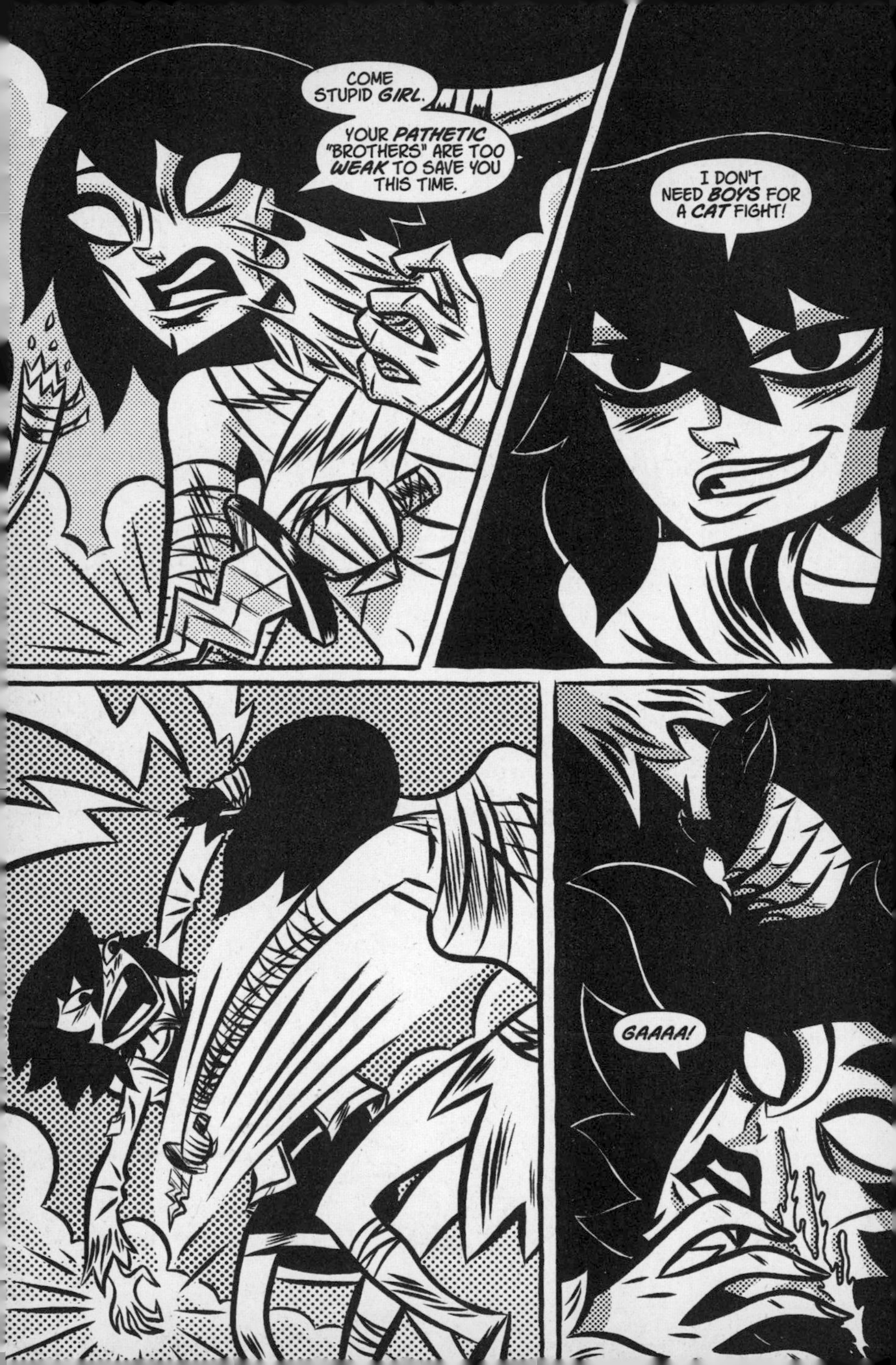
COME STUPID GIRL.
YOUR PATHETIC "BROTHERS" ARE TOO WEAK TO SAVE YOU THIS TIME.
I DON'T NEED BOYS FOR A CAT FIGHT!
GAAAA!

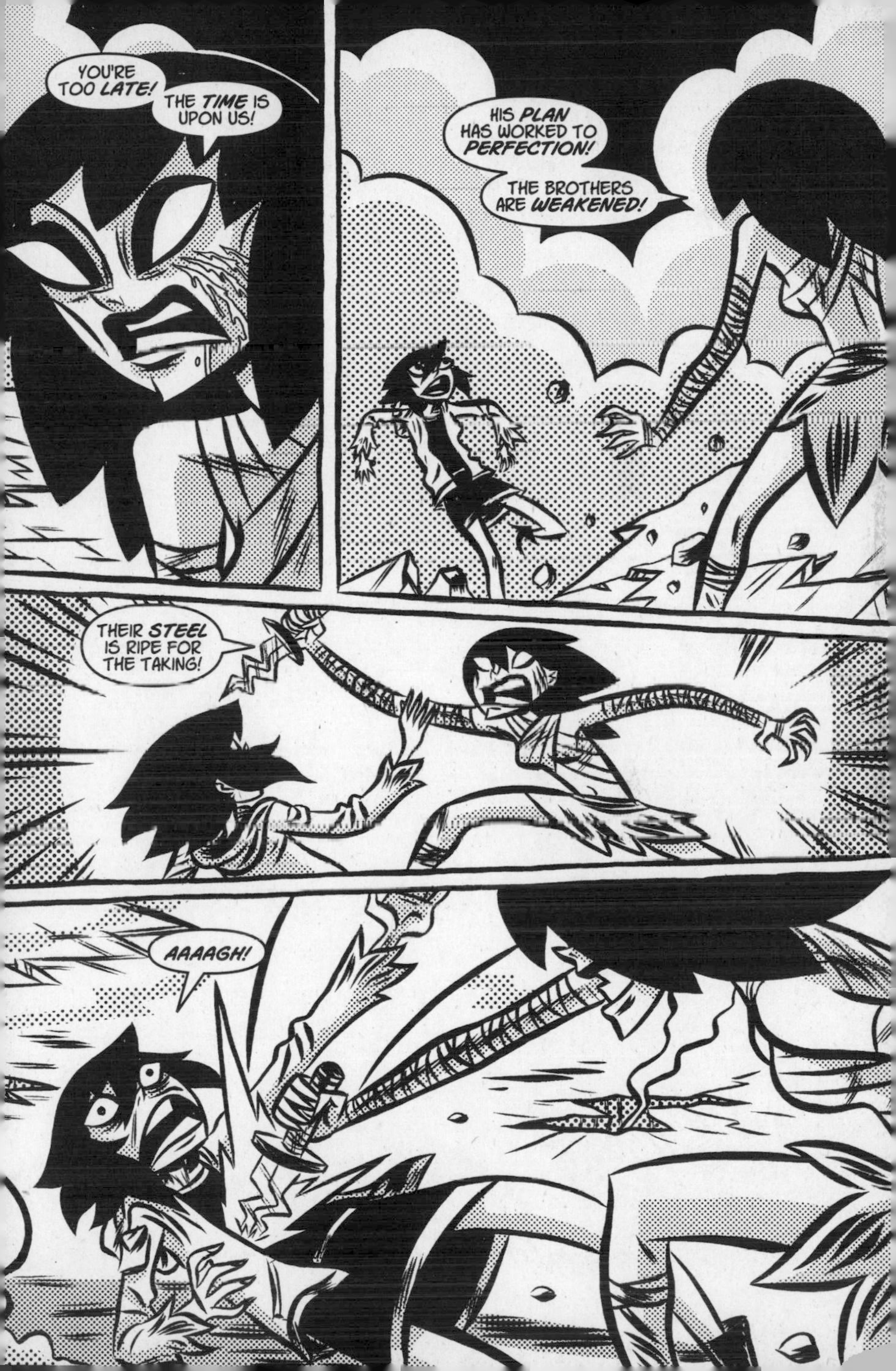
YOU'RE TOO LATE!
THE TIME IS UPON US!
HIS PLAN HAS WORKED TO PERFECTION!
THE BROTHERS ARE WEAKENED!
THEIR STEEL IS RIPE FOR THE TAKING!
AAAAGH!

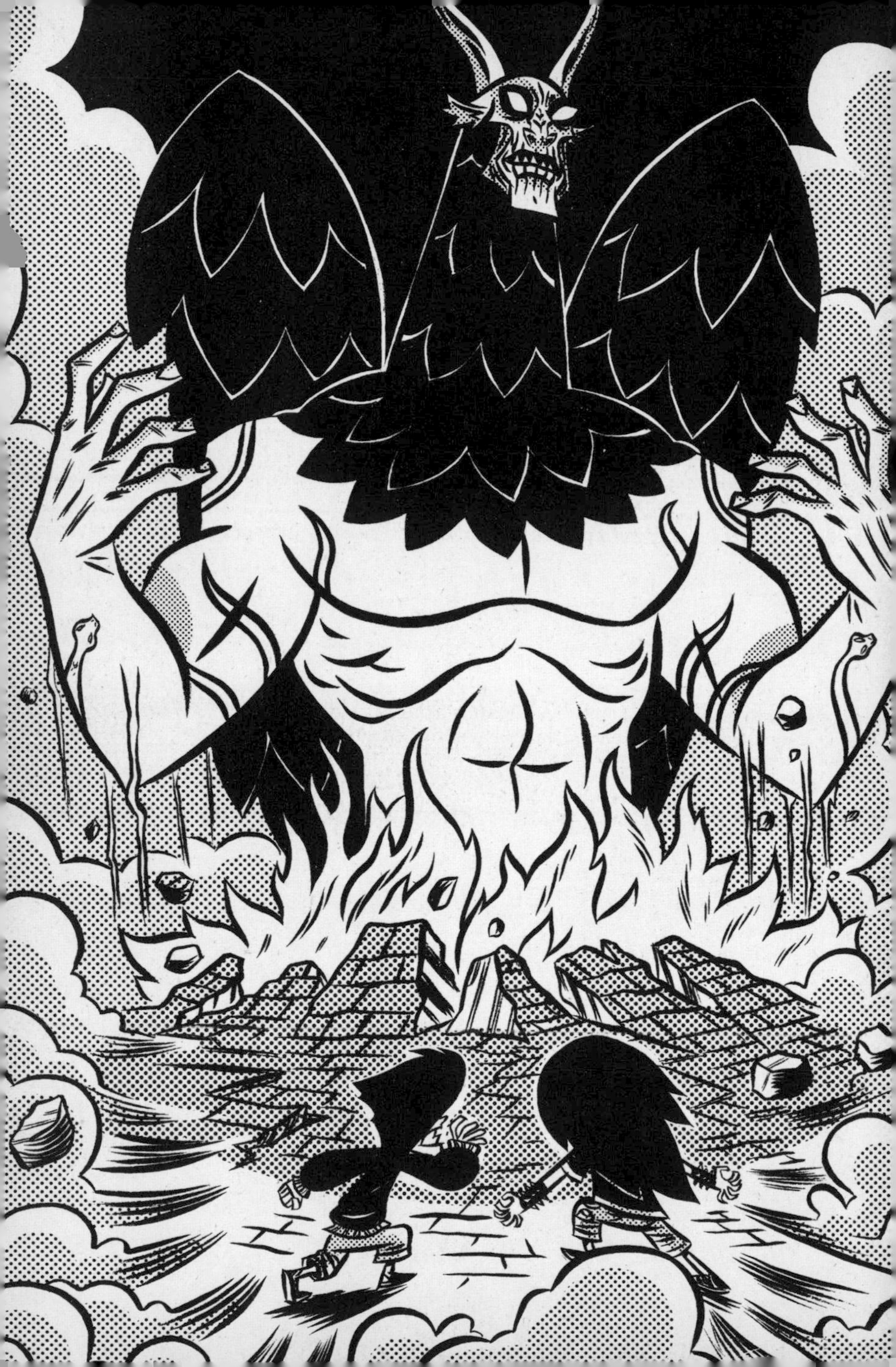

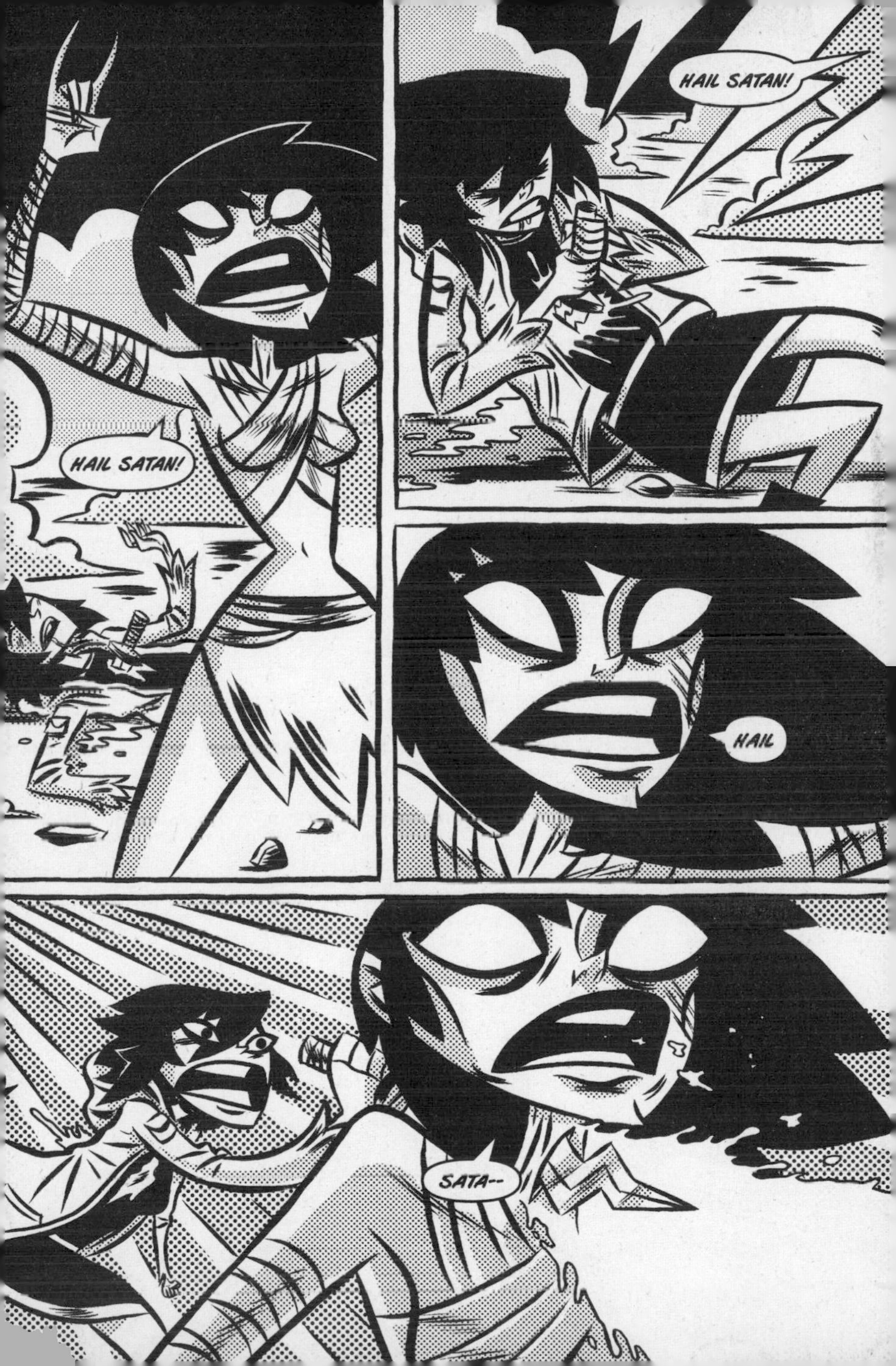
HAIL SATAN!
HAIL SATAN!
HAIL
SATA--

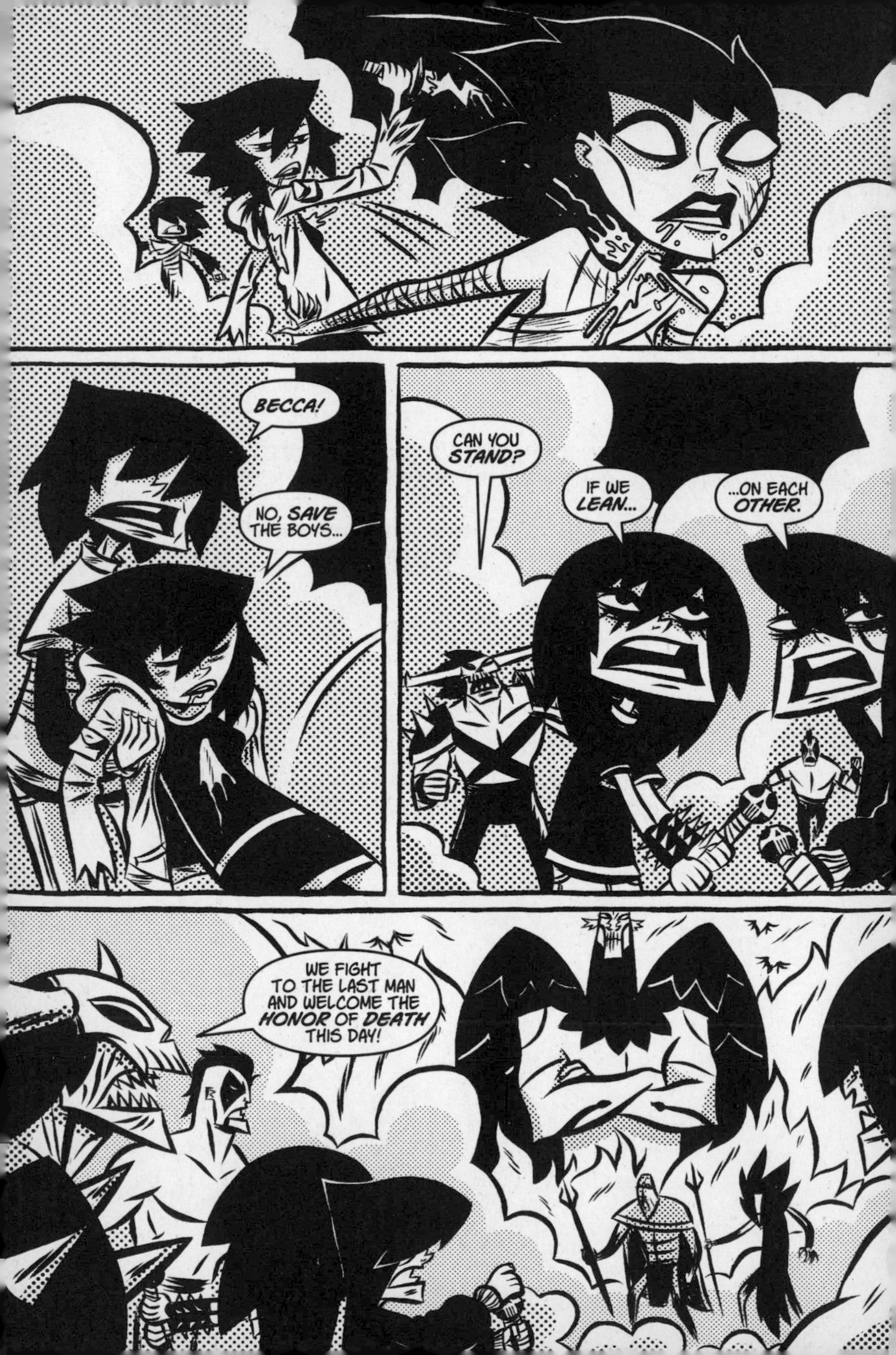
BECCA!
NO, SAVE THE BOYS...
CAN YOU STAND?
IF WE LEAN...
...ON EACH OTHER.
WE FIGHT TO THE LAST MAN AND WELCOME THE HONOR OF DEATH THIS DAY!

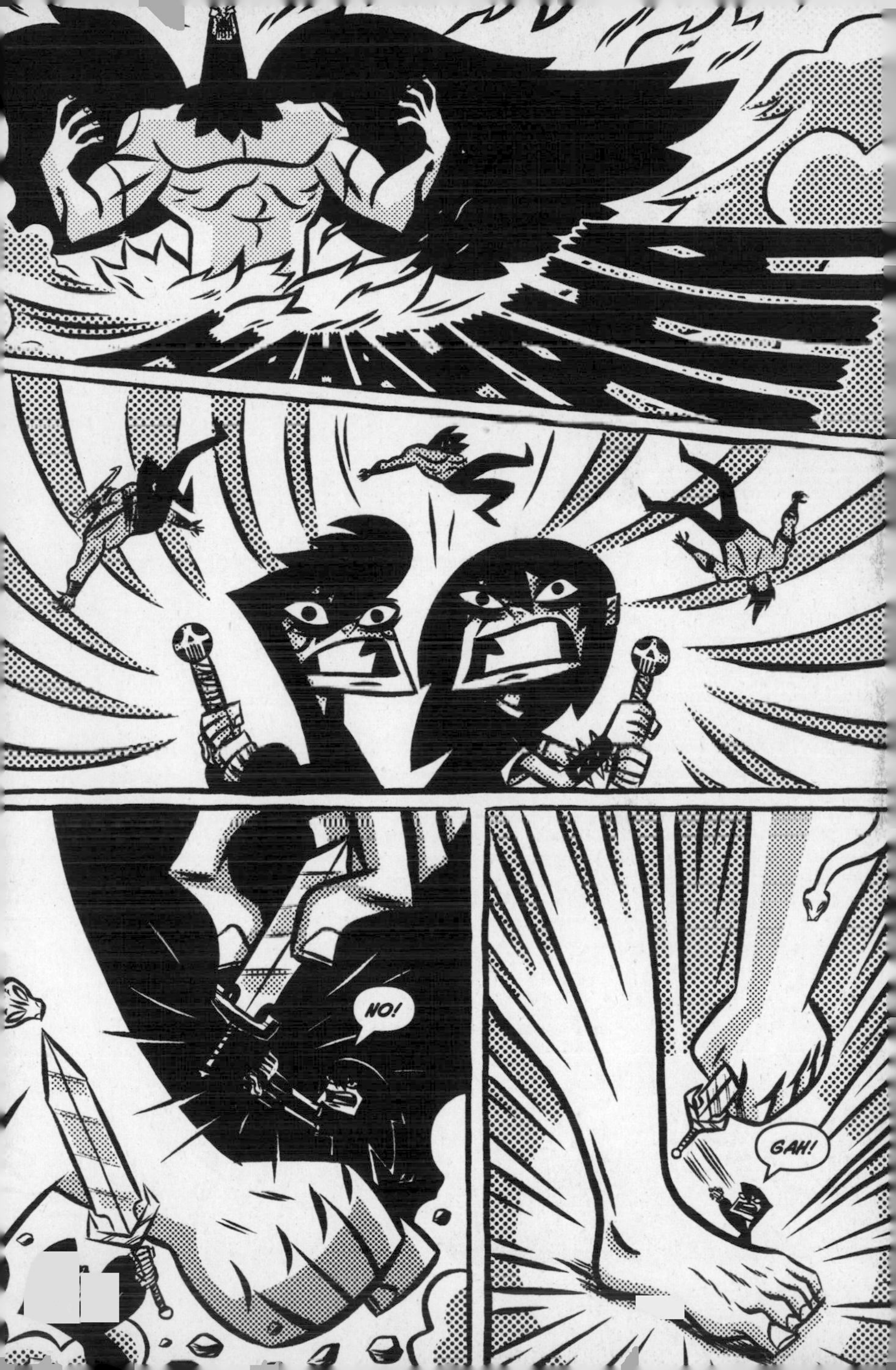
NO!
GAH!

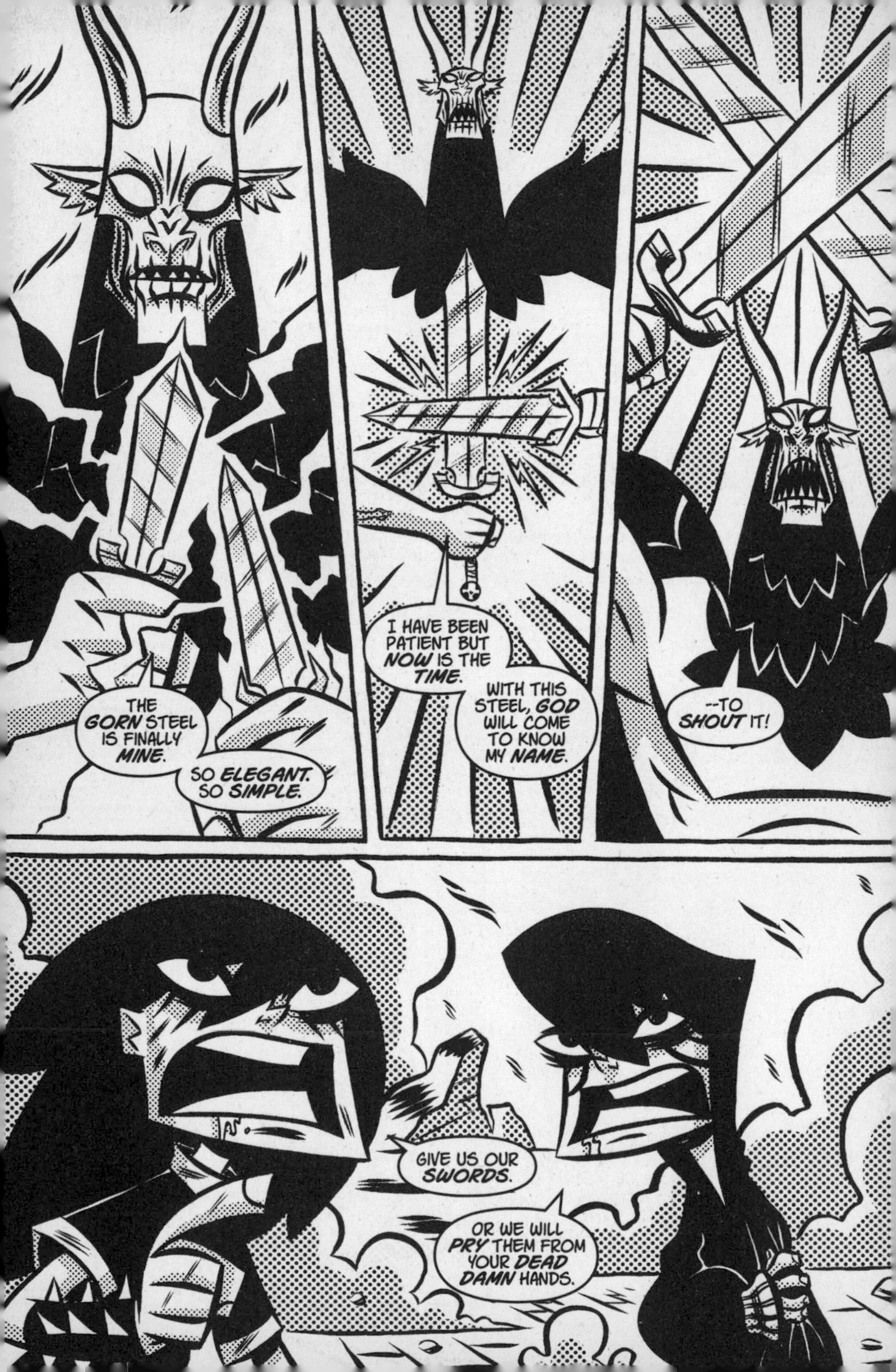
THE GORN STEEL IS FINALLY MINE.
SO ELEGANT. SO SIMPLE.
I HAVE BEEN PATIENT BUT NOW IS THE TIME.
WITH THIS STEEL, GOD WILL COME TO KNOW MY NAME.
--TO SHOUT IT!
GIVE US OUR SWORDS.
OR WE WILL PRY THEM FROM YOUR DEAD DAMN HANDS.

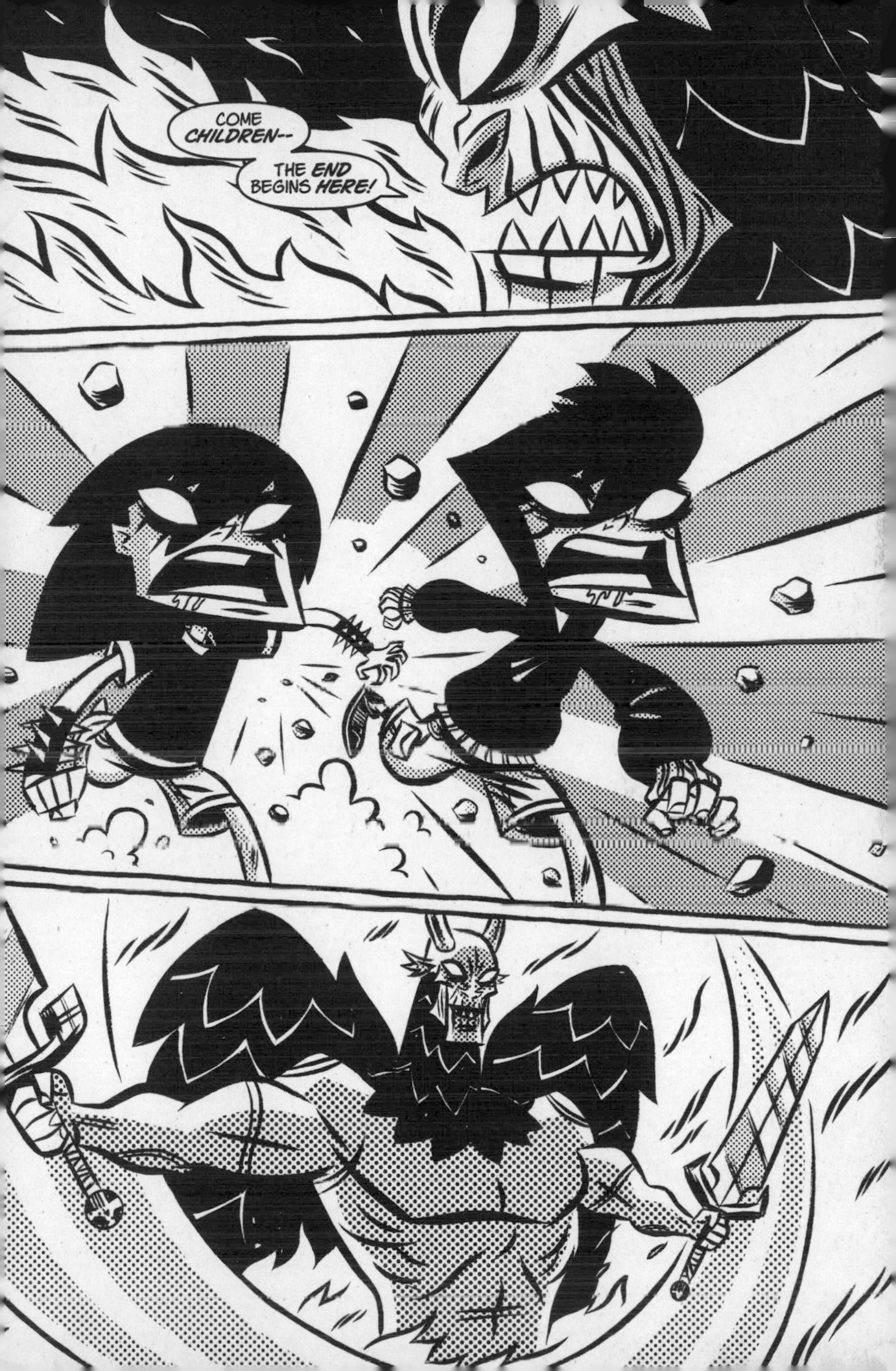
COME CHILDREN--
THE END BEGINS HERE!

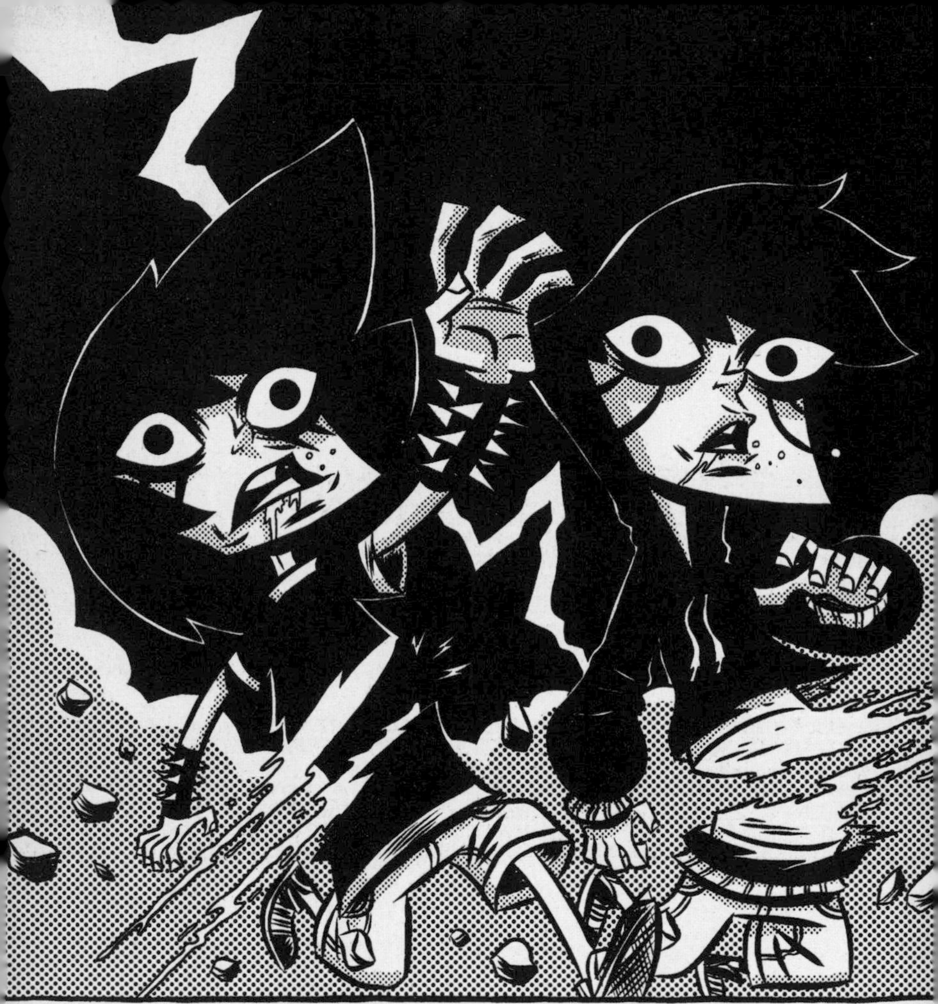
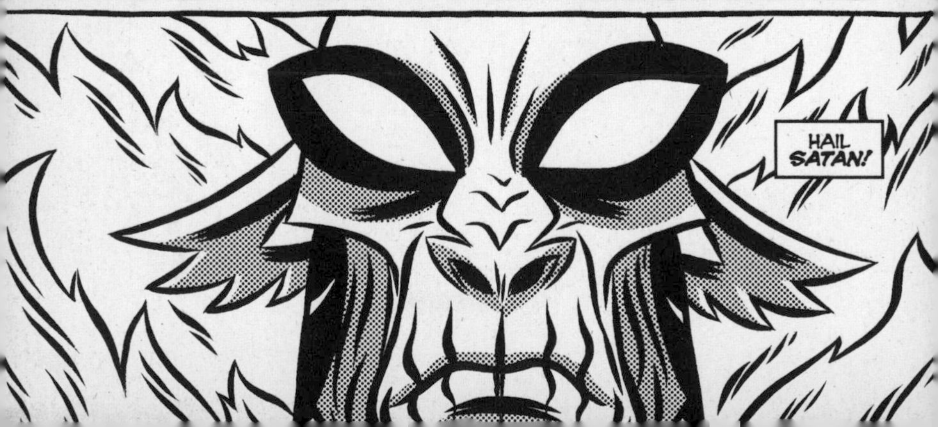
HAIL SATAN!

TO BE CONCLUDED...

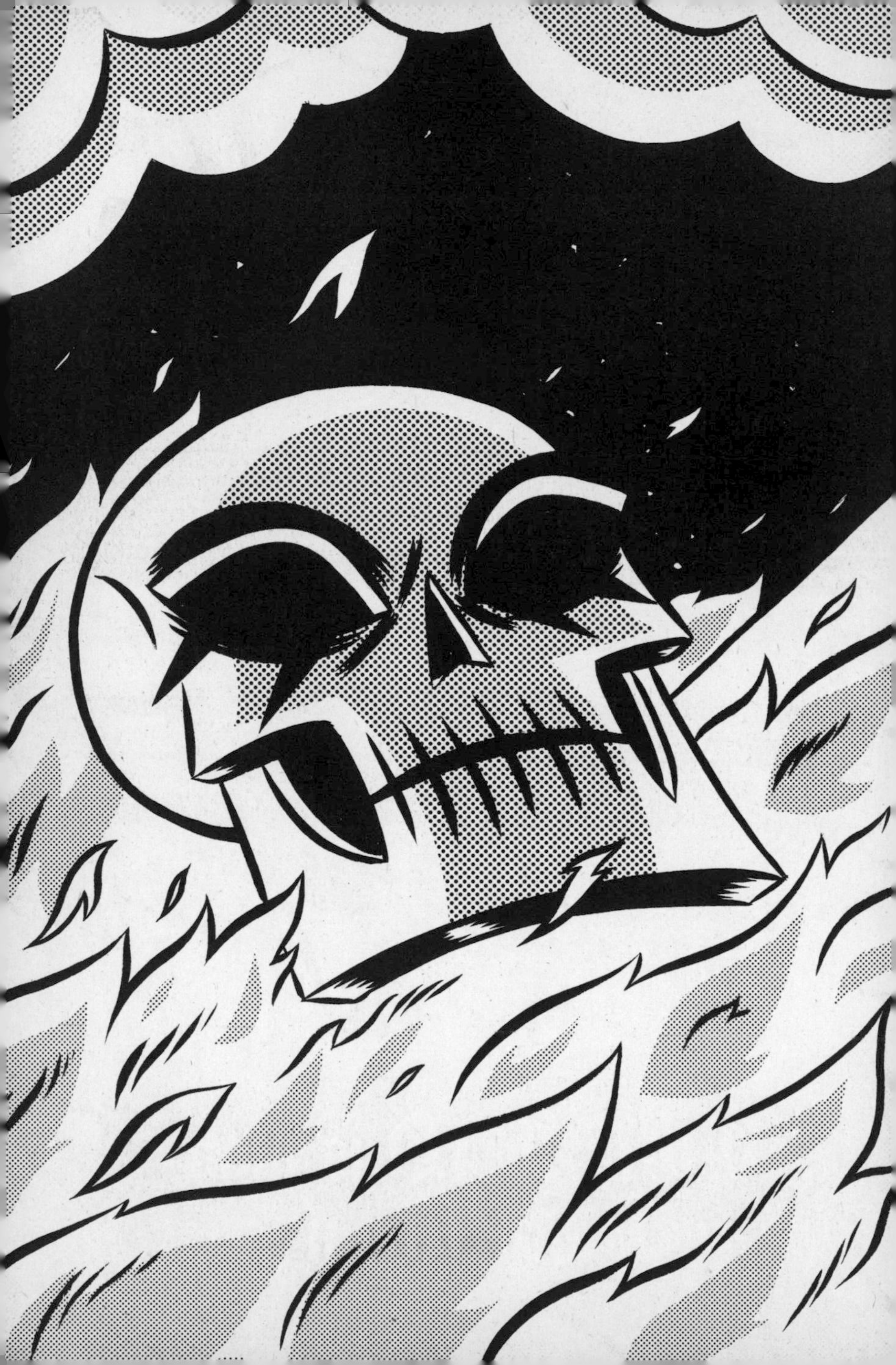

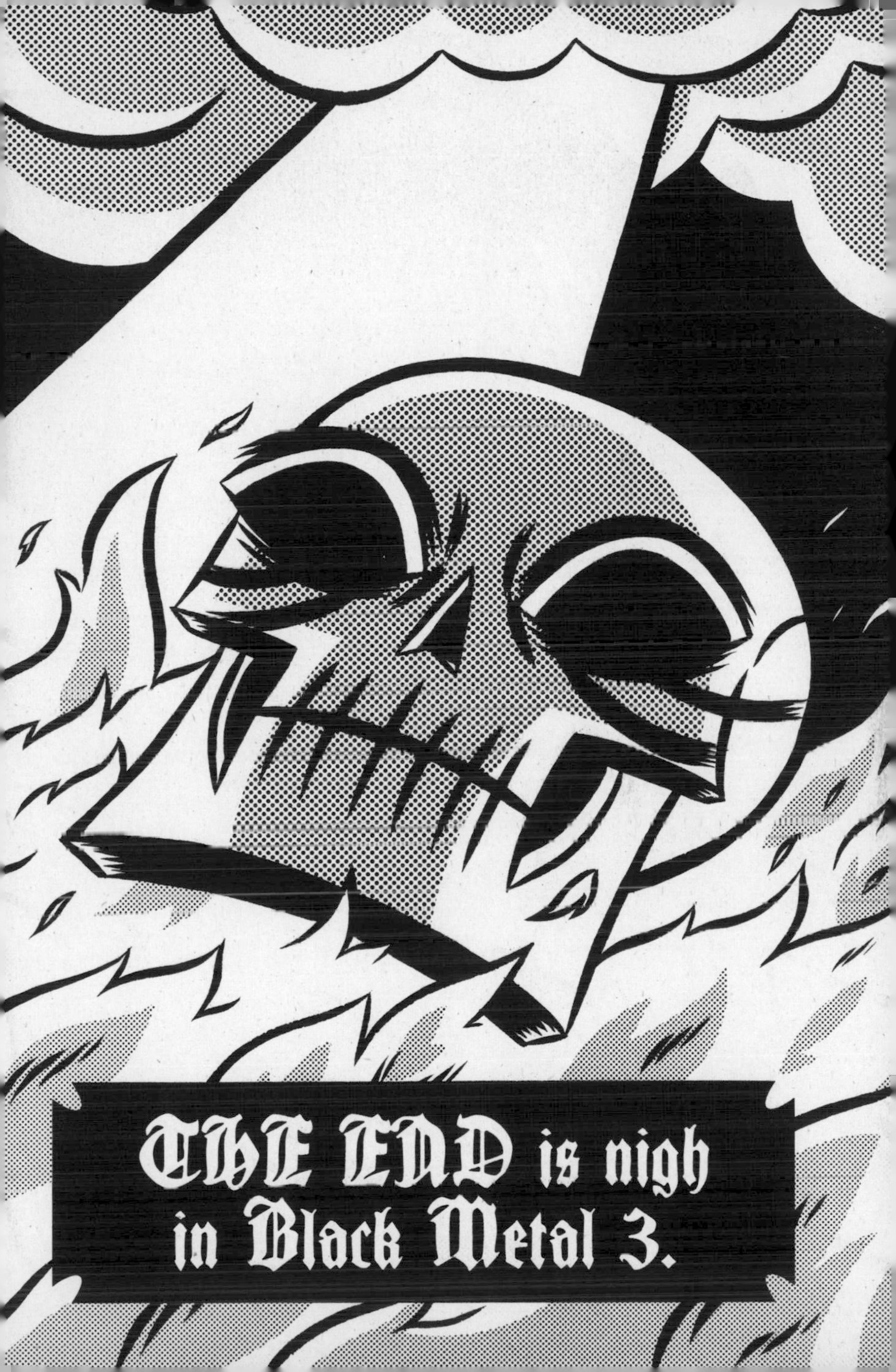
THE END is nigh
in Black Metal 3.

BLACK METAL

2

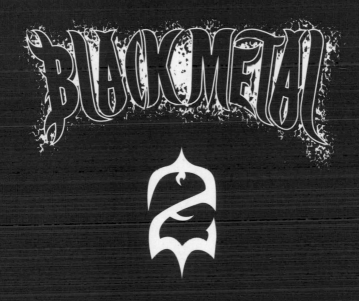

PIN UP GALLERY

PIN-UP BLACK METAL GALLERY

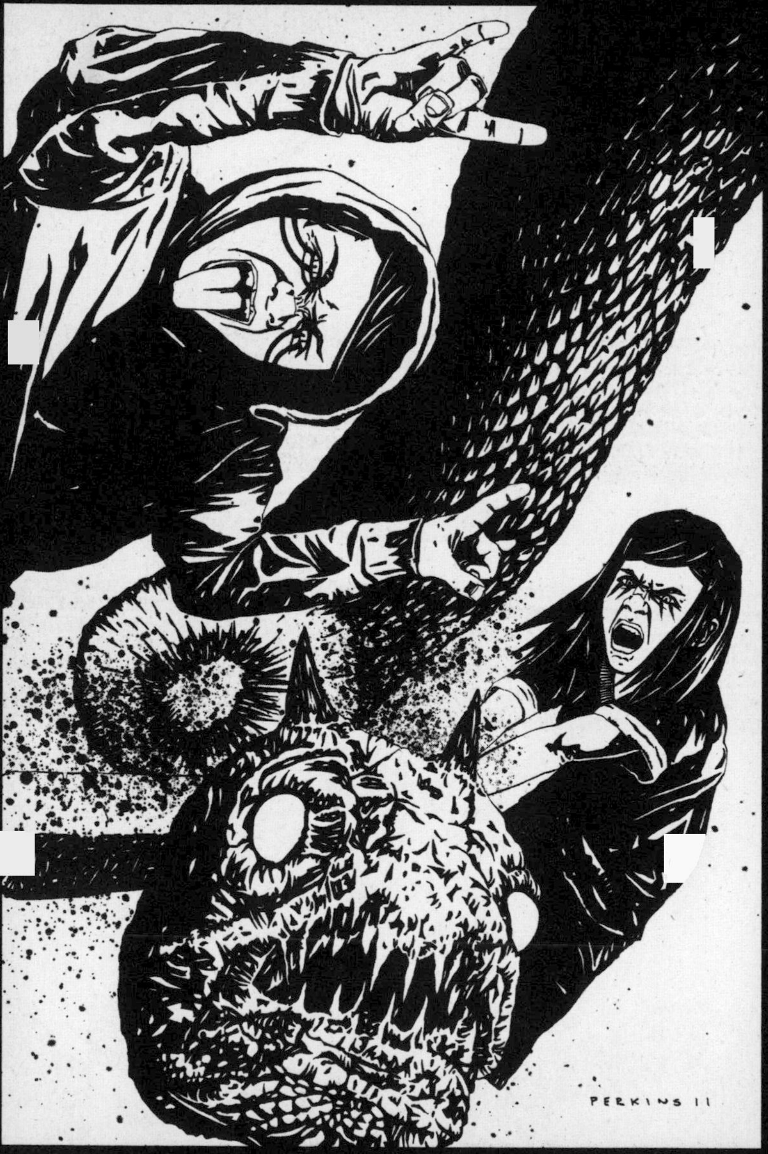
PERKINS 11

STEVEN PERKINS

PIN-UP BLACK METAL GALLERY

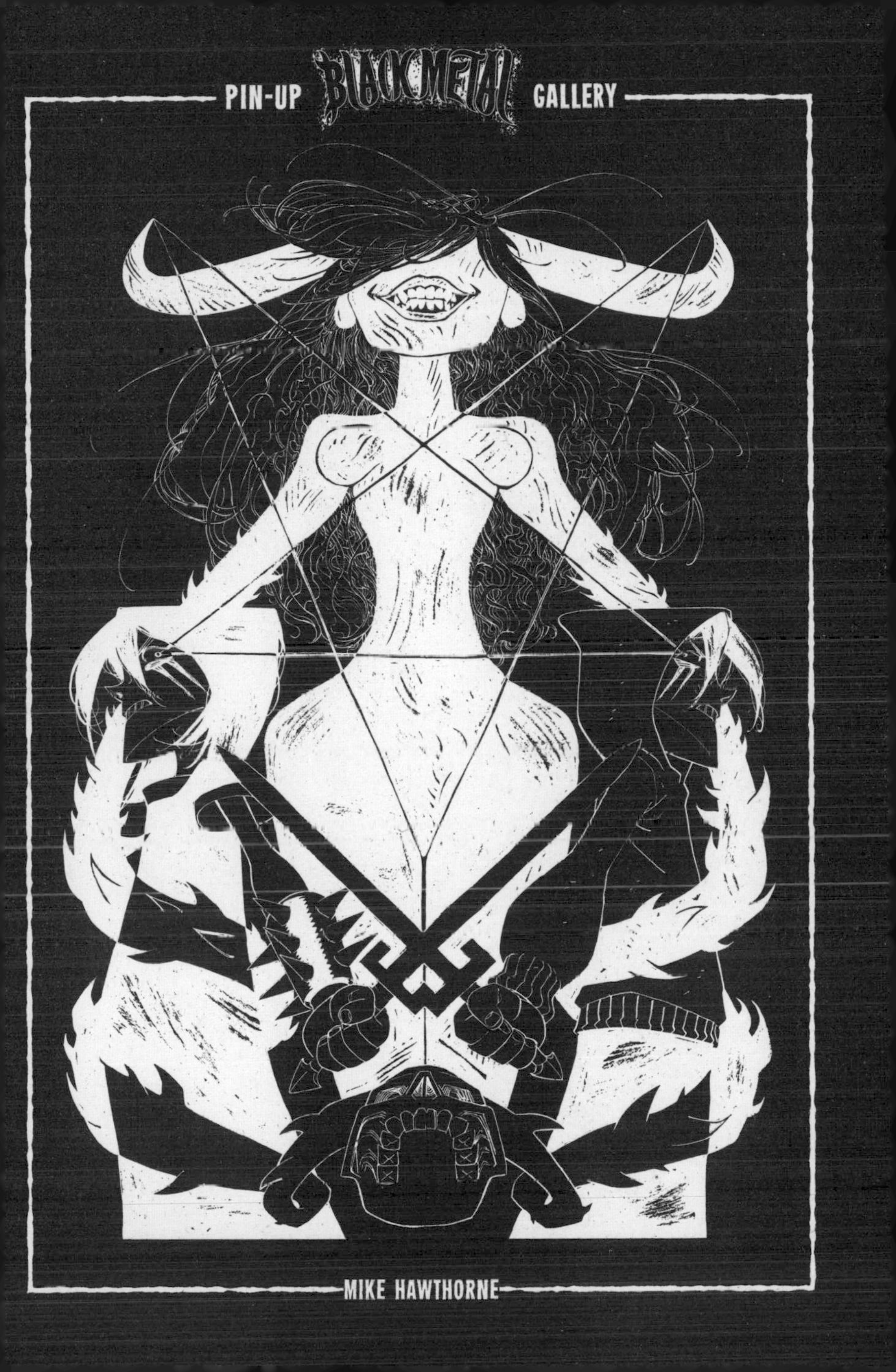

MIKE HAWTHORNE

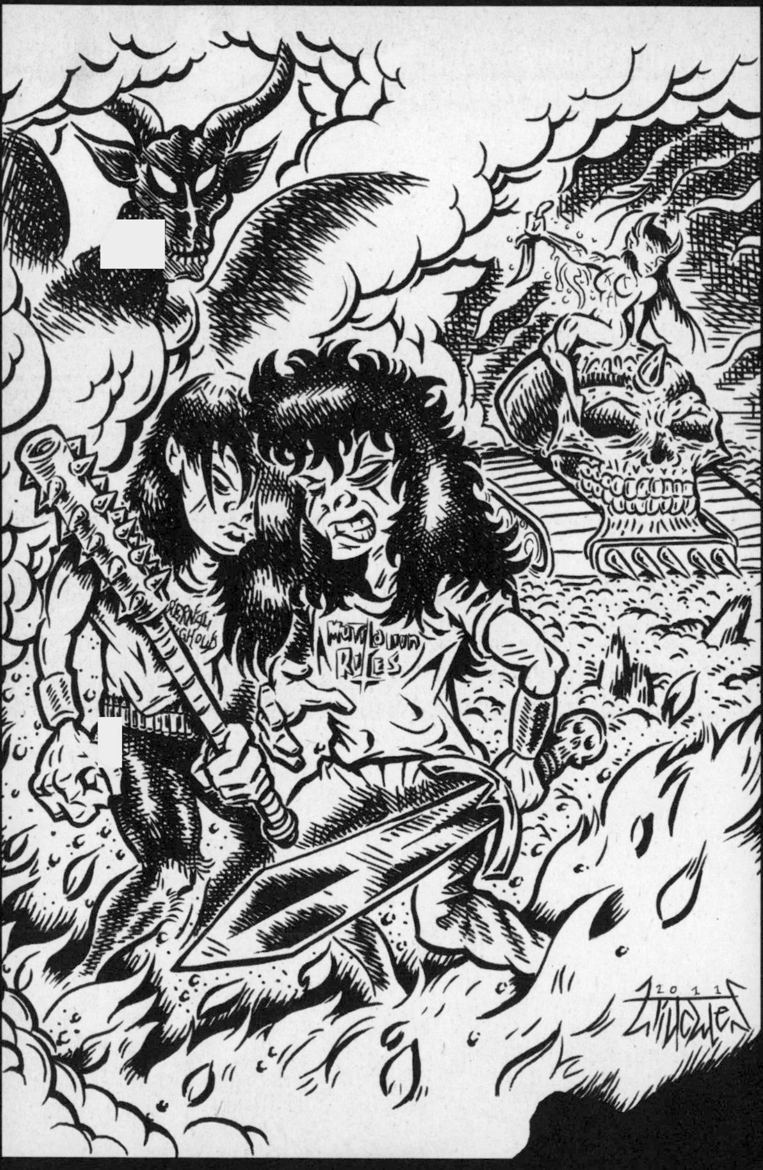
RULES
2011

WILL TOWLES

RICK SPEARS

IS A WRITER OF THINGS
INCLUDING, *TEENAGERS FROM
MARS*, *DEAD WEST*, *FILLER*, *THE
PIRATES OF CONEY ISLAND*,
REPO, VARIOUS PROJECTS FOR
MARVEL AND DC COMICS, AND
THE FORTHCOMING GRAPHIC
NOVEL *MY RIOT* FROM ONI
PRESS. HE LIVES IN
RICHMOND, VA WITH HIS
WIFE AND SCHNAUZER.

RICKSPEARS.COM

CHUCK BB

IS THE ARTIST OF THIS VERY
BOOK YOU HOLD IN YOUR
HANDS. HE IS THE CREATOR
AND WRITER/ARTIST OF *STONE
COLD LAZY* WHICH APPEARS
MONTHLY IN *DECIBEL MAGAZINE*.
HE RECEIVED AN EISNER AWARD
FOR HIS WORK IN THE FIRST
VOLUME OF *BLACK METAL*.
MOST OF HIS TIME IS SPENT IN
LOS ANGELES, NOT
MURDERING ANYONE.

THIS BOOK IS DEDICATED TO
HIS OLD FRIEND, FRISKEY.
1989-2010.

CHUCKBB.COM